# God's Yes to Women

# God's Yes to Women

*Why the Bible's Vision of Partnership Is Good News for Us All*

EDITED BY
Anna Boxwell
Amy J. Erickson
*and* Laura Rademaker

FOREWORD BY
*Aimee Byrd*

WIPF & STOCK • Eugene, Oregon

GOD'S YES TO WOMEN
Why the Bible's Vision of Partnership Is Good News for Us All



Wipf & Stock
An Imprint of Wipf and Stock Publishers
199 W. 8th Ave., Suite 3
Eugene, OR 97401

www.wipfandstock.com

PAPERBACK ISBN: 979-8-3852-6369-1
HARDCOVER ISBN: 979-8-3852-6370-7
EBOOK ISBN: 979-8-3852-6371-4

VERSION NUMBER 05/27/26

# Contents

*For resources and discussion guide see www.godsyes.org*

# Contributors

Dr. Leisa Aitken is a clinical psychologist with a PhD researching the psychology of hope, integrating psychology, theology, and philosophy. For nearly thirty years she has been delivering therapy in private practice as well as talks, seminars, and clinical and pastoral supervision in schools, churches, hospitals, and corporate workplaces.

Bishop Dr. Paul A. Barker is assistant bishop in the Anglican Diocese of Melbourne. He completed a PhD in Old Testament in 1996. From 2009–2016, he was with the Church Missionary Society based in Malaysia, teaching in Seminari Theoloji Malaysia. Paul was consecrated in November 2016 as bishop for Jumbunna, part of the Diocese of Melbourne.

Bishop Vanessa Bennett is assistant bishop in the Anglican Diocese of Canberra and Goulburn. Prior to becoming assistant bishop, Vanessa served as archdeacon of Essendon and vicar of the Parish of Moonee Ponds in the Diocese of Melbourne. She holds a BMin from Morling Baptist College and an MA in theology from Moore Theological College.

Rev. Dr. Michael J. Bird is vice principal and lecturer in New Testament at Ridley College, Melbourne. He is the author of many books, including most recently *Jesus and the Powers* (Zondervan) with Tom Wright.

Rev. Anna Boxwell is a minister at Renew Anglican Church, Canberra; teaches ministry training for St. Mark's National Theological Centre; and is the assistant director of church planting for City to City Australia, training and coaching people who are starting churches across Australia. She holds a BDiv from Moore Theological College.

Aimee Byrd is the author of *Saving Face, Recovering from Biblical Manhood and Womanhood*, and other books exploring gender and spiritual formation. She is currently a graduate student at Hood College, studying clinical mental health counselling. And—fun fact—Aimee is a part-time mixologist at McClintock Distillery in Frederick, Maryland.

Rev. Dr. Andrew Cameron is a minister at St. John's Anglican Church, Reid in Canberra. He has taught ethics and theology for over twenty years in theological colleges. He is the author of several books, largely in the field of theological ethics, including *The Joined-Up Life* (IVP) and *The Logic of Love* (Bloomsbury).

Rev. Dr. Hannah Craven is a lecturer in Christian thought at Ridley College, Melbourne. She was ordained in the Anglican Diocese of Melbourne in 2015 before completing a doctorate in feminist hermeneutics at the University of St. Andrews, Scotland. She currently leads the team for Ridley's biennial Evangelical Women in Academia (EWA) conference.

Dr. Amy J. Erickson is lecturer in theology and ethics at St. Mark's National Theological Centre. She studied under Brian Brock and Stanley Hauerwas at the University of Aberdeen (PhD, 2018). Her research interests include biblical hermeneutics and ecclesiology, with a special focus on church discipline. She is co-author with Greg Wagenfuhr of *Sabbath Gospel: A New Narrative of Time, Rest, and the Work of the Church* (IVP).

Rev. Dr. Jill Firth is lecturer in Hebrew and Old Testament at Ridley College, Melbourne. She has ministered in Western Australia, Victoria, the Northern Territory, and Hong Kong. She is co-editor of *Grounded in the Body, in Time and Place, in Scripture: Papers by Australian Women Scholars in the Evangelical Tradition* (Wipf & Stock).

Dr. Michael Gladwin is a senior lecturer in church history at St. Mark's National Theological Centre in Canberra. He is the author of *Captains of the Soul* (Big Sky) and *Anglican Clergy in Australia* (Royal Historical Society). He is also the editor of *St. Mark's Review*.

Rev. Scott Goode is an ordained Anglican priest serving an evangelical parish in regional New South Wales, Australia. He is currently completing doctoral research on Pauline marriage theology and maintains active research interests in Pauline studies and the historical Jesus.

Pastor Grace Lung is the director of the Centre for Asian Christianity at the Brisbane School of Theology. She is also the Next Generation Bicultural Program coordinator at the Melbourne School of Theology. She is on the pastoral team at Rise Alliance Church in Brisbane. Grace studied at Sydney Missionary Bible College and Fuller Theological Seminary. She writes and lectures on Asian Australian issues and multiculturalism.

Erica Mandi Manga (née Hamence) is a minister at St. Paul's Anglican Church, Castle Hill, in Sydney. For many years she worked as senior assistant minister at St. Barnabas Anglican Church, Broadway, also in Sydney. She founded Common Grace's Domestic and Family Violence Justice team and was a creator and author of their SAFER Domestic and Family Violence resource for churches (www.saferresource.org.au) as well as *Renew: An Australian Guide for Christian Women Survivors of Domestic Abuse*.

Rev. Dr. Megan Powell du Toit is an ordained Baptist minister in Sydney, Australia. She has worked as a pastor, academic, and editor. Her doctoral research focused on tensions within evangelicalism. She is a senior pastor at a Baptist church and co-director of the WADR Project, co-hosting its podcast, *With All Due Respect*, as well as editing its online platform, WADR Online.

Associate Professor Laura Rademaker is an historian at the Australian National University, Canberra, with research interests in Christian missions, gender, race, and religion and the author of numerous prize-winning books. Her husband, Phil Rademaker, is rector of Christ Church Anglican in Belconnen, Canberra.

Dr. David C. Ray is a university scholar at the University of Divinity, St. Francis College, Brisbane, researching the Writings in the Hebrew Bible. He is married to Rev. Suzie Ray, rector of St. James Anglican Church, Sanderson, and ministers under her leadership.

Dr. Jacqueline Service is director of St. Mark's National Theological Centre, Canberra, and senior lecturer in systematic theology at Charles Sturt University, Australia. She holds postgraduate degrees in law and theology, with a PhD specialising in Trinitarian theology. She is the author of *Triune Wellbeing: The Kenotic Enrichment of the Eternal Trinity* (Fortress Academic).

# Foreword

## Aimee Byrd

I'm not Australian. I am not a leader in my church. And, I have no formal theological education. Yet I was asked to write the foreword to this book. I have found myself in this kind of situation numerous times, wondering what I can possibly have to contribute. Unlike many of the authors, I have never aspired to church leadership. My story is one of much disillusionment with the church. And yet, I represent a significant kind of person this book will serve.

I came to church as a young married woman with the assumption that my eagerness to learn about God would be met with encouragement and investment. I wanted to figure out how what is true about God affects the way I live in the everyday life as a wife, mom, and neighbour. And that was exciting. I embraced what was taught as "biblical manhood and womanhood" because being a biblical woman sounded like a godly goal. And yet, it was a lonely station as a thinking woman in the church. I was appreciated as I served in the nursery and made the casseroles, but I was not invited into the creative, intellectual, and theological life of the church. The avenue for that was nowhere to be found. How I longed for some kind of investment and stimulation!

That's how I became an author. Certainly, there had to be other women out there like me. And if not, I wanted to encourage women in the church that theology was for us as well as the men. Through my writing, I found the women. And at first, I received a lot of encouragement from leadership in my denomination and those adjacent to it in its theology. Invitations started coming in for me to speak at women's retreats and conferences.

I thought I found what I was longing for—like-minded women to learn and discuss the faith. But we all realised something. We were siloed—side-armed into the evangelical space for women's ministries. The books marketed to us were full of error. And we were not expected to commingle in the heart of biblical teaching and theological discussion with the men. So I began researching and writing books about investing in women, friendship between the sexes and ancient siblingship, the use of the woman's voice in Scripture, Trinitarian orthodoxy, and anthropology. To make a long and convoluted story short, this got me into a lot of trouble. I began to be harassed online by leaders in my denomination. They were also calling ahead of my speaking engagements to warn churches to guard their families from this dangerous woman (me) and plotting ways to sabotage my Amazon page. Suddenly, I saw pastors and elders calling me things online like "the great whore of Babylon" and saying I should shut up and make them a sammich. I was merely writing about men and women's great honour and responsibilities as disciples. Perhaps I was such a threat to these leaders' system of church leadership because I spoke as an informed and curious lay person. I wasn't trying to become a pastor, but merely asking the question about the agency and gift of women in the church as disciples.

And this is why the teaching in *God's Yes to Women: Why the Bible's Vision of Partnership Is Good News for Us All* is so important. The issue isn't only about women in church leadership and academia, as important as that is. It is about seeing women as gift. It is about being able to walk in the doors of our churches as our full selves. It is about how God sees us and how we are to see one another. What was made plain to me through the disillusionment I went through in my evangelical culture is that when we talk about partners in the gospel, we are talking about both the leadership and the laity. The reason why so many leaders were up in arms about my work as a lay disciple was because of the implications: it closed the gap and built a bridge between the laity and the leadership of the church—men and women co-labouring together, shoulder to shoulder.

I was labelled a troublemaker. At first, I tried to explain. I wore that marker of shame. As I began to visit other churches, I was afraid that the pastor there would google my name and become worried that a troublemaker was attending their church. Eventually, I attended my first church with a woman pastor. I met her for coffee and told her my story. She listened and had empathy for me. As we left, I thanked her for listening and shared my fear of pastors thinking I was a troublemaker, saying, "And no one wants to be a troublemaker." Do you know what she said? "Let me know when you do!"

This pastor completely changed the word around for me. My accusers were right! The implications of my work were huge! But it was a good kind a trouble I was making. In this book, you will become acquainted with numerous women from the Scriptures who were also good troublemakers. We need to learn of their impact with humility and gratitude. One shouldn't set out to cause trouble, but sometimes we need to reveal that the norms we are accepting and living are indeed troublesome.

The gift of this book is the blending of personal stories with biblical studies, church history, and theology. These teachings are not merely intellectual; they affect our everyday lives. And there are big life questions wrapped around where we land on women's agency in the church:

- How is the Bible to be read and interpreted?
- Is leadership masculine?
- How does a woman discern the call of God? Is that mediated by a man?
- What does a woman teaching represent?
- Are men and women merely interchangeable?
- Who do we need permission from to show up as our full selves?

Many do not approach studies on women in the church with good faith because they know it may cost them something: friends, their job, a certain level of privilege, reputation. It may cause some trouble in your life. What if you read this book with curiosity and an open mind because you are beginning to sense how much this matters? Are you ready to see something much more beautiful for God's church? Then I invite you—I dare you—to keep reading.

# Acknowledgements

THIS BOOK COULD NOT have happened without our incredible contributors. It has been a joy to work with such smart, generous, and faithful people, who have given so much for God's church. We know that participating in this project came with personal risk for some, so we are all the more grateful for those who said yes to join us in this work.

This project also could not have happened without a team of readers and advisers. We received thoughtful advice from many people holding a diversity of views, some of whom read many iterations of drafts to help us get it just right. Scott Goode provided detailed advice on some of the more contested passages of Scripture. Andrew Cameron was invaluable for his guidance on how to frame the project. We also thank Kris Argall, Kai Boylan, Honoria Brennan, Geoff Broughton, Aden Cotterill, Catherine Earp, Annemieke Earp, Bonnie Giles, Laurel Moffatt, Christine Murdoch, David Neville, Michelle Philp, Danika Pullar, Philip Rademaker, Fiona Reid, Sue Rice, Victoria Wilkins, Erin Williams, Ellie Shaw, Nathanael Thierry, and the women of the Evangelical Women in Academia Conference of 2025. We are indebted to you for your wise counsel and constant encouragement.

Rachael Bahl, the library manager from St. Mark's National Theological Centre, provided invaluable assistance with some of the research and referencing.

We are thankful to our families and loved ones.

Finally, we are grateful to all those who have prayed for us and for this book. Without prayer, we could do nothing.

# Introduction

## *Even Better News*

Laura Rademaker

*In the Lord, woman is not independent of man, nor is man independent of woman.*

1 Corinthians 11:11

I was going to be a pastor when I grew up.

I was eleven, I was brimming with ideas and idealism about my suburban Sydney church, how we might reach our community with Jesus. I loved the Bible. I ditched Sunday School for the main service at church; I wanted to hear the sermon. I poured over the Koorong catalogue. Christian books beside my parents' bed were pilfered to my room. I was good at public speaking, too, which, as far as I could see, was the main thing pastors did. I felt made for ministry.

I had never seen a woman lead a church, but I assumed this was for the same reason I had never seen a female prime minister. By the time I was a grown up, the whole gender-equality problem would be fixed, I believed. It was the nineties. We were optimistic then.

It came as a shock to discover that this was not the case.

I was twelve when I learned it wasn't just a matter of time until women led churches. The reason I had never seen a woman preach or lead a church was because it wasn't allowed. This was not good news. I found 1 Tim 2:12: "I do not permit a woman to teach or to presume authority over a man, she must be silent." For the first time, I wrestled with Scripture. Could this really mean it would be wrong for me to preach? And is this the main thing the Bible has to say to me, a girl?

Fast forward eleven years and I was still mulling over ministry. We were at Tilley's Devine Café on Canberra's north side. I had just finished a degree at the Australian National University and was meeting with a mentor from my church with a question: do I pursue a PhD in secular academia, or should I begin a ministry apprenticeship, a track that might lead to Bible college and Christian ministry?

"You're smart," she told me, "you could make it as an academic."

I was flattered. *She thinks I'm smart!*

But we both knew the subtext. Put bluntly, any teaching gifts I might have would be wasted in Christian ministry.

That was not the advice my church was giving to bright young Christian men at the time. I know this because my soon-to-be husband was one of them. He had a perfectly good graduate job when our church leaders tapped him on the shoulder and asked him to consider a ministry apprenticeship instead. He would be supported, mentored, encouraged. After all, the harvest is plentiful, and the workers are few.

Today I'm an academic—a historian—and a pastor's wife. My husband is an Anglican minister in a suburban Canberra church. I'm a regular preacher there, and I volunteer a fair bit, but I've got a day job at a university.

I don't blame my mentor for the advice she gave me. It was wisdom for the circumstances. She believed that there was something about the way God made us that meant that it was not right for women to teach men the Bible. Nor should a woman be making decisions at church. If married, she should respect her husband as leader of the home. She should submit.

This meant, if I were to go into ministry, I would teach women. I would provide pastoral care, but any preaching or ministry of the word—the very things I was most passionate about—would be limited to children or rare contexts where it was only women in the room. It wasn't clear how ministry could be a viable job for a woman like me. Although the women in ministry I knew at the time *were* smart, I could also see how they downplayed and even hid their gifting as leaders and teachers.

They made themselves smaller to make room for the men. I didn't think I could follow.

These teachings about gender always jarred. They clashed with everything else I knew and loved about God and the gospel. What of the dignity Jesus gave to women, the first witnesses to his incarnation and resurrection? What of the abundant gifts of the Holy Spirit, poured out on women and men alike? What of the power of the cross to do away with hostility, hierarchy, and exclusion—not only when it came to Jews and Gentiles—but also men and women? What of the upside-down kingdom of Jesus, where the first are last and the last are first? How could the exclusion of women from particular ministries fit with any of this? And what was it about how God made women that meant they were unsuited to teach or lead men anyway?

I didn't know.

But I had read a handful of passages in the New Testament. I wanted to be faithful to what I was told that the Bible "plainly" taught, even though it was never "plain" to me. Nearly every Christian leader I knew held that these gender distinctions were God's will. It felt inescapable.

This is the book I wish I'd had then.

What my churches taught is a theology developed in the late 1980s known as complementarianism. Complementarianism is a position often contrasted with egalitarianism. These labels aren't great. We don't find them particularly helpful (for an explainer of how they're used, skip forward to the FAQs chapter by Erica Mandi Manga). We don't use the egalitarian label because we don't think equality is the main idea the Bible uses to capture the relationship between men and women. What we see in the Bible are ideas like *partnership, interdependence, oneness in Christ* (especially in our differences), but most of all, *love*.

It's been a while since complementarians and egalitarians have talked to each other. When the Anglican church was debating women's ordination as priests[1] (a move that would allow them to be senior ministers) in the 1980s and 1990s, I didn't participate. That was because I was too busy finger-painting and playing in the sandpit: I was in preschool.

My hometown of Sydney turned out to be one of the few Anglican dioceses in Australia that chose not to ordain women as priests. It's a

1. In Sydney, Anglican priests are more often referred to as presbyters.

powerhouse of Australian evangelicalism, training Anglican clergy for Sydney and beyond, but also missionaries, youth and university student workers, and many who go into other denominations and para-church ministries.

I'm a product of Sydney Anglicanism. I was baptised a baby Sydney Anglican in the late 1980s, just as complementarianism was becoming a "thing." I went to Anglican churches, an Anglican school, and attended Anglican conferences. We even holidayed with other Sydney Anglicans. I am indebted to all those who pastored me, especially for their love of Scripture and their passion for introducing people to Jesus. But I never heard another view.

Soon after that conversation with my mentor in Canberra, I married my husband. We tried out the gender roles we thought God required of us. But they didn't fit. Why should he make the final decisions when we work better as equal partners? Neither of us knew. We felt clumsy and encumbered, as if we were pretending to be someone else.

A couple of years later my husband began theological study in Sydney. His enrolment came with a library card. This was where I found books that helped me see that what I had been taught was mistaken. My husband, too, reached the conclusion that being a good husband is about exercising sacrificial love, not authority, and that the gifts of the Holy Spirit determine ministry, not gender. I had been told that Christians with different views on gender either hadn't read the Bible or had chosen to ignore it. This, I found, was simply untrue.

The books I encountered challenged me to be *more* thoroughly biblical in the way I thought about gender, not less. What surprised me most was that it was the very principles of how to understand the Bible that my husband was learning—especially the principles of biblical theology—that led me to different conclusions about what the Bible says about gender. These are principles such as:

- Using a biblical theology or narrative approach to the Bible. That is, when you come to a passage, you need to know where you are in the overarching story of the Bible and God's unfolding plan to save us through Jesus.
- Using a Jesus-focused interpretation of the Bible where his death on the cross and rising to life are what make the difference for us.

- Using the clearest teachings of the Bible to help us understand the less-than-straightforward bits.
- Appreciating the ways the Bible was written for us, but not directly to us. We need to understand its meaning for its original hearers before we can work out what it means for us.

I found a message that was better than I had ever heard: freedom and hope for women, and of true partnership and reconciliation with men, because of what Jesus has done at the cross.

Today it's my daughters who are playing in the sandpit; a whole generation has passed since the debates of the eighties and nineties. We are witnessing new challenges for churches that are constantly confronted with hard questions about gender, power, and abuse. It's time we learned to have better conversations about gender and the gospel.

So, in this book, we've gathered some of the best and brightest Bible nerds and pastors Australia has. These are faithful people who love Jesus and his word. Although there are a lot of academics on our list, it isn't written for academics. It you're after something more like that, we'll point you to scholarly resources in the footnotes. We hope this book might be your starting point for more exploration and learning.

There are lots of good reasons to support women ministering in all kinds of ways, according to their gifts. For some, it's a matter of justice: they've seen women wronged and excluded and want to put this right. For others, it's a matter of the health of the church: they're concerned that the church is hampered without women's full service. Some are worried about our witness to the world: it's hard to hear good news from a church that can be dismissed as sexist. These are all important concerns, and I share them.

But for me, and for the contributors to this book, one fundamental reason undergirds all of these:

It's biblical.

We're convinced that the Bible's vision is of women and men working together as servants of Jesus, as equal partners, without hierarchy or exclusion, and that this is *good news for women and men*: ultimately for everyone. We don't think men and women are the same, or interchangeable. Quite the opposite. It is *because* we are differently embodied and encultured—gender touches all of us—that *true partnership* is all the more necessary and beautiful.

This is a book about Christian ministry, especially ministries of teaching and leading. Of course, there are all kinds of other important ministries that women do. We don't want to diminish these. But nor do we consider the valuable work women do in other capacities any reason to exclude them from ministries of leading and teaching. These are the ministries where we see women most likely to be excluded, so they are our focus. We'll touch on other issues to do with gender, including marriage and singleness, but the book is not mainly about these. Nor are we going to address every verse in the Bible about gender and ministry, or all the many gifts and ministries of women. It's more of a "taste and see" situation.

The book is in two main parts. The first is a deep dive into the Bible's story with a focus on how this story touches on women in particular. We start in Genesis, move through the Old Testament, and arrive at Jesus, the gift of his Spirit, and the hope that we have through him. Spoiler: this story is good news for women (and actually for all of us). The second section is a collection of stories and testimonies about *how* people have lived this out on the ground, in the face of real-world challenges, and seen the Bible's vision bear fruit. We finish with frequently asked questions about complementarianism, egalitarianism, and women's ministries—we hope this will be a useful reference—followed by a pastoral note for women considering they might serve in ministry. Our prayer is that the chapters of this book might lead you to see that the Bible's invitation to women, men, indeed the whole church is even better than you thought, because the gospel of Jesus is more wonderful than we might imagine.

# Part 1

# Reading the Story of the Bible

# Reading the Bible as God's Over-Arching Story

Amy J. Erickson

I grew up in a Presbyterian church in the United States that fully supported women in ministry. I saw female pastors and preachers at the pulpit from a young age. At eighteen I was recruited to preach a sermon for our annual Youth Sunday. But I was aware of other perspectives. I wrestled with certain odd passages in Scripture, so much so that I considered myself a complementarian for a brief time.

I studied theology at a small Christian university where I became reconvinced that the Bible's witness is a resounding yes to women. But I continued to respect that other faithful, thoughtful Christians read Scripture differently. After a move to Scotland to continue study, I chose to worship with a church who did not permit female preachers or ordained leadership. I wanted to practise relinquishing my own sense of gospel freedom in deference to the convictions of others in my family of faith, and as a sign that our unity was not grounded on a uniform interpretation of Scripture but on a shared faith in the Christ to whom Scripture points, and who holds us in his truth despite our differing perspectives.

That respect for my brothers and sisters in Christ who hold different convictions remains. And yet my concern for the danger of their position has only grown. To be clear, that concern does not arise from their intent. For these siblings in the faith, the stakes are high: allowing female leaders and preachers amounts to sheer rebellion against God's design. Their conviction arises from a desire for faithfulness which I also share. Yet that faithfulness relies on a certain conception of what God's design is. There are profound costs if this design has been misunderstood.

At the end of this chapter I will outline some of these costs. But first, I want to show why there is ample biblical evidence that they are unnecessary. The symphonic theme that resounds throughout Scripture is of *unity in diversity*, of God uniting himself to humanity and the thrumming variety of all his creation. A beautiful microcosm of God's desire for union with all things is the manner that men and women image and labour for him *together*. The nature of the "togetherness" by which men and women both reflect and serve God matters. It is an organic byproduct of the gospel story by which they seek to be transformed.

To tune into this story we need to turn to Scripture. But we don't just need to turn to Scripture. We need to examine *how* we approach Scripture. How we approach it will determine how we interpret it, and how we interpret it will determine how we live. So before we turn to Scripture, we need to consider how we read.

## How to Read (and Not Read) the Bible

We live in an information age that loves to collect and plot data points for analysis and optimisation. It's an impulse that serves us well when we are seeking the most effective medical interventions or developing the best public policy on a complex issue. But when it comes to reading and studying the Bible, this posture does not always help.

Reading Scripture like a dataset—instead of as a unified story of God's plans for humanity which culminate in Jesus—often supports interpretations that exclude women from certain activities and spheres in Christ's body. In this chapter I'm going to refer to these kinds of interpretations, which maintain that there are some roles or actions in the church's life which should be taken on only by men, as "male-only interpretations."

What I hope to show is how the beautiful arch of God's story leaves no room for these interpretations. To quote Graeme Goldsworthy, "grasp[ing] the unity of the Bible, of its one overall message from Genesis to Revelation, is necessary for a right understanding of the meaning of any individual text."[1] If we read the Bible like this, we see that one of the patterns through which God showcases his own reconciliation with humanity is the reconciliation and mutual labour of men and women, brought together into a single body under one head: Jesus Christ.

1. Goldsworthy, preface of *According to Plan*.

But what do I mean when I say that today we often tend to read Scripture like a dataset instead of as this unifying story? The thing about data points is that they're linear. They form lines when plotted against x and y axes defined by certain criteria. If we treat Scripture like a dataset, we'll reduce it to a collection of data points to be searched for select variables to generate lines of interpretation that will bypass significant portions of Scripture from consideration. There are obvious verses that are flagged when we search them for the controlling variables "women" and "speaking" or "teaching."

One is 1 Cor 14:34, which reads:

> Women should remain silent in the churches. They are not allowed to speak, but must be in submission, as the law says.

Another is 1 Tim 2:12:

> I do not permit a woman to teach or to assume authority over a man; she must be quiet.

You only need two data points to form a line. Our job is done: two verses clearly ban women from roles that entail speaking or teaching in church.

But Scripture is not a dataset to be plotted. It is more like a building to inhabit. It has the architecture of a story bracing and sturdy enough for us to make a home in with our very lives. And its cornerstone is Jesus Christ (Matt 21:42). Goldsworthy explains it this way: as Christians, we should always interpret the Bible, not as isolated pieces of data, but in view of the whole story of what Jesus has done:

> Jesus Christ in his life, death and resurrection is the fixed point of reference for the understanding of the whole of reality. We must apply this fact to our doing of biblical theology. The gospel is the fixed point of reference for understanding the meaning of the whole range of biblical revelation.[2]

In keeping with Goldsworthy here, when I say that we should interpret Scripture less like a dataset to graph and more like a building to inhabit, I mean that we should avoid reading it two-dimensionally and aim to read it three-dimensionally. When we read parts of the Bible we also need to keep in mind its whole driving plotline, remaining sensitive to its theologically significant structural features. If you're trying to appreciate a cathedral but get drawn into only examining the brickwork, you'll miss

2. Goldsworthy, *According to Plan*, 60.

the overall effect. That's not to say that paying attention to the details of Scripture isn't important. Subsequent chapters in this volume will do just that, including chapters that will address the two critical verses above. But individual verses must be examined in their context. My focus is on getting a grasp of the main architecture of the Bible, so that any part of it is situated in the light of its whole and in light of the gospel.

So let's consider together the full story of the Bible in relation to the place of women in God's work to save all humanity. The story that unfolds is a gripping tale about the unrestricted and surprising ways that God's Spirit moves through both women and men. Together, they proclaim the good news of the reconciling grace that comes only through Jesus Christ.

## Women in the Whole Story of Salvation

To examine the architecture of the biblical story, we should start at the beginning. If you want to explore a building, you need to get through the front door. So the first book of the Bible, Genesis, is a natural starting place.

In Gen 1 we are told that men and women image God together (Gen 1:27). Their tasks aren't differentiated by their gender. Instead, their mission is the same: both are instructed to be fruitful and to rule over the earth (Gen 1:28). Some people claim that the fact that man was created first in Gen 2 means that men should take on the mantle of leadership. However, chronology doesn't necessarily denote authority.[3] If anything, God favours the second-born when cultural norms would privilege the first (Isaac over Ishmael, Jacob over Esau, Ephraim over Manasseh).[4]

When both Adam and Eve rebel against God, male domination is identified as a *negative* consequence of their sin. Men ruling women departs from the original goodness of their created relationship (Gen 3:16). Again, the opening chapters of Scripture make it clear that male domination of women is *not* God's original design for humanity. Instead, it is a negative outcome of human rebellion. This is a key architectural feature of the Bible that male-only readings often overlook. *Male dominance—and*

3. In fact, some read Eve as the pinnacle of creation. This explains why the man is instructed to leave his parents and cling to his wife (Gen 2:24). See Brock, *Joining Creation's Praise*, 543.

4. Adam (the "human" in Hebrew) functions for Paul as a representative of all humanity (1 Cor 15:22). Some may appeal to 1 Cor 11:3, but Paul's discussion of the "head" is conditioned by his statement that men and women are *interdependent* (1 Cor 11:11–12).

*the female deference to this dominance—is a feature of our fallen condition which is undone in Christ.*

We get a hint of that undoing right here in the opening pages of Scripture. God tells the serpent, with Eve in earshot, of his ultimate plan: "I will put enmity between you and the woman, and between your offspring and hers; he will crush your head, and you will strike his heel" (Gen 3:15). Throughout the Old Testament, we get glimmers like this that foreshadow Jesus's ultimate redemption, including how he will repair and restore the relationship between men and women. In the meantime, God's people wait in hope for the One who fulfills this promise. As they wait, women like Deborah, Ruth, Esther, and the prophet Huldah bear witness to the place of female initiative in God's redemptive purposes, even as they work against the grain of the patriarchal conditions that were set by the fall.

When that promised Saviour arrives, a key aspect of his work is the undoing of male domination of women that came from the fall. Jesus's life, death, and resurrection are the key that unlock the whole Bible. Let's examine each in relation to women.

## Women in Jesus's Life, Death, and Resurrection

At the start of Jesus's human life we are struck with the immense role of a woman. The Bible is at pains to stress that "when the set time had fully come, God sent his Son, *born of a woman*, born under the law" (Gal 4:4). God could have done otherwise. God did not have to be born. God could have shown up on scene as a full-grown male. But God decided to go through the whole gamut of human development and existence, including full gestation *in utero*.

There is something else remarkable. God not only decides to rely on a woman, he even actively elects *not* to use any contribution from a man. Scripture stresses that Jesus is born of a *virgin* woman, Mary. Jesus has a human mother, but no earthly father. Theologically, this is important. Because Jesus has no earthly father, through him we can be adopted directly into God's family, with God as our Father (John 1:13; Gal 4:4).

Neither should we miss this astounding fact: a woman literally bears the Word Incarnate, God himself, in flesh (Luke 1:35). This is a profound endorsement of God's resounding trust in women to handle not just the word of Scripture, but the Word himself.

The significant role of women does not end at his conception and birth. It continues in his ministry. Jesus consistently elevates women, who directly receive (Luke 10:39), follow (Luke 8:2), finance (Luke 8:3), and share (John 4:39) the word of his gospel without any male oversight or mediation. Jesus's engagement with women is revolutionary and culture shattering (John 4:1–27). His interaction with Mary and Martha tells us in no uncertain terms that a woman's primary place is as a theology student, a disciple at the feet of her rabbi, over and above any domestic obligations and in the face of cultural expectations (Luke 10:38–42).

That Jesus's ministry brought good news directly to women is seen most dramatically at his death. At the very moment that Jesus died, the curtain of the inner sanctuary of the temple was torn in two (Matt 27:5). At that time in history, the Jewish temple complex was comprised of concentric areas known as the Court of Gentiles and the Court of Women. Gentiles were not allowed past the Court of the Gentiles, and women were not allowed past the Court of Women.[5] Only Jewish men were permitted in the area immediately around the holy of holies, and only one Jewish male—the high priest—was allowed inside, and this just once a year (Lev 16). By tearing open the inner curtain, Jesus erupts the holy of holies to flood God's presence onto all people, who now only require *his* mediation. As a consequence, there need no longer remain "male-only" domains of the life of God's people any more than there are "Jew-only" ones (Gal 3:28; Eph 2:14–18). Some may contend that this only signifies that women are saved in Christ and does not mean much practical difference for the life of God's people. But this denies the real social impact that the reality of the gospel should and does have on our life and relationships with one another.

This is why in Gal 3:28 Paul states that "there is neither Jew nor Gentile, neither slave nor free, nor is there male and female, for you are all one in Christ Jesus." In Galatia, the Jewish Christians were excluding Gentile Christians, looking down on them and not eating with them. Paul corrects them, teaching that there can be no second-class Christians because we are all saved by faith in Jesus. The old hierarchies have been overcome. A crucial point of Paul's letter to the Galatians is that our relationships with each other must reflect that unity. And just as it does for Jews and Gentiles, Jesus's death also breaks down hostility between men and women, forging one new humanity from the two. Now the only

5. See Eph 2:14, which makes direct reference to this boundary between Jews and Gentiles. See also Bailey, *Jesus*, 250.

qualification for full participation in God's people and their ministries is not gender or race; it's faith in the mediating work of Jesus Christ.

That brings us to one final, critical aspect of that mediating work of Jesus: his resurrection. Just as with his birth, life, and death, we cannot escape the profound role of women. It is not his male disciples who are recorded as witnesses to his resurrection, as would have been expected in a culture where women were considered unreliable sources of evidence. Instead, surprisingly, Scripture insists that it was Jesus's female disciples who first bear witness to the resurrection (Matt 28:8; Luke 24:9–10).[6]

Jesus's resurrection garden scene is a redo of the disastrous garden scene in Eden. John's opening line to this scene echoes the opening chapters of Genesis, hinting that we should read this as a moment of re-creation (John 20:1). And get this: the very first recorded word out of the resurrected Jesus's mouth is "woman" (John 20:13). The woman to whom he was speaking, Mary, is then sent directly by Jesus to proclaim the best news to the disciples—"*He is Risen*"—for the very first time. Because *apostle* just means "sent" in Greek, and given that Mary Magdalene was the first one "sent" to proclaim the news, there is a long-standing tradition in the church of giving her the title *Apostle to the Apostles*.

Let's marvel here at the monumental place of women in Jesus's life and work, from the virgin Mary to Mary Magdalene. It is women who ultimately bear the good news of the risen Jesus, from which derive all sermons and evangelical ministry. All gospel messages, every true sermon or work of ministry, depend on the Incarnate Christ who did not shun a woman's womb and point to the resurrected Christ who was not ashamed to send a woman to first proclaim his victory over death to his male disciples. Women were the first to teach these truths to men. The story of Scripture is a resounding testimony to the qualification of women to handle and convey the deepest truths of Scripture and of God's reconciling work.

6. These two facts overcome suggestions that only men should teach and lead because Adam should have told Eve about the command not to eat from the tree of life (Gen 2:16). If God's speech failed to come through a man at his creation, it has now resounded through women at his re-creation. In fact, we may read 1 Cor 14:36 as a warning to early Christian women not to get too smug about their starring role in the drama of redemption.

## Women in the New Testament Church

Christ's reconciling work continues in the New Testament, which consistently depicts women and men ministering together. In 1 Cor 12, Paul gives his most robust account of spiritual giftings and identifies specific roles, including apostles, prophets, and teachers. Nowhere in this letter does he indicate that either these giftings or roles are distributed by gender, even when he does give instructions specifically relating to gender (which we'll consider more closely in another chapter). This is consistent with what we find elsewhere in the Bible. Old Testament prophecy fulfilled at Pentecost specifies that God's Spirit is unleashed on all his people, men and women (Joel 2:28; Acts 2:17). If gender discrimination were crucial to the organisation of the church and obedience to God, we would be right to expect to receive such instruction here.

But instead, there are direct New Testament examples of women filling the role of prophets in Philip's seven daughters (Acts 21:9), and also of apostle in Junia (Rom 16:7), to say nothing of Mary Magdalene serving as an apostle to the apostles.[7] There is also the New Testament's cumulative evidence of women in active roles: the deacon Phoebe (Rom 16:1), Nympha and her house church (Col 4:15), and Priscilla's instructing Apollos (Acts 18:26). Phoebe is not only identified as a deacon but was tasked with delivering the book of Romans (Rom 16:1). As its courier, she also likely had the authority to act as its first interpreter.[8] There is also reason to believe that John's second letter is addressed to the female leader of a house church.[9] Women were so active in the early church that when Paul was still persecuting it, he found it strategic and necessary to target women as well as men (Acts 8:3).[10]

Each of these instances may be protested. *"Phoebe simply indicates that women can be deacons, but not elders"; "Nympha was only hosting the church at her house, not leading it"; "Priscilla instructed Apollos under Aquila's headship."* And so on. But here's the problem with these arguments: they presume that they are protecting a clear male-only account

7. For evidence that Junia was a female apostle, see Sprinkle, *From Genesis to Junia*, 138–48.

8. McKnight, *Blue Parakeet*, 200–202.

9. McKnight, "Elect Lady." While some argue that the "elect lady" references the church itself, this does not account for the way in which the "elect lady" is distinguished from "her children" (2 John 1). Moreover, she is addressed in the same manner that John greets Gaius, to whom he writes 3 John.

10. Wright, "Women's Service."

found elsewhere in Scripture. There isn't one. These arguments are also pregnant with the risk that by limiting women's activity, we also hinder the capacity of one half of Christ's body to gift the church with the very offerings that they are commanded to bring (Rom 12:6–8; 1 Cor 14:26). What is more, if we read the New Testament as requiring male-only leadership, then it will be essential to determine different forms of ministry and leadership in order to assign only the latter to men. But the New Testament does not seem overly concerned with distinguishing leadership from other ministries. Paul—and Scripture as a whole—is vastly less concerned about leading than with serving (Matt 23:8–10), about what belongs to men and what belongs to women (1 Cor 11:12) than with *unity in difference* (John 17:21; Rom 12:5; 1 Cor 12:12–26).

In other words, the Bible doesn't directly lead to the assumption that ministries of leading and teaching are only for men. But more than that, such an assumption resists the redemptive story of Scripture, the trajectory of Jesus's ministry, and the New Testament portrait of the life of the early church. The thrust of the story of the Bible is one of reconciliation of both men and women, with God and with each other, and of ministry together, *in Christ*. Male-only readings are against the grain of Scripture. They also persist with enormous cost to the church's ongoing witness to the gospel.

## Theological Concerns with Male-Only Readings

First, they encroach on Jesus's role as the only mediator between humanity and God. Jesus's work on the cross destroyed the layers of separations that humans put up between one another and God. Christ is the unrestrained access to God's presence for all humans, without mediating structures like temples and their patriarchal priestly systems. The problem with male-only readings is that they effectively reinstate the Court of Men, setting up a priestly caste of male leaders and teachers as necessary to mediate between God and women, even if they don't always call themselves priests. In making women dependent on men, they trespass on territory that has been claimed solely by Christ.

The second concern I have with male-only readings relates to the mutual service to which the Bible invites us. What male-only readings often fail to account for is the profound cost to the body of Christ (i.e., the church) by depriving us of the gifts that we are commanded to bring to one another, to build one another up and to witness to the gospel. Male-only readings fail to give sufficient exegetical evidence to merit disqualifying half the church from roles and actions of mutual service and ministry, especially when the harvest is plentiful and the workers perennially few. There is not only the cost of disabling the body, but of the wasted energy diverted into endless debates deliberating what, exactly, women can and can't do. That is to say nothing of the psychological toll these debates place on women and girls simply wishing to serve their Lord, but rendered unsure of what offerings, under what conditions, they are "allowed" to bring.

Some may protest that, even though women are free—scripturally speaking—to lead or preach or offer their gifts, women should exercise restraint out of deference to the conscience of another sister or brother in Christ for whom this is a scandal. There are certainly grounds—even commands—to refrain from exercising one's freedom for the sake of one another (Rom 14:15). But the biblical examples are of an individual bearing the cost of the others' conscience in their own self. To extend this to the matter of women's giftings for the church is to require the entire body to be deprived. And this is to say nothing of the cost of our gospel witness to a watching world desperate for winsome examples of men and women working together in reconciled relations. Can these costs be justified by the available biblical evidence?

My final concern with male-only readings is that what they ultimately deny is not the freedom of women, but the freedom of God. Male-only readings constrain the movement of God's Spirit through women in a manner that flatly denies the biblical witness. These readings say effectively, "God would never—or should never—move through women in *this* way—or at least, not under *these* conditions, or not with *this* audience, or not with *this* title, or not through *these* particular actions." But such assumptions deny a biblical understanding of the Spirit of God, who blows where *he* wills, (John 3:8) and who appoints whatever mouthpiece *he* ordains, just as we see in figures like Deborah, Huldah, or Mary, to name but a few. Some might counter that these women are exceptions to God's normal pattern. But what is taken to be a normal pattern is constructed not from the load-bearing plotlines but instead from the brickwork; from isolated verses treated as data points that can be extracted and removed from their whole.

What *is* the ideal pattern for human relations? There are a number of social configurations that Scripture rejects. One is uniformity (see the story of Babel). Another is division ("I hate divorce," God says). Another is authoritarianism ("The son of Man came not to be served, but to serve"). When it comes to the genders, the Bible's vision is neither interchangeability, nor segregation, nor delegated hierarchy. Instead, the Bible casts a vision of unity in diversity, of reconciled men and women serving together—just as it was at the beginning.

## Bibliography

Bailey, Kenneth E. *Jesus Through Middle Eastern Eyes: Cultural Studies in the Gospels.* Downers Grove, IL: IVP Academic, 2008.

Balfour, Alan. *Solomon's Temple: Myth, Conflict, and Faith.* Malden, MA: Wiley-Blackwell, 2015.

Brock, Brian. *Joining Creation's Praise: A Theological Ethic of Creatureliness.* Grand Rapids: Baker Academic, 2025.

Goldsworthy, Graeme. *According to Plan: The Unfolding Revelation of God in the Bible.* Nottingham, UK: Inter-Varsity, 1991.

McKnight, Scot. *The Blue Parakeet: Rethinking How You Read the Bible.* 2nd ed. Grand Rapids: Zondervan, 2010.

———. "That Elect Lady." Jesus Creed on Patheos, last updated March 13, 2015. http://www.patheos.com/blogs/jesuscreed/2014/09/18/that-elect-lady/.

Sprinkle, Preston. *From Genesis to Junia: An Honest Search for What the Bible Really Says About Women in Leadership.* Colorado Springs: Cook, 2026.

Wright, N. T. "Women's Service in the Church: The Biblical Basis." Paper presented for the symposium "Men, Women and the Church," St. John's College, Durham, UK, September 4, 2004. http://ntwrightpage.com/2016/07/12/womens-service-in-the-church-the-biblical-basis/.

# Partnership from Page One

PAUL A. BARKER

GOD MADE MEN AND women to be different. But created differently does not require a difference in hierarchy or spiritual leadership.

The first chapters of the Bible—Gen 1–3—are foundational for so much of the Bible, not least in what they declare about the sovereign and sole God of the universe. They show us God's original good and perfect intentions and, so succinctly, humanity's catastrophic fall. The rest of the Bible's trajectory goes on to tell of the redemption and reconciliation of all things, through Christ, and the culmination of a new heaven and earth. So, as we turn to Gen 1–3, with our particular focus on women and men in relationship and ministry, we need to be aware of what is God's good design, and what is part of our fallen world.

## Genesis 1:26–28—Made Equally in the Image of God

Many years ago, I lived opposite a vacant block of land. One day, machines arrived; the block was cleared and levelled. Then followed trenches, pipes, concrete, a wooden frame, roofing, windows and doors, and then internal fittings out of my sight. The pinnacle, though, and what it was all created for, was the arrival of my new neighbours, a family with two young children.

Likewise, the six days of creation in Gen 1 are the creation of a universe in preparation for the pinnacle, the creation of humanity, on the sixth day, in verses 26–28. It was all created for human beings.

That humanity is the pinnacle of creation is seen in the poetic way our creation is described. This is the only act of creation in which God reflects on what he will do: in verse 26, "Let us make humans . . ." The plural "us" is surprising. It implies loving relationship at the heart of God (see Jacqueline Service's chapter in this book) and is tied then to the importance of relationship among humanity.

Then, there are three poetic lines in verse 27:

> So God created mankind in his image,
> in the image of God he created them;
> male and female he created them.

Poetry slows the narration and therefore draws attention to itself and, in this instance, to the creation of humanity, over and above all other creation acts in the chapter. Only humanity is made in the image of God. The word *image* suggests a strong resemblance, the word *likeness* is more general. In verse 26 "likeness" eases the closeness of "image," so it is clear humanity is not also god. There has been long debate over what that image is precisely, but it seems most likely to indicate that inherent in humanity is a capacity to relate to God, morally, wisely, and righteously.

Flowing from this, as a consequence of being made in God's image, humanity is to rule over the creation, a point which immediately follows the first occurrence of "image" in verse 26 and is also in verse 28. So humanity represents God on earth. Note that it is both men and women together who are to rule over and indeed fill the earth (Gen 1:26–28). This is the only command with a sense of authority before the fall. We also should note that "rule" is not exploitative but is to be a reflection of God's good rule over the whole creation.

There is no indication of differentiation of role or function for men or women here. The third line of the poetic verse 27, which mentions male and female, is not so much to distinguish them as it is to be explicitly inclusive. Women are equally made in the image of God. In the first two lines of verse 27, a more generic word is used than the word "male" in the third line, more like *humans*. The NIV uses "mankind," some older translations have "man" in the first line and "him" in the second. But these lines are not limited to male humans. They apply to all humans. The third line makes that point also.

Genesis 1 makes no distinction in role or authority between male and female. Equally they are both fully made in the image of God, tasked together to rule for God in his creation.

## Genesis 2—Made Equally for Each Other

Genesis 2 is a second story of creation complementing Gen 1, which itself functions as a prologue for the whole of the book of Genesis. There is little reason to see these accounts as alternative or contradictory. They are addressing the creation from different but complementary angles.

The description in chapter 2 of the relationship of men and women continues the focus on their oneness and similarity. That the woman is made from the man's rib or "side" evokes their unity, as does the man's declaration in verse 23, "Bone of my bones and flesh of my flesh," and the "one flesh" statement about marriage in verse 24. There is an equality and unity—yet a similarity and not identical being—being highlighted here, a mutual kinship, with no sense of male superiority or authority.

The two, male and female, belong together equally and need each other. This is also suggested by the Hebrew words *ish* and *ishhah*, man and woman or "husband" and "wife." In Gen 1, *adam* is used for "human" (both male and female). But now, the similar words, *ish* and *ishhah* (from the same root word), and the bones, flesh, and "one flesh" language in verses 23–24, all indicate equality and belonging together.

This equality is also reflected in the language of a "suitable helper." By itself, the idea of a helper could indicate inferiority or being under authority. However, that is not the idea in Gen 2.

The word for "helper" is about matching the man, not being under his authority. This is underscored by the language of "corresponding to him." This last phrase makes it even clearer that correspondence, a partner or companion, is the key idea.

Indeed, in the Old Testament, the one described most often as helper is God, who frequently acts as helper for Israel. God is hardly subservient to Israel! God is in charge but takes initiative to serve Israel by doing what Israel could not do for itself. *Helper* often refers to a powerful figure, like God, who comes to help or save someone in trouble.

So, the woman is created here to help or save the needy man.[1] Nothing is said here about the woman's role as child bearer. She's simply the man's counterpart and is valued for herself alone. Those who base an argument for men having authority over women on this word *helper* are failing to grasp the language and its context.

The problem being solved by the creation of woman is the man's aloneness, not any need to be served or to exercise authority. So the

1. Bailey, *Paul Through Mediterranean Eyes*, 310.

helper, one fit for the man, is to match him equally as a companion, for company and with him for procreation, in order to fulfil the command of 1:28 to be fruitful and multiply as well as to have dominion together. That command is given to both male and female, equally and without distinction.

Naming sometimes demonstrates authority and, in 2:23, some interpret the man's words as naming the woman. After all, the man has named the living creatures earlier in chapter 2. That reflects the call in Gen 1 to rule over all the animals and living things.

But when it comes to naming Eve, that naming does not actually occur until 3:20, when the woman is given the name Eve. This takes place only after the sin and its punishment is given. It belongs, then, to a different era, one tainted by sin. In 2:23, rather than saying that she shall be called "female" because she was taken from "male," there is a poetic alliteration, *issha* from *ish*, woman from man. Hamilton suggests the possibility that "by using two words which sound alike the narrator wished to emphasise the identity and equality of the primal couple."[2] This verse is more a joyful delight in having someone fit for the man rather than a specific name denoting authority.

There is no call in Gen 1 for the man to have authority over the woman. It is the man and woman together in God's image who are to rule, or have dominion, over the living things. In Gen 2:23, the man rejoices in one to equal him, to be his fit companion so he is no longer alone. This is not an act of authority.

Calling her "woman" in 2:23 is poetic, a statement of joy and praise, of equality and belonging because she corresponds so perfectly to "man." There is no expression of delighting to have someone beneath him over whom he has authority. The delight is in mutual belonging, that she is flesh and bones of his flesh and bones.

What follows is quite surprising; the man leaves his family to cling to his wife, rather than his wife becoming part of his own family under him. This is not what you would expect in ancient patriarchal societies. If the man saw his wife as under his leadership, we might expect the woman to leave her family to join his. Verse 24 continues, therefore, the emphasis on equality and mutuality with no hint of subordination. The two become "one flesh," a sense of completeness and belonging together.

2. Hamilton, *Genesis 1–17*, 180.

Of course there is difference, deliberate and significant difference, between male and female humans, but Genesis does not include authority of one over the other as one of those differences.

Some assume that having been created first, the man has some leadership, if not also authority, over the woman. Andrew Reid says, without explanation, that man created first shows a particular ordering of existence which he calls "an ordained order of authority."[3] Claire Smith says that in Gen 2, the differences show there is an "order in the relationship" and that the man "has a responsibility of leadership" and she has a responsibility "to accept his leadership."[4]

This is reading too much into the text. Their argument depends on a particular understanding of Paul in 1 Timothy (dealt with later in this book). But Gen 2 itself does not make this point. Indeed, animals are created before humans in Gen 1, but that does not give them authority over humans! Some also suggest that since firstborn have greater rights in inheritance, so the creation order of man and then woman must suggest greater authority. However, inheritance rights of the firstborn are a completely different issue.

Genesis 1 and 2 describe the good and perfect world and creation. Together, the man and woman are naked and unashamed in 2:25. At the end of these chapters there is no sense of authority or leadership of the man over and above the woman.

## Genesis 3—The Sin

The prohibition about eating the fruit is given to the man in 2:16–17, before the creation of the woman in verse 22. Clearly the woman is aware of this prohibition when she is approached by the serpent in 3:1–5. However, it is not necessarily the case that the man told her of this command (which some suggest could be a sign of his authority over her). God himself may have told the woman separately—the text does not say either way.

Though not obvious in English, when the serpent addresses the woman, his "you" is plural (like the colloquial Australian *youse* or the American *y'all*); the serpent addresses both the man and the woman.

Her replies to the serpent are not fully accurate in comparison with the words of the Lord God in chapter 2. She leaves out the word *freely* in

3. Reid, *Genesis*, 43.
4. Smith, *God's Good Design*, 177.

3:2 and adds an additional prohibition against touching the fruit in 3:3. Both changes, though small, point toward a view of the Lord God as less than generous and more forbidding.

The blame for this cannot be apportioned. It could be that the woman has distorted God's words and is at fault. It could also be that if the man had indeed told her, that he got it wrong and is at fault. We simply don't know.

It is true that the serpent deceived the woman. The serpent begins with questions seeking to cast doubt about the Lord God's commands. "Did God really say . . . ?" (3:1). Then comes an outright denial of God's words. In 2:17, the Lord God is adamant that whoever eats the fruit "will certainly die." The serpent denies that in 3:4. The woman is deceived and eats the fruit.

Though it appears she eats first, the man is right there with her (v. 6) and simply eats when she gives him the fruit. Since the man was with her, he knew where the fruit was from and quite likely heard the conversation with the serpent. The man makes no objection to eating the fruit handed to him. He does not refute the serpent or check the fruit's origin with the woman. That he is to blame as much as the woman is seen in the fact that the eyes of both of them were opened (v. 7) and also in the serious aftermath of the sin; God's judgment is against them both.

Is it that the serpent has approached the woman because she is weaker or easier to deceive? Nothing in the text of Gen 3 points in that direction. Given the man's ready acceptance of the fruit from the woman, it is hard to argue that the man would have withstood the temptations of the serpent.

## Genesis 3—God's Judgment

God's response to the sin in the garden addresses the man first, both in his question to the man in 3:9, even though the woman is with him, and in his accusation in 3:11. So can we assume God addresses the man alone because the man has authority over the woman, or is there some other reason? Biblical narrative does not always make clear motives and reasons for behaviour. In the end, I do not think we can be dogmatic on this question.

Given that God gives the prohibition to the man in chapter 2, before the woman is even made, it seems appropriate that God addresses the man. He has, after all, broken the command given explicitly to him by the

Lord God. That alone does not necessarily imply leadership or authority of the man over the woman.[5] Nor does it imply that the man is responsible for the woman or that she has to obey him.

There is what scholars call a chiastic structure in God's response to the sin. That is, the narrative is structured like a sandwich; parallel slices of bread on the outside, parallel butter, and filling in the middle. So the chiasm structure, which is an artistic device, is:

- God addresses the man
    - God addresses the woman
        - God addresses the serpent
    - God addresses the woman
- God addresses the man

God addresses the man first, who blames the woman. When she is addressed by God, she blames the serpent (who has no leg to stand on, according to the old joke). To the serpent there is no question. Simply the Lord God issues punishment, then punishment to the woman and then to the man.

This chiastic pattern does not in any way highlight the sin or culpability of the woman as worse than that of the man. Usually in chiasms, the midpoint (the central filling) and the beginning and end (the pieces of bread) are the key points.

So this chiasm highlights the serpent in the middle. The order of man and then woman in the chiasm reflects their order in being created, but the chiasm does not point to a difference in authority.

All three, man, woman, and serpent, have basic functions made harder, with more pain and difficulty:

- The basic function of the serpent is troubled as he will now move on his belly.
- For the woman, her task of bearing children, reflecting the command to multiply and fill the earth in Gen 1, will continue but now be full of pain, in 3:16a. The task given to humanity, both male and female, in Gen 1:28, to fill and subdue the earth, remains their task but will be exercised under difficulty.

5. In contrast to Collins, *Genesis 1–4*, 173, for example.

- For the man, his task of tilling of the ground, a task given in 2:15 and reflecting the dominion entrusted to humanity in Gen 1, will continue but now be difficult, full of hard work and sweat, in 3:17–19.

So there is an equivalence in punishment here. The woman is not blamed for leading the man into sin, nor is the man blamed for not stopping her (which might be the case if she were under his authority). Each is equally at fault for the sin that each committed. The man is addressed first, not because he has more authority but because it was to him that the prohibition was first made. His punishment is the climax of the sequence, and not an anti-climax.

We need, though, to comment on 3:17a. The statement of punishment addressed to the man begins, "Because you listened to your wife." Presumably this refers to 3:6, even though there is no mention of the woman saying anything to the man. A similar expression is used with Abram before his sin with Hagar in Gen 16:2. In Hebrew, the word for "listen" has a connotation also of heeding or obeying.

Some interpret this accusation against the man as implying that his rightful leadership over the woman has been usurped by her, and that this is her sin. However, that is reading too much into these words. The man ought to have listened to the voice of God. Instead, he has disobeyed, not by listening to a woman per se, but by following her sin. The wrong is not in heeding a woman because she is a woman, but in heeding her in doing wrong and in not heeding God.

On top of punishment affecting the basic functions of each, the serpent, woman, and man, there is also relational punishment affecting each:

- The relations between the serpent's offspring and the woman's offspring will be fraught (3:15).
- The relationship between the man and the woman is also damaged (3:16).
- The relationship between the earth and the man is fraught (3:17–19).
- Clearly, there is now a fractured relationship between humans and God, as the man and the woman are expelled from the garden (3:23–24).

We need to look carefully at Gen 3:16b. This verse says, "Your desire will be for your husband, and he will rule over you." What does this mean? This cannot be understood as the ideal, for a man to rule over a woman. All the other relational and functional punishments speak of something less than ideal, whether pain in childbirth, hard toil in tilling the earth, or in the ongoing enmity with the seed of the serpent. The ruling of the man over the woman is not a new ideal, and certainly not what the original creation aimed for.

What about the "desire" of the woman? Is that a good desire? The word *desire* could imply either. If it is the woman's good desire for the man, then it will be frustrated by him ruling over her. But it could be that her desire for him is also wrong, after this sin, in which case both her desire and his ruling are signs of fractured relationships.

There is a parallel in Gen 4:7, which speaks of sin's desire for Cain and his need to master it. This parallel shows again broken relationships in a fallen world. But we should not use chapter 4 to force an interpretation back onto chapter 3. So, we do not need to say that because it would be good for Cain to master sin, then it is good for the man in chapter 3 to master the woman. Nor do we need to say that because sin's desire is to dominate, that the woman's desire was also to dominate.

We need to be careful not to read too much into the word *desire*. It only occurs here, in 4:7, and in Song of Solomon.[6] The direct context in chapter 3 is that frustrated and broken relationships abound post-sin. This means that 3:16b is a reflection of a fractured relationship that is now less than perfect. Woman's desire is therefore a good desire that will sadly be thwarted, "leaving the woman vulnerable to exploitation."[7]

## Equality as God's Image-Bearers

Nothing in Gen 1–3 tells us that man is made to be an authority over a woman, in general or in marriage. Quite the opposite, these chapters show:

- our equality as image-bearers;
- our equality in the call to have dominion and multiply;
- our equality in relationship;
- and our equal blame for sin.

Genesis 1–3 shows that men and women are not the same, and the difference between them is no basis for any hierarchy between men

6. Wenham, *Genesis 1–15*, 81–82.
7. McKeown, *Genesis*, 36.

and women. Men and women equally are divine image-bearers, equally called, under God, together to exercise dominion over the earth and to multiply.

But the perfection of relationship before Eden's sin ends with frustrated and skewed relationships as part of the relational punishment for both disobeying God. As the story of the Bible unfolds, we will eventually see how God repairs these broken relationships in the person and work of Jesus Christ, restoring his ideal for humanity—male and female—as equal partners in his work.

There is therefore nothing in Gen 1–3 that demands subservience or submission of a woman to a man in family or faith communities.

## Bibliography

Bailey, Kenneth. *Paul Through Mediterranean Eyes: Cultural Studies in 1 Corinthians*. Downers Grove, IL: IVP Academic, 2011.

Collins, C. John. *Genesis 1–4: A Linguistic, Literary, and Theological Commentary*. Phillipsburg, NJ: P&R, 2006.

Hamilton, Victor P. *The Book of Genesis Chapters 1–17*. New International Commentary on the Old Testament. Grand Rapids: Eerdmans, 1990.

McKeown, James. *Genesis*. Two Horizons Old Testament Commentary. Grand Rapids: Eerdmans, 2008.

Reid, Andrew. *Genesis: Salvation Begins*. Sydney: Aquila, 2000.

Smith, Claire. *God's Good Design: What the Bible Really Says About Men and Women*. 2nd ed. Newtown, Australia: Matthias Media, 2019.

Wenham, Gordon J. *Genesis 1–15*. Word Biblical Commentary 1. Waco, TX: Word, 1987.

# Disney Princesses, Superheroes, Influencers, and Women of the Old Testament

Jill Firth

The women of the Old Testament are sometimes presented to young girls as Disney princesses or superheroes, and teenagers may be encouraged to become influencers to their friends and maybe to a wider audience. It's worth taking a closer look at the biblical text to gain some clearer ideas about the lives of Old Testament women, before considering the women of Genesis, the saviours, judges, and prophets from Exodus to Esther, the influencers, and the other women and girls whose lives are honoured by being recorded in Scripture. This record of the lives and ministries of women and girls in the Old Testament points to God's delight in their place in his work in the world. Some stories highlight God's care for women in complex and difficult life circumstances.

## The Everyday Lives of Women

The everyday lives of women in ancient Israel had some differences from New Testament times, and from today. This reminds us to look carefully at the cultural context of biblical texts so that we can apply the Bible's teaching faithfully in our own context.

Some people might think that women and men were segregated in ancient Israel, but in Old Testament times, women mixed with men in public life, in the household, and in the palace. Women were specifically included in public gatherings from the early days of the nation through to the resettlement of Jerusalem after the exile (Deut 31:12; Josh 8:35; 1 Chr 16:3; Neh 10:28). The public roles of women include Miriam and women singers announcing God's salvation (Exod 15), wise women weaving for the tabernacle (Exod 26:35), and the women who, along with men, make donations for the work on the tabernacle (Exod 35:22; 38:8). Women also serve at the entrance to the tent of meeting (Exod 38:8; 1 Sam 2:22), sing victory chants, as when David and Saul return from battle (1 Sam 18:6–7), play hand drums in procession (Ps 68:25), and rejoice at the dedication of the wall of Jerusalem (Neh 12:43). God gives wise women a lament to sing when the nation is in danger (Jer 9:20–21), and the words of the women of Zedekiah's palace are incorporated into prophecy (Jer 38:20–23). Both men and women singers lament for King Josiah (2 Chr 35:25).

In the household, women and girls ground grain, baked bread, and spun and wove cloth, typically working together and surrounded by other family members. Archaeologists have found that, in a typical house, men and women ate and worked together in a public area on the ground floor and slept in an upper storey. The Proverbs 31 woman shows an example of the life of a wealthy woman who imports household supplies, buys land, plants a vineyard, gives to the poor, carries on a textiles business, supervises a large household which includes servants, and was respected by her husband and sons. In the palace, ordinary women along with men had access to the king of Israel including an enemy's wife (1 Sam 25:20), an unknown mourner (2 Sam 14:1–5), and two prostitutes (1 Kgs 3:16).

## Disney Princesses and the Women of Genesis

Like Disney princesses, the women of Genesis are often exceptionally beautiful. They are typically fourteen to twenty-one years old like the princesses, as the typical age for marriage in the ancient world was fourteen to twenty. But unlike Disney princesses, their stories do not usually end with a magnificent wedding or a spectacular triumph against impossible odds. Disney princesses face difficulties with courage and strength of character. However, though the women in Genesis sometimes trust in God, they are also devious, fearful, or selfish, and sometimes their character flaws persist into old age. In the same way, the men in Genesis (unlike the male lead characters in princess movies) are also neither completely good nor evil.

The writers of the Old Testament show their (and God's) interest in and concern for women in their nuanced depiction of women in the Genesis narratives. God's promise of a son to Abraham and Sarah makes a wonderful story, but both Abraham and Sarah are slow to trust God's plan. Sarah offers her Egyptian slave girl, Hagar, to Abraham as a surrogate mother (16:2), and she mistreats Hagar when Hagar falls pregnant and looks with contempt on Sarah (16:4–6). However, God treats Hagar with compassion. He meets her when she runs away to the wilderness and promises her an honourable future. Responding to God's kindness, Hagar names him *El Roi*, "You are the God who sees me" (16:13). Abraham is commended for his faith but, like Sarah, he also shows serious flaws. He is slow to protect the calling of Sarah even after God specifically names Sarah as the mother of the promise (Gen 17:16, 21). He twice risks Sarah becoming pregnant by other men when he asks her to say, "She is my sister," because she is very beautiful (12:10–20; 20:1–16).

Rebecca is featured in a long and elegant narrative describing her wooing by Abraham's servant in the city of Abraham's brother Nahor (Gen 24). After a romantic beginning to their marriage (24:62–67), Isaac and Rebecca settle in Philistine country because there is a famine in Israel. Rebecca is very beautiful, and Isaac imitates his father by seeking to pretend that Rebecca is his sister (26:6–11), again endangering the promised family line. Later in the story, Rebecca also shows guile when she plots to deceive the aging Isaac into giving his blessing to Jacob instead of to their elder son, Esau (27:1–46).

Judah's childless daughter-in-law Tamar chooses a risky and unsavoury plan to preserve the family line of her deceased husband, Er. When Judah seeks out a prostitute after the death of his wife (Gen 38:1–19), Tamar pretends to be a prostitute so that through Judah the family line will continue (38:13–14). When she falls pregnant, Judah denounces her as immoral, but when his own fatherhood of the child is revealed, he declares, "She is more righteous than I," because she had shown greater faithfulness to preserving the family line (38:26).

These and other stories in Genesis present a warts-and-all depiction of both the women and men of Abraham's extended family, yet Sarah, Rebecca, Rachel, and Leah are respected as "mothers in Israel," and Tamar, who made an imperfect, but brave and faithful choice, is commended. Rachel, Leah, and Tamar are held up as role models by the people of Bethlehem (Ruth 4:11–12).

## Superheroes and Women Saviours, Judges, and Prophets

Like superheroes, women from Exodus to Esther negotiate complex and often dangerous circumstances. They make decisions and act upon them, but unlike many superheroes who have superpowers or exceptional physical abilities, the Old Testament heroines seldom use direct physical force. (Two exceptions are Jael in Judg 4:21 and the woman who drops a millstone on Abimelech in Judg 9:53.) Stories from Exodus to Esther showcase women as saviours, judges, and prophets.

### Saviours

No women have the label *saviour* in the Old Testament, but several took action to rescue family members or the nation. In Exodus, seven women ensure Moses's safety. First, the Hebrew midwives, Shiphrah and Puah, preserve the lives of baby Hebrew boys (Exod 2:15–21). Then four women, Moses's mother, Pharaoh's daughter, Pharaoh's daughter's maid, and Moses's sister ensure his survival (2:21–10). Interestingly, God uses only women and girls to save baby Moses. Neither Moses's father nor his elder brother Aaron nor any other men have a role in this story of rescue. Later, Zipporah, the Midianite wife of Moses, saves Moses's life after he disobeys God by failing to circumcise his sons (Exod 4:18–26).

In the book of Joshua, Rahab, a local Canaanite woman, protects Joshua's spies by hiding them from Jericho's soldiers. After the fall of Jericho, she and her family accept the invitation to remain with the Israelite community (Josh 2:1–24; 6:17, 22–25). The faithfulness of Rahab (Josh 6:25) is contrasted with the disloyalty of a man from the tribe of Judah in the next chapter. Achan's greed endangers the nation, resulting in losing his own life and forfeiting his family line's inheritance in the promised land (Josh 7:1–26). Rahab marries Salmon of the tribe of Judah and becomes a great-great-grandmother of King David (1 Chr 2:11–16; Matt 1:4–6).

Women rescuers including Michal and Abigail are highlighted in 1 Samuel. Michal, David's first wife, helps David escape when Saul sends men to kill him (1 Sam 19:8). Abigail is the only woman in the Old Testament described as both wise and beautiful (1 Sam 25:3). Abigail first meets David when her foolish husband Nabal insults David. David sets off to attack Nabal, Abigail hears of her husband's dangerous mistake, and skillfully pacifies David (1 Sam 25:32–25) who later marries her.

Wise women also counsel and rescue David in 2 Samuel. A wise woman advises David to be reconciled to his son Absalom, who had fled after murdering his elder brother Amnon (2 Sam 14:1–24). David forgives his son but does not take any action to reconcile, or to prevent Absalom from rebelling against him. Subsequently, a Benjamite named Sheba also rebelled (2 Sam 20). He was besieged in the northern city of Abel Beth-Maacah by David's commander, Joab. A wise woman of the city offered to throw Sheba's head over the wall. Joab agreed and the city was saved (2 Sam 20:14–22).

In the book of 2 Kings, Queen Athaliah planned to destroy the whole of Judah's royal family. Princess Jehosheba rescued baby Joash and hid him away for six years, until a palace coup restored Joash to the kingship (2 Kgs 11:1–12). By saving Joash, Jehosheba enabled the restoration of the line of Davidic kings, which culminates in the birth of Jesus.

Four hundred years later, Queen Esther rescues the Jewish people. Esther subtly uses a series of feasts to gain the king's sympathy for the Jews. Meanwhile, a series of "coincidences" lead to the downfall of Haman, the plot leader, and Esther and her uncle Mordecai become important officials in the Persian administration. They are then able to work together to avert the genocide of the Jewish people so that God's people and the Davidic line are preserved.

## Judges

In the book of Judges, Deborah (Judg 4:4) and eight other people are described with the verb *judging* (also translated as "led," "serve as judge," "became judge," and "held court"): Othniel (3:10), Tola, Jair (10:2–3), Jephthah (12:7), Ibzan, Elon, Abdon (12:8–9, 11, 13–14), and Samson (15:20; 16:31). No specific leaders, whether men or women, are described with the Hebrew singular noun *judge* in the book of Judges, but the plural noun *judges* is mentioned several times in the introduction (2:16–19).

In Judges, Deborah is the only *prophet* who also *judges* Israel (Judg 4:4). Her role is similar to Moses and Samuel, who are described both as *prophets* (Deut 18:15; 34:10; 1 Sam 3:19–20) and as *judging* the people (Exod 18:13; 1 Sam 7:15). As with Moses and Samuel, the Israelites came to Deborah to settle disputes (Judg 4:1–5). Like Moses and Samuel (Exod 17:8–16; 1 Sam 7:5–14), Deborah gives leadership to the army, and, like them, she does not engage directly in battle.

Deborah was *judging* Israel when Jabin, a Canaanite king in the north of Israel was oppressing the Israelites (Judg 4:1–24). When Barak, the army commander, is reluctant to trust in God without Deborah's support, she further prophesies that God will give Sisera into the hand of a woman. The woman turns out to be Jael, who lulls Sisera to sleep in her tent and kills him with a tent peg (Judg 4:17–22).

## Prophets

Five women are described with the Hebrew word *prophetess* (also translated as "prophet") in the Old Testament: Miriam (Exod 15:20), Deborah (Judg 4:4), Huldah (2 Kgs 22:14; 2 Chr 34:22), the wife of Isaiah (Isa 8:3), and the false prophetess Noadiah (Neh 6:14). Miriam declares God's salvation in Exod 15, and Deborah gives God's word to Barak. Noadiah is critiqued with other false prophets by Nehemiah (Neh 6:14).

Huldah's prophecy occurs after the High Priest Hilkiah finds the book of the law during temple renovations in the time of King Josiah (2 Kgs 22:1–10). When the king hears the contents of the book, he sends his officials to inquire of the Lord. The priest and the officials go to the home of the prophetess Huldah, and she delivers a substantial prophecy of judgment and mercy that they convey to the king (2 Kgs 22:11—23:3). Huldah's prophecy is respected by Hilkiah and Josiah and recorded in Scripture. The prophets Jeremiah and Zephaniah were also active at this time, and perhaps Nahum, yet Huldah was chosen for this significant prophetic role.

## Everyday Influencers

Like twenty-first-century influencers, women of the Old Testament impacted the lives of other people and became exemplars, but unlike today's female icons, some of these Old Testament women were not well-known public figures during their lifetimes. These Old Testament women influenced others by speaking up for what they believed was just, right, or brave. They include the daughters of Zelophehad; a Syrian general's servant girl; King Belshazzar's mother; Caleb's daughter, Acsah; and the beloved woman in the Song of Songs.

The five daughters of Zelophehad influenced inheritance laws for Israel. In Num 27, Maiah, Noah, Hoglah, Milcah, and Tirzah address the leaders and the people who are gathered at the entrance of the tent of meeting. These women are concerned that their clan will die out because their father died without leaving any son to inherit his land. Moses consulted God, who agreed that the daughters could inherit their father's land if there were no brothers (Num 27:1–11). Later, the elders of the tribe of Manasseh were anxious that the land allotted to Zelophehad's daughters could pass out of the tribal allotment when they married. After consulting God, they agree that the daughters of Zelophehad should marry men from their own tribe of Manasseh so that the land would continue to belong to Manasseh (Num 36:1–13).

The wife of Naaman, the commander of the army of Syria, had a young Israelite serving maid, who alerted her mistress to the healing reputation of Elisha the Israelite prophet. Naaman had an incurable skin disease, perhaps leprosy. Though initially offended by Elisha's advice, Naaman washed in the Jordan and was healed. He returned to Syria, vowing to worship only the God of Israel (2 Kgs 5:1–19).

When God caused a mysterious message to appear on the wall of King Belshazzar's banqueting hall, the king and his court were terrified and perplexed because no one could read the writing (Dan 5:1–9). Belshazzar's mother reminded him that his father, King Nebuchadnezzar, trusted the advice of the prophet Daniel (Dan 5:10–12). Daniel interpreted the writing and was honoured by Belshazzar (Dan 5:13–30). Neither Naaman's wife's serving girl or Belshazzar's mother are named, but they used their influence for the benefit of Naaman, Daniel, and God's kingdom.

Caleb's daughter, Acsah, is presented as a woman with agency who requests a water source so she can enthusiastically take up residence in the promised land (Judg 1:14–15). In the Song of Songs, the beloved woman is given 53 percent of the dialogue, and she is warmly described as boldly showing agency and desire. These women, along with others, are presented as exemplars in the Old Testament.

## Memoir: Women Who Are Chosen and Remembered

Some Old Testament stories remind us of God's care for ordinary women who are chosen and beloved, and the names and sometimes tragic stories of other women are told that they may not be forgotten.

## Chosen

In three significant stories, God relates chiefly to a woman rather than to her husband. The angel of the Lord twice chooses to address the wife of Manoah about the birth and upbringing of her son Samson (Judg 13:3–5, 9) and he repeats the instructions to her in Manoah's hearing (Judg 13:13–14). Manoah's wife shows wise insight when her husband fears that they will die (Judg 13:22–23).

Ruth, the daughter-in-law of Naomi, is a young Moabite widow, who "as it turned out" (Ruth 2:3) went to work in the field of her relative Boaz, who marries her after a series of other coincidences. Ruth thus becomes an ancestor of King David (Ruth 4:17).

Hannah is a childless wife whose son Samuel is a gift from the Lord. Hannah offers a prayer celebrating God's power which introduces the message of the whole book of 1 Samuel. She predicts that God "will give strength to his king" (1 Sam 2:10) before there are any kings in Israel. Mary's song in Luke 1:46–55 has many similarities to the prayer of Hannah, as she also praises God who cares for the poor and humble.

Two clusters of stories about the prophets Elijah and Elisha focus on God's love for ordinary women. In the Elijah narratives, God's mercy to the widow of Zarephath includes miraculously feeding her household during a famine and later bringing her son back to life (1 Kgs 17). After Elijah ascends to heaven, God shows mercy to two women through Elisha. First he provides for a poor widow, miraculously enabling her to pay her debts and keep her children out of slavery (2 Kgs 4:1–7). After this, God brings the child of a wealthy woman back from death (2 Kgs 4:8–37).

In these texts, the faith of women is clearly shown through their actions and speech. Stories featuring God's choice of women are highlighted, and women with agency are admired. The final group of texts are more sombre, yet these stories of suffering women are also respected and remembered in the Old Testament narratives.

## Remembered

The names of the mothers of the kings of Judah are remembered in 1 and 2 Kings, there are two hundred or so women mentioned in genealogies, and other women and girls appear in crowd scenes in both poetry and prose (e.g., 2 Sam 6:19; Jer 31:13; 40:7; 41:16). God's care for women who are widows or landless immigrants is frequently mentioned in the Old Testament (e.g., Deut 10:18; Jer 22:3).

Some stories about women in the Old Testament are disturbing or downright frightening, gaining the label "texts of terror." These include the rapes of the unnamed concubine (Judg 19) and of David's daughter Tamar (2 Sam 13:1–22), the killing of Jephthah's daughter (Judg 11:34), and the mourning of the concubine Rizpah for her sons (2 Sam 21:7–14). It can be noted that these rapes are condemned in their context (Judg 19:30; 2 Sam 13:12), and Old Testament law allows that foolish vows like Jephthah's can be rescinded (Lev 5:4–13). King Saul's error in killing the Gibeonites results in bereavement for Rizpah (2 Sam 21:1–14). As is usual in Hebrew narrative, the stories are told with a minimum of commentary by the narrator, but action, characterisation, and dialogue reveal the biblical writer's awareness of and sympathy for the tragedy in the lives of these women. The trauma of women is honoured by retaining these stories in the text of Scripture.

## Reading and Preaching in Context

Some aspects of women's and men's lives changed between the old covenant, based on the law given to Moses on Sinai, and the new covenant, given by Jesus through his death and resurrection. For instance, in Old Testament times, the scope for ministry was limited for both men and women. The priesthood was only for the men of one tribe out of the twelve tribes. The priests had to be bearded males from the tribe of Levi, thirty to fifty years old, without disability, blemish, or leprosy, and not married to a divorced woman or a widow (Lev 21:1—22:9). In the new covenant, however, the sacrificial priesthood is fulfilled only by Jesus, our Great High Priest (Heb 7–10). In the New Testament, both Jesus and Paul welcomed women as fellow workers, accepted their help, and entrusted their messages to them (Matt 28:1–10; John 20:11–19; Rom 16:1–16).

Some references to feminine language can be missed in English translations of the poetic sections of the Old Testament, for example in speeches by metaphorical female figures such as Lady Wisdom in Prov 8 and personified cities including Babylon and Jerusalem in Isaiah, Jeremiah, and Lamentations. In the ancient Near East, the word *city* was grammatically feminine, so personifying a city as a female figure was part of the culture. Isaiah uses feminine imperative language inviting Zion to "arise, shine, for your light has come" (Isa 60:1). This difference between the original Hebrew and English translations can conceal feminine references in the Old Testament.

English translations can also unintentionally misrepresent Scripture by adding headings which are not part of the original Hebrew text. Some English translations add the word *adultery* to the heading of Ps 51, but the Hebrew word for adultery is never used about Bathsheba anywhere in the Bible, and she is never condemned in Scripture for what was done to her. Instead of condemning her, the prophet Nathan champions Bathsheba in his allegorical parable convicting David of his sin (2 Sam 12:1–15). In a later story in 1 Kgs 1–2, Bathsheba is the respected and trusted ally of King David and the prophet Nathan, helping Solomon receive his promised crown (1 Kgs 1:1–31), and King Solomon honours her by seating her at his right hand (1 Kgs 2:19).

Bathsheba's place in Jesus's family tree in Matthew's Gospel (Matt 1:2–7, 16), often and unfortunately described in commentaries or social media as due to her "sinfulness," more likely represents her fellowship with Mary, who also falls pregnant outside marriage, risking shame and disgrace along with Tamar who showed faithfulness to the line of Judah, and Rahab whose daring faith in welcoming the spies is commended in Heb 11:31.

Preachers today can give an unbalanced emphasis on female sinfulness. Both men and women sinned in Bible times, as today. The term "Jezebel spirit" is never found in the Old or New Testament. Alongside the wicked women of the Old Testament, such as Jezebel and Athaliah, there are many men who become icons of evil such as the men of Sodom, and the wicked kings Ahab, Manasseh, and Jehoiakim. In the New Testament, a prophetess code-named "Jezebel" is described as guilty of eating food offered to idols and sexual immorality (Rev 2:20), and similar sins are linked to a male prophet code-named "Balaam" in the same chapter (2:14). On closer reflection, we see that both Old and New Testaments present men and women as alike in their sinfulness.

## Written for Our Learning

Compared with the Disney princesses, the personalities of the women of Genesis are complex, and their stories don't always have straightforward endings. Unlike superheroes, Old Testament women from Exodus to Esther achieve their ends through trust in God, not by physical force. Compared with modern day influencers, some Old Testament women may not have had a huge fan base, but they made a difference to individuals and to the nation. The women of the Old Testament are saviours, judges, prophets, influencers, exemplars, chosen by God, beloved, and remembered for their great suffering. Their inspiring and sometimes tragic lives are held in honour by being recorded in Scripture. Read in context, their stories benefit us by showing us more of God's view of women.

## Further Reading

Durgin, Celina, and Dru Johnson (eds). *The Biblical World of Gender: The Daily Lives of Men and Women*. Eugene, OR: Cascade Books, 2022.

Meyers, Carol. *Rediscovering Eve: Ancient Israelite Women in Context*. Oxford: Oxford University Press, 2013.

Mowczko, Marg. "Old Testament Women." https://margmowczko.com/tag/every-ot-woman/

# What Have the Romans Ever Done for Us?

## *Women, the Christian Gospel, and the Greco-Roman World*

Michael Gladwin

What was life like for women in the first-century Greco-Roman world? What do we know about their roles, social status, and involvement in religious life? By focusing on the historical context of ancient Roman society and women's subordinate place within it, my aim in this chapter is to show just how revolutionary the teachings and practices of the early church were—in championing women's essential equality and religious leadership, in undermining men's almost unlimited power (and potential for abuses of that power), and in challenging sexual double standards.

I'm approaching this topic as a professional historian who has taught and read early church history for nearly twenty years; and as a historian and Christian who has long been deeply impressed by women's prominence in the leadership and life of the church in its formative centuries. Although the primary focus is on women in the first century AD, the early part of the chapter looks further back to influential Greek precedents.

### The Greek Philosophical Background

It is said that although the Romans conquered the empire of the Greeks, the Greeks conquered the Roman mind. Romans absorbed much of the philosophy, religion, and culture of ancient Greeks, while adding their own unique twists. Greek assumptions about women have a long backstory. Plato (429?–347 BC) argued in his *Republic* (around 375 BC) that women could by nature do what men do, whether serving in the armed forces or exercising and wrestling naked to maintain fitness.[1] Where men and women differed for Plato was in their sexual roles. Both, for example, had a soul capable of wisdom, and so women might therefore be eligible to act in a leadership role within the republic/city-state.[2]

A generation later, Plato's student Aristotle (384–322 BC) stressed fundamental differences between men and women, with implications both for their subordination in society and state, and for the long conversation about women in Western thought. In his *Politics* Aristotle declares that men are natural rulers:

> Most instances of ruling and being ruled are natural. For rule of free over slave, male over female, man over child, is exercised in different ways, because, while the parts of the soul are present in all of them, they are present in them in different ways. The slave is completely without the deliberative [rational] capacity; that female has it, but it has no authority; the child has it, but undeveloped.[3]

Aristotle contended in another work that women were more compassionate and prone to tears; more jealous and complaining and prone to scold; more dispirited and despondent than the male; more shameless and lying; and more inclined to deceive.[4] Aristotle added that women were "less spirited" than men and therefore not equipped for political life. On a faintly more positive note, Aristotle saw women on a par with men in relation to moral virtue, friendship, and the capacity to contemplate (and therefore be happy).[5]

## Ancient Rome

Moving westward and forward in time, we find assumptions among writers in the Roman Republic that are closer to Aristotle than Plato. The

1. The key text is *Republic*, 5.451c–457c.
2. McAleer, *Plato's "Republic,"* 134–40.
3. Aristotle, *Politics*, 1.13.1260a8–14; author's own translation.
4. Aristotle, *History of the Animals*, 8.1.608b8–18; author's own translation.
5. Connell, *Aristotle on Women*, 7 (conclusion).

historian Livy (59 BC–AD 17) recounted a remarkable scene in 195 BC in which Roman women protested laws that were prohibiting jewellery and luxuries during a period of wartime attrition. Speeches before the Senate are revealing of conventional attitudes. Cato, a powerful magistrate, declared:

> Our ancestors permitted no woman to conduct even personal business without a guardian to intervene in her behalf; they wished them to be under the control of fathers, brothers, husbands; we (Heaven help us!) allow them now even to interfere in public affairs, yes, and to visit the Forum and our informal and formal sessions.[6]

In the Roman Republic of the first century BC, the influential orator and philosopher Cicero (106–43 BC) echoed Aristotle in observing that women possessed weak judgement, were overly emotional, lacked self-control, and were cautious and sentimental (although, he conceded, they could be loyal).[7]

## Change Over Time

Only sixteen years after Cicero's death in 43 BC, the Roman Republic was transformed, after a bloody civil war, into the Roman Empire. In the subsequent century the prevailing view of women's nature and roles remained largely unchanged, though with some important legal exceptions. Before the imperial period, women were legally obliged to have a tutor, a nominated male family member, acting in their interests. By the first century AD, however, tutelage was largely a thing of the past, although both men and women still had to wait until their father's death to inherit property. Women also retained their property rights in marriage unless marriage was accompanied by *manus* (where a wife's property transferred to the husband and she remained under his authority). But by the first century *manus* marriages had mostly disappeared.[8] An estimated one-third of all property in the Mediterranean was owned by women.[9]

6. Livy, *History*, 34.2.11.
7. Culver, "Cicero," 88.
8. Grubbs, *Women and the Law*, 40–43.
9. Hylen, *Phoebe*, 19.

## Womanly Virtues in Ancient Rome

What had not changed, however, were the virtues expected of a respectable Roman woman. These can be summarised as: *pietas*, *pudicitia*, *prudentia*, and *industria*. *Pietas*, one's obligation to the gods, was expected of all citizens, but especially of women—in relation to elders, those in authority, and the gods. This virtue was exemplified in statues portraying women with their heads covered. *Pudicitia* represented chaste behaviour, while *prudentia* expressed modesty and discretion.[10] Finally, *industria* was the virtue of diligence, hard work, and productivity, embodied in statues of a chaste matron working wool at her loom.[11]

## Women and the Household

These virtues were closely identified with women's primary roles of being wives and mothers—bearing and nurturing legitimate children (*pietas familiae*) and overseeing the household (*domus*). Roman households usually included the nuclear family as well as a larger extended family of members, servants, and slaves. In her household sphere the Roman woman was described as the *materfamilias* (mother of the family), which meant a respectable matron, whether single or married, of virtue, modesty, and upright character. She attended to the running of the home and its slave workforce, and perhaps worked on handicrafts.[12] A woman property owner might play a role in civic life as patron and benefactor, and oversee the commercial production of goods (such as looms). The *materfamilias* might attend the evening dinner party (*convivium*), although guests would be predominantly male and focused on socialising and politicking. In Greek households, however, women did not attend the equivalent dinner party (*symposium*) if unrelated men were present.[13] Few women had access to formal education, though a few upper-class women might study literature and philosophy (the upper class represented less than 2–5 percent of the population; the middle class around 8–10 percent; and subsistence level, or below, around 85 percent).[14]

10. Winter, "'New' Roman Wife," 292–93.
11. Cohick, "Women, Children," 229–30.
12. Grubbs, *Women and the Law*, 40–41.
13. Cohick, "Women, Children," 228–29.
14. Merdinger, "Roman Empire," 21; Wright and Bird, *New Testament*, 172–73.

The household was the basic unit of Roman society. Conventional household codes (rules for a well-ordered household) were male dominated: the head of the household, the *paterfamilias* (father of the family), was the most senior male figure who wielded absolute authority (*potestas*) over his household. This extended to power over life and death, although his wife and her property usually remained under the legal authority of her father while he was still alive. Even so, a tragic reality was the prevalence of domestic violence and, in the worst cases, the killing of wives (Emperor Nero notoriously killed two of his wives with impunity). The later church father John Chrysostom reported the nightly screams of women echoing through the cobblestoned streets of Antioch (in modern-day Turkey).[15]

A father's authority extended to choices about the fate of children. Roman society was one where the killing or discarding of infants—by abortion, infanticide, or exposure—was accepted and legal. The *paterfamilias* might decree this if the infant were a result of poor contraception; if there was a poor omen; if children were deformed or the product of rape or incest; or if their legitimacy were in question. There is evidence that males were preferred and that girls were more likely than boys to suffer abortion, infanticide, or exposure. A poor family, for example, might leave a baby girl to die to spend limited resources on a male. In contrast, Jews and Christians condemned such practices.[16]

Most ancient men and women married. For ancient Romans the primary purposes of marriage were progeny (producing legitimate heirs) and partnership (harmony or *concordia* was the ideal, though this was still based around a husband's priorities and preferences, and his wife's submission). Divorce was relatively easy to obtain, in part to secure property when heirs were needed, and the father took custody of children. The abovementioned womanly virtues of *pudicitia* and *prudentia* (fidelity, chastity, and modesty) meant that access to extramarital relations was tightly controlled. Marriage for most Roman women was young: somewhere between twelve and twenty.[17] Given high rates of maternal mortality, the life expectancy of a Roman woman averaged twenty-five to thirty-five years. A woman surviving to fifty was likely to have given birth to six children, with only two or three surviving to adulthood.[18]

15. Cowan, "Domestic Violence."
16. Merdinger, "Roman Empire," 19–21.
17. Merdinger, "Roman Empire," 19.
18. Cohick, "Women, Children," 233–34.

Women married young to ensure legitimate heirs and that no sexual history might embarrass a future husband. In contrast, it was accepted that a Roman man could fulfil his sexual wishes with his wife, mistresses, sex workers, and slaves of both sexes.[19]

These realities help to explain why the New Testament's household codes (Col 3:18—4:1; Eph 5:21—6:9; Titus 2:1–10; and 1 Pet 2:18—3:7) were so subversive (see also Scott Goode's chapter in this book). Unlike pagan household codes, Christian household codes prescribed male monogamy and fidelity, and curbed the *paterfamilias's* potential abuses of power; they addressed women, children, and slaves directly, giving them unprecedented dignity; and they taught submission and sacrificial love for one another out of reverence for Christ.

## Women and Work

We have seen above how women worked on handicrafts or oversaw slaves and commercial production. Women also ran their own financial affairs and owned businesses (such as Lydia, an early Christian convert who was also a businesswomen dealing in expensive purple cloth [Rom 16:11–14, 40]), acted as benefactors and ran estates (especially after being widowed). Lower-class women had a more visible role in the marketplace because they worked for a living—typically in agriculture, weaving, markets, crafts, shopkeeping, trades, in family businesses, or as a midwife, wet-nurse (*nutrix*), or nurse (*nutritor*). Slaves often took on the latter roles. Some women had the role of *pedagogus*, the servant assigned as guardian to look after children until they reached maturity.[20]

In a society with no welfare safety net, however, the life of a lower-class widow could be extremely precarious. Below her on the bottom of the social rung were slaves and women who worked as actors or in the sex trade.[21] The vulnerability of widows, slaves, and sex workers is a reminder that women's experience differed significantly across social status and class. As one Roman man put it, "It is accepted that every master is entitled to use his slaves as he desires."[22] Lower-class women had far fewer rights and protections than women (especially citizens) of higher social

19. Flemming, "Sexuality."
20. Cohick, "Women, Children," 234–35.
21. Merdinger, "Roman Empire," 19.
22. Holland, *Dominion*, 115.

status. Sex workers and waitresses, for example, could not prosecute for rape, while the rape of slaves was considered property damage sustained by the owner.[23]

## Women in Public and Political Life

Roman women could be citizens, but they could not attend political assemblies, vote, or hold office. Yet by the first century AD the increasing importance of the imperial family diminished the influence of the Senate, the popular assembly, and political franchise. This gave increased political influence to women through family connections. Strong-minded women—like Livia Drusilla (58 BC–AD 29), the wife of Emperor Augustus, or Iulia Agrippina (AD 15–59), the mother of Emperor Nero—might influence the hereditary succession, the emperor, and even imperial policy.[24] Even so, such women were usually represented in conventional terms of female spite, treachery, or a lack of self-control.[25]

Women might fulfil traditional feminine virtues and yet act in ways that seem surprising, such as speaking up on various causes as patrons and advocates, and even serving in civic roles.[26] Patronage was woven deeply into the socioeconomic fabric, where a wealthy or powerful individual (patron) supported a less-powerful individual (client), usually in exchange for loyalty, gratitude, and votes. Or a patron might commission local public works. The New Testament mentions several patrons: for example, Mary Magdalene, Joanna, and Susanna, who financially supported Jesus (Luke 8:1–3); and Phoebe, who supported the apostle Paul (Rom 16:1–2). Yet women in these positions were always expected to respect norms of deference to those of a higher social class: in the context of the family, for example, a modest woman should defer to the speech of her husband while in his presence, especially in public.[27] "Patronage bridged the gap between public and private," explains Lynn Cohick, "and clarified how public women were esteemed with 'private' virtues of modesty and chasteness."[28]

23. Winkler, *Constraints*, 22.
24. Bauman, *Women and Politics*, 13–16.
25. Roberts, *Oxford Dictionary*, s.v. "Women."
26. Hylen, "Modest," 3–12; Hylen, *Phoebe*, 139.
27. Hylen, "Modest," 3–12.
28. Cohick, *Earliest Christians*, 23.

## The Jewish Context

What about Jewish women's experience, given the Christian movement's early Jewish centre of gravity? Not surprisingly, Jewish views of women resembled the patriarchal norms of those around them. Like other Roman women, Jewish women were expected to act in keeping with womanly virtues of fidelity, modesty, and chastity. This was the case within Judaism's two major streams: the more traditional Rabbinic Judaism and the Hellenistic Judaism that was more influenced by Greek culture and philosophy. First-century Hellenistic Jewish philosopher Philo of Alexandria (ca. 20 BC–AD 50) observed that "in their nature men take precedence over women" and that

> market places, and council chambers, and courts of justice, and large companies and assemblies of numerous crowds, and a life in the open air full of arguments and actions relating to war and peace, are suited to men; but taking care of the house and remaining at home are the proper duties of women; the virgins having their apartments in the centre of the house within the innermost doors, and the full-grown women not going beyond the vestibule and outer courts . . . the men having the government of the greater, which government is called a polity; and the women that of the smaller, which is called *oeconomy* [the household].[29]

Yet we also know that Jewish women could own their own homes, appear in public gatherings, and enjoy freedom of travel. Some had access to their own funds; served as patrons; worked in clothing, baking, and textile industries; and purchased goods at market. Most of a typical Jewish family's economic activities—usually involving both men and women—took place in the home or its adjacent courtyard.[30]

Rabbinic Jewish men were taught to pray the prayer: "Blessed are You . . . King of the universe, for not having made me a woman." Rabbis taught that divorce could be initiated only by the husband. Likewise, the rabbinic marriage contract recognised a wife's rights in the face of divorce or widowhood, but it named the husband as sole actor in his wife's property.[31] The first-century Jewish historian Josephus (AD 37/38–100) reported that women were excluded as witnesses in Jewish courts of law,

29. Philo, *Special Laws*, 3.31.169–170.

30. Cohick, "Women, Children," 228–29.

31. Ilan, "Women, Ancient," 651; Ilan, *Integrating Women*.

owing to "the levity and temerity of their sex."[32] Nevertheless, there is some evidence from the Qumran community (a Jewish sect living at Qumran on the Dead Sea into the first century AD) that married women over twenty were able to bear witness.[33]

## Women and Religious Leadership

What do we know about ancient Roman women and religious leadership? Here *leadership* is defined broadly as some kind of formally acknowledged service—not necessarily ordained—within a religious tradition.[34] While the *paterfamilias* was a kind of priest in the Roman household, women participated with men in household religious rites, observing festivals, prayers, and sacrifices to the household deities of the *paterfamilias's* ancestors.[35] In the public expression of the Roman state religion, which largely consisted of offering public sacrifices to avoid misfortune and appease the Roman world's many gods, men held most major priesthoods—even of female deities! Nevertheless, some wives of priests held a quasi-priestly office by virtue of marriage: for example, the wife of the *flamen dialis*, the high priest of Jupiter, assisted at certain public rituals.

There were also vestal virgins, unmarried women who served the cult of Vesta (goddess of home and family) for thirty years from before puberty. Vestal virgins were required at many public sacrifices and rites normally barred to women. A vestal virgin was free of her father's authority and of marriage ties, although the grim penalty for breaking her virginity was entombment alive.

Women were more conspicuous in cults and mystery religions that had a "foreign" tinge—like *Mater Magna* (Great Mother of the Gods, or Cybele), the cult of Ceres (goddess of harvests, served by a priestess), Sibylline oracles, and the religion of the ancient Egyptian goddess, Isis (goddess of dying, healing, and motherhood).[36]

32. Josephus, *Jewish Antiquities*, 4:219.
33. Ilan, "Women, Ancient," 651.
34. Following Taylor and Ramelli, *Women's Leadership*, 19–20.
35. Cohick, "Women, Children," 228–29.
36. Takács, *Vestal Virgins.*

## Jewish Women and Religious Leadership

Although Jewish women were excluded from religious leadership as rabbis, they had important roles in synagogues, which became the focus of Jewish religious life after the Roman military's destruction of Jerusalem's temple in AD 70. Officeholders were laypersons, including women, and synagogue inscriptions tell us that female donors played important roles in financing construction and administration. Women attended synagogues, though there is some debate about whether women were segregated from men. Interestingly, many leadership titles were held by women. Female heads of synagogues appear, for example, on inscriptions in Crete and modern-day Turkey; and female elders were present in Italy and North Africa (though not in Palestine).[37] These women must have had some education.

There is some ancient evidence for women praying publicly in temples, shrines, homes, and even arenas: Judith, in the apocryphal books of the Bible (3 Macc 5:49–51), and a Greek woman named Anthia praying in the temple of Isis. Women also prophesied in public, which we know from the shrine of Apollo at Delphi in Greece and the famous group of prophets known as the Sibyls.[38]

## Conclusions: Women, the Christian Gospel, and the Greco-Roman World

Throughout the period noted here—from around 400 BC to the first century AD—Greco-Roman women lived in patriarchal societies where the expectations included subordination, meekness, and a sphere of authority primarily in the household (*domus*) as a *materfamilias*: wife, mother, and household manager under the authority of the male head of the household (*paterfamilias*). While women were expected to embody virtues of piety, modesty, and chastity, this did not rule out semi-public roles in civic life as advocates, patrons, and benefactors, so long as they met expectations of womanly virtue. Women were also visible in a wide range of occupations and in the marketplace. In the sphere of religious life, both Jewish and non-Jewish women had opportunities to be involved

37. Ilan, "Jewish Women's Life."

38. Hylen, *Phoebe*, 116–17.

in household and public worship, but they had few opportunities for religious leadership beyond patronage and the synagogue.

Just like the many paintings and sculptures in Roman theatre backdrops that set the scenes for plays, understanding this historical "backdrop" of Greco-Roman women's lives can help us set the scene for understanding just how radical Christian teachings were in their context: in according dignity and spiritual equality to women; in challenging sexual double standards, licentiousness, and potential abuses of the *paterfamilias's* power in marriage and the household (Christians added monogamous male fidelity to female, hence the significance of the term *one-woman man* in 1 Tim 3:2); in dignifying singleness as a genuine vocation for women; and in opening new opportunities for women's religious leadership beyond patronage—as missionaries, martyrs, house-church leaders, deacons, prophetesses, and even apostle (as seen in the New Testament, later church history, and in other chapters of this book). As historian Tom Holland has pointed out, Christian concepts of male-female and sexual equality, humility, and self-sacrificial love set a depth charge under Greco-Roman culture that has rippled through history as a powerful and transformative force, especially for women.

## Bibliography

Bauman, Richard A. *Women and Politics in Ancient Rome*. London: Routledge, 1992.

Cohick, Lynn H. "Women, Children, and Families in the Greco-Roman World." In *The World of the New Testament: Cultural, Social, and Historical Contexts*, edited by Joel B. Green and Lee Martin McDonald, 227–37. Grand Rapids: Baker Academic, 2013.

———. *Women in the World of the Earliest Christians: Illuminating Ancient Ways of Life*. Grand Rapids: Baker Academic, 2009.

Connell, Sophia M. *Aristotle on Women: Physiology, Psychology, and Politics*. Cambridge: Cambridge University Press, 2021.

Cowan, Eleanor. "Domestic Violence and Vulnerability in the Roman World." University of Sydney, November 1, 2024. https://www.sydney.edu.au/arts/news-and-events/news/2024/11/01/domestic-violence-and-vulnerability-in-the-roman-world.html.

Culver, Edith Ethel. "Women in the Life and Works of Marcus Tullius Cicero." MA thesis, University of Montana, 1950.

Flemming, Rebecca. "Sexuality." In *The Oxford Handbook of Roman Studies*, edited by Allessandro Barchiesi and Walter Scheidel, 797–814. Oxford: Oxford University Press, 2010.

Grubbs, Judith Evans. *Women and the Law in the Roman Empire: A Sourcebook on Marriage, Divorce and Widowhood*. Oxford: Taylor & Francis, 2002.

Holland, Tom. *Dominion: The Making of the Western Mind*. London: Abacus, 2020.

Hylen, Susan E. *Finding Phoebe: What New Testament Women Were Really Like*. Grand Rapids: Eerdmans, 2023.

———. "Modest, Industrious, and Loyal: Reinterpreting Conflicting Evidence for Women's Roles." *Biblical Theology Bulletin* 44 (2014) 3–12.

Ilan, Tal. *Integrating Women Into Second Temple History*. Tübingen: Mohr Siebeck, 2001.

———. "Jewish Women's Life and Practice in the World of the New Testament." In *The Oxford Handbook of New Testament, Gender, and Sexuality*, edited by Benjamin H. Dunning, 220–37. Oxford: Oxford University Press, 2019.

———. "Women, Ancient: Second Temple Period." In *The Cambridge Dictionary of Judaism and Jewish Culture*, edited by Judith R. Baskin, 651–52. Cambridge: Cambridge University Press, 2011.

Josephus. *Jewish Antiquities, Volume II: Books 4–6*. Translated by H. St. J. Thackeray and Ralph Marcus. Loeb Classical Library 490. Cambridge: Harvard University Press, 1930.

Livy. *History of Rome*. Translated by Evan T. Sage. Cambridge: Harvard University Press, 1935.

McAleer, Sean. *Plato's "Republic": An Introduction*. Cambridge: Open Book, 2020.

Merdinger, Jane. "The World of the Roman Empire." In *Early Christianity: Origins and Evolution to AD 600*, edited by Ian Hazlett, 17–27. London: SPCK, 1991.

Philo of Alexandria. *The Special Laws*. Translated by Charles Duke Yonge. 4 vols. London: Bohn, 1854–1890.

Roberts, J. W., ed. *The Oxford Dictionary of the Classical World*. Oxford: Oxford University Press, 2007.

Takács, Sarolta A. *Vestal Virgins, Sibyls, and Matrons: Women in Roman Religion*. Austin: University of Texas Press, 2008.

Taylor, Joan E., and Ilaria L. E. Ramelli, eds. *Patterns of Women's Leadership in Early Christianity*. Oxford: Oxford University Press, 2021.

Winkler, John. *The Constraints of Desire: The Anthropology of Sex and Gender in Ancient Greece*. New York: Routledge, 1990.

Winter, Bruce W. "The 'New' Roman Wife and Timothy 2:9–15: The Search for a *Sitz im Leben*." *Tyndale Bulletin* 51 (2000) 285–94.

Wright, N. T., and Michael F. Bird, eds. *The New Testament in Its World: An Introduction to the History, Literature, and Theology of the First Christians*. Nashville: HarperCollins Christian, 2019.

# “Blessed Are Those Who Hear the Word of God and Obey It!”

## *Women’s Discipleship in the Gospels*

Hannah Craven

It was not until my late teens that I first encountered Christians who believed it was right to limit the ministry and leadership of women. I was a committed Christian, already involved in ministry in my local church, and I was baffled. In all I’d ever read and understood of Jesus’s call and instructions to his disciples, I’d never seen Jesus teach that there was one track for men, and another for women. Jesus’s call to follow him, his commission to make disciples, and his empowering by the Spirit were for everyone. As a young woman discerning my future and seeking to live for Christ, I’d sought to answer these kinds of questions: “Where is Jesus leading me? Where does he call me to go and to serve? How is he equipping me by his Spirit?”

In 2 Tim 3:16–17, the apostle Paul writes that “all Scripture is God-breathed, and is useful for teaching, rebuking, correcting, and training in righteousness so that the servant of God may be thoroughly equipped for every good work.”[1] *All of Scripture* is both relevant and necessary for training in righteousness. The interpretative principle “Scripture interprets Scripture” means that the Bible does not contradict itself but is the guide to its own interpretation. This means that when it comes to the ministry and roles of women, we have to keep the whole Bible in view.

1. When he wrote this Paul was referring to the Old Testament, but Christians understand these verses to refer to the whole of Scripture—both Old and New Testaments.

Whatever Paul meant in 1 Tim 2:12 or 1 Cor 14:34, it can't forbid what Paul himself actually practiced, or what Jesus modelled and taught.

John 1:18 says, "No one has ever seen God, but the one and only Son, who is himself God and is in closest relationship with the Father, has made him known." Jesus makes God known. He shows us what God is like. His acts are the acts of God, his words the words of God. Hence, the way that Jesus treats, teaches, talks about, and instructs women shows us the way that God relates to and thinks about women. So, seeking to find out for myself and to live in obedience to God, in my year twelve Texts and Traditions class I wrote my first essay on "Jesus and Women in the Gospel of John." What I found delighted, encouraged, and emboldened me. Nearly thirty years later, I hope it will encourage you. For in the Gospels we see women's wholehearted yes to Jesus met with an equally wholehearted yes from Jesus in return!

## Jesus's Conception and Birth; Mary, the Mother of Jesus

Jesus was conceived by the Holy Spirit in the womb of his mother Mary. The virginal conception was particularly important to the earliest Christians as a way of affirming and holding together both Jesus's humanity and his divinity. At the same time, this emphasis on Jesus's birth from Mary was often coupled with views about women—and particularly their bodies—which introduced a tension to this discussion. This mixed history has meant that many Protestants (and many women) have been reluctant to emphasise the importance of Jesus's birth from Mary. In modern theology, particularly in liberal theology and in some schools of feminist theology, the truth of the virginal conception has been challenged—rejected as not only far-fetched but also as damaging.

But Jesus's virginal conception and his birth from his human mother Mary *are* important—and not just for our understanding of Jesus. They tell us something about God's view of women, of women's bodies, and of women's discipleship. First, consider women's bodies. God himself has entered a woman's body—to be nurtured and grown in her uterus, birthed through her vagina, and fed at her breast. In a tradition in which women's bodies have too often been viewed negatively, the incarnation offers divine affirmation of the goodness of women's bodies, including their reproductive organs and processes. Pregnancy, birth, blood, milk—these attendants to motherhood have been used to exclude women from society, from leadership, and from participation in the life of God's people.[2] But the incarnation puts a stop to any view which holds that there is something inherently wrong or inferior about women's bodies, anything shameful about her bodily fluids, or anything about her role as mother which makes her unfit for service or worship. God is not squeamish about women's bodies, and neither should we be.

But God doesn't just "use" Mary's body, as though she is a passive vessel for Jesus's gestation and birth. No, in this event God invites Mary into active discipleship and obedience through faith. Mary's Yes! to God (Luke 1:38), her faith and trust in God (Luke 1:45), her awareness of Israel's history and its hopes (Luke 1:46–55), and her courage, commitment, and cooperation are all part of her role too. And what we see clearly in this story is that Mary's discipleship and relationship with God is unmediated by a man—neither husband nor father are involved. So while the role that she takes up (motherhood) is traditionally feminine, the discipleship on display here is also a rejection of stereotypical "femininity." In her reply to the angel Gabriel, Mary risks expulsion from her father's household, rejection by her fiancé, and shunning by the community. By naming herself the Lord's servant (Luke 1:38) Mary defines herself first and primarily as a member of God's household instead.

And it doesn't stop there. Instead of spending her pregnancy in seclusion, Mary travels to visit Elizabeth—seemingly alone. In a beautiful scene that contains no adult male characters, just two women and their unborn babies in the presence of the Holy Spirit, the cousins pray and bless each other, and Mary sings a song of praise. We don't know yet that Joseph will accept Mary as his wife and take the child as his own, and Mary's courage does not rely on it. Mary is one who finds her status, role, and even family identity, solely in relation to God.

Mary is also a prophet and a teacher of God's word. In Mary's Song—known as the Magnificat (Luke 1:46–55)—Mary is "the first authoritative

2. For example, some Orthodox traditions still suggest that women ought not receive communion when they are menstruating. In 2017 Pope Francis made news by encouraging women to breastfeed in church, acknowledging that many have been discouraged from doing so. Under Mosaic law, menstruation was one of a number of bodily fluids considered "unclean" which prevented persons from entering the tabernacle (Lev 15). It is important to note that "uncleanness" does not signify sin or moral failing, but it might prevent one from engaging socially to an extent, and it did prevent one from participation in worship. Much early Western thinking about women was influenced by Aristotle's teaching that women were biologically and rationally inferior to men, in part due to their bodily fluids.

interpreter of Scripture in the light of God's new work [in Christ]."[3] That is, she is the first human person to know the significance of the coming of Jesus, how it relates to Israel's history and their hopes, and the first to tell of it to others. In doing so, Mary interprets Israel's Scriptures, interprets the person of Christ, and interprets the meaning of these events for her people. Mary's song provides the foundation for the presentation of Jesus found throughout Luke's Gospel. But more than that, now part of Scripture, Mary's teaching remains authoritative for Christian men and women today. Mary is a sound teacher, approved by God (see 2 Tim 2:15).[4]

## "Blessed Are Those Who Hear the Word of God and Obey It!"

Later in Luke come two more scenes which involve Jesus and his mother, Mary, and prompt a reconsideration of ideas of discipleship, women's roles, and of family:

> Then his mother and his brothers came to him, but they could not reach him because of the crowd. And he was told, "Your mother and your brothers are standing outside, wanting to see you." But he said to them, "My mother and my brothers are those who hear the word of God and do it." (Luke 8:19–21)
>
> While he was saying this, a woman in the crowd raised her voice and said to him, "Blessed is the womb that bore you and the breasts that nursed you!" But he said, "Blessed rather are those who hear the word of God and obey it!" (Luke 11:27–28)

Following Jesus demands a reorientation of life so significant that it disrupts even our closest allegiances. It is nothing less than a redefinition of family (Luke 8:19–21). In light of this teaching, we can see Mary as the first to recognise this reorientation: her identification of herself as "servant of the Lord" (Luke 1:38) is a claim to membership in God's family which supersedes all other allegiances and roles.[5] The woman in the crowd (Luke 11:27) sees Jesus's mother in traditional cultural terms: defined by her role as mother, and worthy of honour due to the status

3. Forbes and Harrower, *Raised from Obscurity*, 51.

4. For more on Mary in the Gospel of Luke, see Forbes and Harrower, *Raised from Obscurity*; also Green, "Blessed Is She."

5. Green, "Blessed Is She," 15–16.

of the child she has borne.[6] Jesus's reply does not imply that Mary is not blessed nor worthy of honour, but it is a sharp critique of the values expressed by the woman from the crowd. Jesus indicates that it is not by virtue of motherhood that women are blessed or honoured: "Blessed rather are those who hear the word of God and obey it!" (Luke 11:28). Mary is praiseworthy not because of the child she bore, but because she responded to the word of God with faith and obedience.

God's work in Mary's life demonstrates that cultural values and norms for women's lives are not necessarily God's values and norms. We see in Jesus's birth an affirmation of women—and specifically of women's bodies; and later we also see Jesus's refusal to reduce the value of those bodies to the role of motherhood alone. Mary is not defined by her femaleness, her femininity, by marriage, or by her role as mother, and Mary is not simply a "woman-disciple" or an "ideal example" for women. As a disciple, Mary is an example for both women and men, married or single, parents or not. What is pertinent about Mary as an example for *women* then, is not what she reveals about a woman's nature, but what she reveals that God makes possible for women in a world which would deny or limit them. That is, Mary reveals that in God's economy there is another, countercultural, way of being woman—both in Mary's day and in ours. The blessed woman, the woman-disciple, is the one who "hears the word of God and obeys it."

## Luke—The "Gospel for Women"

Much of this portrait of Mary, and of discipleship, comes from Luke's Gospel, which has often been affectionately known as the "Gospel for Women." Luke includes more stories about women than any other Gospel. He gives sustained attention to Jesus's birth, giving prominence and voice to Mary and Elizabeth (chs. 1–2). Plus, there is Luke's habit of pairing stories about men and women. In Luke, women feature alongside men as disciples (Luke 6:13, 17; 8:1–3; 21; 10:1, 38–42), as prophets (Luke 1:39–45, 46–55; 2:25–38), as recipients of Jesus's healing (Luke 4:31–39; 7:1–17; 8:2, 40–56; 13:10–17), as figures in his parables (Luke 13:20–21; 15:3–10; 17:34–35; 18:1–8), as those who receive his teaching (Luke 10:38–42), and as those who financially support his ministry (Luke 6:13; 8:1–3). The story of Mary and Martha of Bethany (Luke 10:38–42)

6. E.g., Gen 29:31—30:24.

explicitly affirms that women's discipleship need not only take the form of practical service—administration, hospitality, or behind-the-scenes tasks—but also that of student and learner. Mary sits in a place ordinarily reserved for men.

Luke also tells us that the group of disciples who travelled with Jesus was more than the twelve apostles, and routinely included many women, several of whom are listed by name, including Mary Magdalene, Joanna, and Susanna (Luke 8:2–3). Many women consistently travel with Jesus, witness his ministry, and hear his teaching. And it makes sense that women are sent out amongst the seventy-two to preach the kingdom of God (Luke 10:1–12). In Luke's Gospel, women are presented equally alongside men in all aspects of following Jesus.[7]

## Matthew and Mark

Not all the Gospels include as much material on female disciples as Luke, but each has its own emphasis and important contribution. For example, although genealogies are not usually considered exciting reading, Matthew's presentation of Jesus's genealogy (Matt 1:1–17) is striking for its unusual inclusion of four women: Tamar (v. 3), Rahab (v. 5), Ruth (v. 5), and Bathsheba, though she is named as "Uriah's wife" (v. 6). The first three women are non-Israelites, and all have complex and painful stories. Though their stories are already significant as told in the Old Testament, their inclusion in Jesus's genealogy elevates the place of these women in Israel's story, highlighting their faith, righteousness, and courage amid their vulnerability. Israel's—and Jesus'—story depends on the faith of women as well as men. The genealogy also ends unconventionally—with Joseph being named not as the father of Jesus, but as the husband of Mary, and Mary as "the mother of Jesus who is called the Messiah" (Matt 1:16).[8]

Matthew also includes the story of a woman anointing Jesus with perfume (Matt 26:6–13), anticipating Jesus's death and preparing his

7. Why then are the twelve apostles all men? Jesus connects his choice of twelve disciples with the twelve tribes of Israel (Matt 19:28; Luke 22:29–30) suggesting that the twelve represent Israel somehow. However, we have already seen that these were not Jesus's only disciples, nor the most exemplary. And after the coming of the Holy Spirit at Pentecost, we see no evidence that the church needed to or chose to elevate twelve Jewish males as overall leaders, but that leadership was taken up by both men and women, just as by Gentiles and Jews.

8. For more on the women in Jesus's genealogy, see Clements, *Mothers on the Margin?*

body for burial.[9] In this act, and at this point in the story, the woman is shown to see more truly than the male disciples, and her anointing of Jesus is immediately followed by and contrasted with Judas's betrayal. The woman recognises who Jesus is and what he must do, and her response to Jesus exemplifies discipleship. Jesus's own words highlight the significance of her act: "Truly I tell you, wherever this gospel is preached throughout the world, what she has done will also be told, in memory of her" (Matt 26:13).

The Gospel of Mark tells the story of the healing of the woman with bleeding, and of Jairus's daughter (Mark 5:21–43). Jairus is a synagogue leader whose twelve-year-old daughter is unwell, and soon dies. While Jesus is on his way to Jairus's house, he is approached by a woman who has been bleeding for twelve years. The characters in these stories are intentionally contrasted: young and old, prominent and marginalised. And yet, both Jairus and the bleeding woman exhibit faith which brings healing. And in both cases, Jesus touches and is touched by a person who is—according to Jewish law—unclean. Jesus's ministry extends to young girls and to older women, and demonstrates his inclusion of those who are marginalised. It shows that women's bleeding and gynaecological concerns are not outside of God's care.

The power of this story for women and girls became particularly evident to me when I noticed that it was my daughter's favourite story from the *Jesus Storybook Bible*.[10] If we asked her which story she would like us to read, she would always respond: "Jesus and the little girl!" This was the story in which she saw herself, and so saw herself as important to Jesus. These stories show women and girls, young and old, no matter how vulnerable or marginalised, that they matter to Jesus.

## John

The Gospel of John includes a number of important stories about women at key points in its narrative, often also in male/female pairs. In chapters 3 and 4 we find two such paired stories, in Jesus's encounters with Nicodemus (John 3:1–15) and a Samaritan woman (John 4:1–42). Both stories treat common themes, and centre around the symbol of water. But

9. Despite stubbornly persistent confusion, the woman who anoints Jesus should not be identified with Mary Magdalene. For more, see McNutt, *Mary We Forgot*.

10. Lloyd-Jones, "A Little Girl and a Poor Frail Lady," in *Storybook Bible*, 214–21.

the characters and their responses to Jesus are dramatically contrasted. Nicodemus is a Jewish teacher, Pharisee, and ruler—and yet he comes to Jesus at night, and remains metaphorically as well as literally "in the dark." The Samaritan woman, on the other hand, is an "outsider" and a regular person, but she meets Jesus at midday, the "light" mirroring her recognition of Jesus's identity. The Samaritan woman not only believes, but she also becomes the first apostle, sharing about Jesus and bringing others to faith in him (John 4:28–30, 39–42). Both characters struggle with misunderstanding in their conversation with Jesus, but it is the Samaritan woman, not the male Jewish teacher, who eventually "sees" Jesus and understands who he is. In John's Gospel, she is the first character to name Jesus as the Christ (Messiah; John 4:29).

John 11:1—12:11 is a powerful story about which there is much to say—both about the ministry of Jesus and the story's female characters. Its foreshadowing of Jesus's own resurrection gives it an important place in John's narrative and theology, but here we might simply note the friendship that is displayed between Jesus and the two women. Mary and Martha are likely both single women and, along with their brother Lazarus, are disciples of Jesus. The text tells us that Jesus not only loved Lazarus (John 11:3) but also Martha and her sister (John 11:5). Both women express their grief and pain honestly to Jesus, who is deeply moved (John 11:33). We see here that Jesus experienced close friendship and emotional intimacy with women as well as men.

## Witness to and Proclaimers of Jesus's Resurrection

We have already seen that women were routinely present in most crowds and large groups during Jesus's ministry, but one point at which all four Gospel authors make the presence of women explicit is at the death, burial, and resurrection of Jesus. At this crucial moment in each Gospel narrative, each author makes a point of noting that women were present, that they looked after Jesus's needs during his ministry, that they remained with Jesus at his suffering and his death (Matt 27:55–56; Mark 15:40–41; Luke 23:27, 49; John 19:25), and that they cared for his body after he died (Matt 2:1; Mark 16:1; Luke 24:1–3; John 20:1). The quiet faithfulness of Jesus's female followers is contrasted with Judas's betrayal, with Peter's denial, and with those who mock and insult Jesus. At Jesus's death and burial, women are present *alongside* male followers. But at the resurrection, it is women *alone* who are first to discover the empty tomb (Matt 2:1; Mark 16:1; Luke 24:1–3; John 20:1), first to hear that Jesus has risen (Matt 28:5–6; Mark 16:6; Luke 24:4–8), first to meet the risen Jesus (Matt 28:9–10; Mark 16:9; John 20:14),[11] and first to proclaim the resurrection of Jesus to the other disciples (Matt 28:7–8, 11; Mark 16:10; Luke 24:9–11; John 20:18).

The resurrection of Jesus changes everything for Jesus's first disciples, and for the whole world. That Jesus entrusts this message first to women—sometimes considered unreliable witnesses, and later disbelieved even by the male disciples—is monumental. That he gifts his female followers with this discovery, with this intimate moment of grief turned to joy, and with this world-transforming message, is surely an affirmation of their full and equal status in his ministry and a rejection of any attempt to sideline women in the proclamation of the gospel. John's extended narrative in which Mary Magdalene is first to meet Jesus and is sent to proclaim his resurrection to the other disciples (John 20:11–18) led her to become known as the apostle to the apostles (see Erickson's chapter in this book).

## Called, Taught, Transformed and Sent

In each of the Gospels we see an intentional and consistent inclusion of women in all aspects of Jesus-discipleship, including a particular focus on women's involvement at key points in Jesus's life and ministry—namely, his incarnation and birth, his death, and resurrection. By pointing out women at these key moments, I don't imply that women are better or more important than men. But certainly, if women were *not* participants in these stories, I suspect that the narratives could and would be interpreted to show that they are not required, and perhaps excluded. The pairing of women and men in all aspects of discipleship, and the intentional inclusion of women at key points in Jesus's story, show that Jesus himself, as well as the Gospel writers, want us to see that women are called to be active disciples of Jesus, and called to the same path of

11. In Luke, Jesus appears first to two disciples on the road to Emmaus (Luke 24:13–27). Though we usually assume that these two disciples are men (though it is not stated in the text), they could also be a married couple. Verse 18 names one of these two as Cleopas. Some think this is Clopas, whose wife, Mary, is named in John 19:25 as also present at Jesus's death.

discipleship as men: to recognise his identity, to turn and follow him, to take up their cross, and to be Jesus's witnesses in all the world.

Women's lives and words witness to the good news of God's love for his world, shown in the life, death, and resurrection of Jesus, and offered to all people, regardless of sex, status, or ethnicity. Women's discipleship includes their sexed embodiment, includes their lives as wives and mothers, but also takes up their intellectual, spiritual, social, and public selves, married or single. That women—and only women—are so central to key moments of Jesus's life and ministry defies attempts to suggest that women's discipleship is of a different nature to men's, or that women have a subordinate role in the ministry of the church. These stories of women show us that cultural values and norms for women's lives are not necessarily God's values and norms.

As we see what Jesus does in the lives of these Gospel women, and what he calls them to, I pray that we, too, are able to image who we ourselves might be in Christ and his kingdom. I recall the questions I explored as a young woman: "Where is Jesus leading me? Where does he call me to go and to serve? How is he equipping me by his Spirit?" In my own life, it seemed that the answer to those questions was teaching and leadership. What is Jesus leading you to?

Called, taught, transformed, and sent—women are inheritors of God's kingdom, heirs of his promises, and sent to proclaim the good news of his Son, Jesus Christ our Lord.

## Bibliography

Clements, E. Anne. *Mothers on the Margin? The Significance of the Women in Matthew's Genealogy*. Eugene, OR: Pickwick, 2014.

Forbes, Greg W., and Scott D. Harrower. *Raised from Obscurity: A Narratival and Theological Study of the Characterisation of Women in Luke-Acts*. Eugene, OR: Pickwick, 2015.

Green, Joel. "Blessed Is She Who Believed: Mary, Curious Exemplar in Luke's Narrative." In *Blessed One: Protestant Perspectives on Mary*, edited by Beverly Roberts Gaventa and Cynthia L. Rigby, 9–20. Louisville: Westminster John Knox, 2002.

Lee, Dorothy A. *The Ministry of Women in the New Testament: Reclaiming the Biblical Vision for Church Leadership*. Grand Rapids: Baker Academic, 2021.

Lloyd-Jones, Sally. *The Jesus Storybook Bible*. Illustrated by Jago. Anglicised ed. Grand Rapids: Zondervan, 2012.

McNutt, Jennifer Powell. *The Mary We Forgot: What the Apostle to the Apostles Teaches the Church Today*. Grand Rapids: Brazos, 2024.

# Interdependence in the Spirit

## *Love, Gifts, and the Body of Christ in 1 Corinthians*

Amy J. Erickson & Laura Rademaker

What difference does the Holy Spirit make for the ministries of women and men? Does the Holy Spirit give some gifts to women and others to men? Or, more to the point: do men get gifts of leading, teaching, pastoring, and prophecy while women get gifts of children's ministries, pastoral care, preparing the roster, and doing the washing up? Or does the Holy Spirit only intend women's gifts for some contexts, for only a subset of the church (i.e., other women and children)?

This chapter looks at passages in 1 Corinthians (chs. 11 and 14) that are often used to limit women's public ministries in some way. These are difficult passages to comprehend, and even the best scholars disagree on what they mean.

But a good rule of thumb when reading the Bible is, when you come across something that's not clear, look to *what is clear* and work back. That's our plan here. We'll look at 1 Cor 11 and 14 in light of what is abundantly clear in the chapters in between (12–13) and, of course, in the message of the gospel itself.

When you do that, the message is unmistakable. *Paul wants every believer—men and women alike—to use their Spirit-given gifts for the good of the whole church.* In 1 Corinthians, Paul doesn't argue *whether* women can speak publicly in church—he assumes it. Instead, he gives guidance on *how* they should do it, making sure that it's done in a way so that the whole church is built up. In other words, the main constraint that Paul puts on us is that our gifts should always be given out of love.

So let's begin at that cataclysmic moment, when the Holy Spirit came to that first generation of Jesus-followers: men and women alike, empowered to speak, serve, and lead.

## Signs of the Times

Long before Jesus came, the prophet Joel spoke of a great and glorious day of the Lord. This would be when God restored his people, bringing peace and justice to the land. God's people waited in hope. A sign that the day had finally arrived would be that men and women alike would prophesy, filled with the Spirit:

> I will pour out my Spirit on all people.
> Your sons and daughters will prophesy,
> your old men will dream dreams,
> your young men will see visions.
> Even on my servants, both men and women,
> I will pour out my Spirit in those days. (Joel 2:28–29)

It wasn't only men in the room on Pentecost. Luke, the author of the book of Acts, took care to mention that women were always part of the gatherings (Acts 1:14). When the Holy Spirit came on the morning of Pentecost, the apostles recognised the sign: the Holy Spirit had come to men and women without distinction.

In his sermon that day, Peter turned to Joel's prophecy (Acts 2:16–21). He recognised that the promised times in which God's Spirit was given to all people—both men and women—had now begun. Of course, women and men had both received the Spirit at particular times for particular purposes throughout the Old Testament. But this outpouring was on a radically new scale and was for *all who turned to Jesus*.

The book of Acts tells the story of the expansion of the news of this kingdom. As men and women received the gospel, so, too, they received the Holy Spirit (Acts 2:38). And the Holy Spirit did not discriminate by gender. Women not only received the Spirit, along with men, they also gave of their gifting in this shared Spirit, including in ministries of teaching (Acts 18:26), prophecy (Acts 21:9), and leadership (Rom 16:1, 7).

As the community of believers grew, they established churches—gatherings—in people's homes. As would be expected in this movement of the Spirit, many of these churches were led by or with women. Lydia led the church in her home in Philippi (Acts 16:40). Priscilla and Aquila, a married couple, led the church in Ephesus; Priscilla is likely named first to reflect her primary teaching and leadership role, with her husband as her support (Acts 18:16; Rom 16:3; 1 Cor 16:19; 2 Tim 4:19). Nympha led a church in Laodicea (Col 4:15), and Philemon and Apphia were leaders in Colossae (Phlm 2). Chloe may also have led a house church and was certainly a household leader (1 Cor 1:11). These homes were not the private spaces of retreat we have today. They were living places, but also businesses. They were homes to the extended family unit—not just the nuclear family—but also likely enslaved people and freed slaves. The head of the household was therefore also the manager of the family business. In terms of the churches, these women were ministers, patrons, hosts, and sometimes all three. The modern-day role of pastor didn't exist, but women were certainly leaders.

But not everything was fair sailing. The early church was still discerning what the implications were for this radical, Spirit-driven reconfiguration of their social life and relationships. And there's nowhere better to read of the challenges these communities faced than in the apostle Paul's letters to the early church in a city called Corinth, where he explains to them how to live as Spirit-filled people in their social and cultural reality.

## Spirit-Filled Ministry in 1 Corinthians

There are two particularly difficult and controversial passages in 1 Corinthians (1 Cor 11:2–16 and 14:33–35) that contain some of Paul's specific instructions related to gender. But the key to understanding the logic behind these passages is the chapters in between, chapters 12 and 13. These are famous words; if you've ever been to a Christian wedding you'd know chapter 13 as the "love" passage. They also lay out the guiding principles when it comes to spiritual gifts:

1. Although there are different gifts, there is one Holy Spirit who gives gifts for the building up of God's people (gifts like prophecy, wisdom, healing) regardless of social class or race (1 Cor 12:4–13).
2. Because there is one Spirit, there is one body—God's church—made up of all Christians. There are not separate churches for different classes or groups of believers: we are one (1 Cor 12: 12–14).
3. All gifts are vital for the well-being of the whole church, just as all members of the church are needed. No one can say they don't

need a particular person (or group of people) or their gifts (1 Cor 12:15–30).

4. Whatever gift someone has, the important thing is they use it in a way that is loving to others and builds them up. Love is what determines how and when we use our gifts because our gifts are not for ourselves but for the common good (1 Cor 12:7; 13:1–13).

In 1 Cor 12, the gifts Paul mentions include prophecy, wisdom, knowledge, healing, miracles, and tongues, as well as roles: apostles, prophets, and teachers (1 Cor 12:8–10, 28). Nowhere does he indicate that these might be reserved for a subset of Christians. Quite the opposite. He is emphatic; just as we all receive the same Spirit, we all share in the gifts of the Spirit (1 Cor 12:4–6).

The gifts are given indiscriminately, without regard to gender, for the good of the whole body. Paul is explicit: to suggest that one part of the body should not minister to another part would be like the eye telling the hand it doesn't need it, or the head saying it doesn't need the feet (1 Cor 12:21).

If any theology or church practice prevents one part of the church contributing to, or receiving ministry from, others, something has gone badly wrong.

But it's not easy to bring together a bunch of people from different classes and racial backgrounds, as well as different genders. Yes, they're one in the Spirit, but there's still cultural and social conventions that need to be kept in mind if they're going to experience that oneness without anyone getting hurt. The early Corinthians lived in a city obsessed with social status. They would need to work out how to live the truth of the gospel in their world. They would need to learn to use their spiritual gifts to show love to one another, and that is not always straightforward or easy.

With that foundation, we can look at some of the more challenging passages of that letter.

## 1 Corinthians 11:2–16

This passage is about how women and men should behave in the Corinthian house churches when they got up to prophesy publicly. But first, what's prophecy? It's not about predicting the future. Prophecy here is about speaking God's word for particular people in a particular place, a bit like what preachers today do when they not only explain the Bible but apply it. Paul considered prophecy one of the most important gifts for the building up of the church (1 Cor 14:4–5).

There's a lot of debate about what might have been going on in Corinth around gender and prophecy. These debates tend to focus on two things: what Paul means about head coverings, and what Paul means by the term *head*. We won't resolve all these puzzles. Instead we'll focus on what *is* clear. The Corinthians seemed to have been openly flouting their culture's gender norms in ways that caused offense. Paul's message to the congregation is to exercise good judgment about how to respect social convention *when* they share their gifts so that they can better build up the whole body of Christ.

## What's Unclear

So let's take a look at some of the interpretive challenges in 1 Cor 11.

1. Scholars have different ideas about the meaning of *head*. In English, *head* is normally a metaphor for "boss" or "leader," and it's tempting to assume that here. But scholars debate what exactly the metaphor means in New Testament Greek (see Scott Goode's chapter next).
2. Scholars don't agree on what cultural practice Paul is referring to. Is he talking about women's hairstyles (tied up or let loose), or what they wear on their head, or even a veil?
3. The Greek words for *man* and *husband* as well as *woman* and *wife* are the same, so it's not always clear if he's referring to men and women in general, or specifically to husbands and wives.
4. Whether his concern is hairdo or headwear, it's also not clear what the cultural significance of it was. Was it a sign of marriage—equivalent to today's wedding ring—such that taking it off was a disrespect to their partner? Was it a sign of sexual availability that was somewhat risqué?
5. Scholars even disagree on what Paul's conclusion is! If he's referring to head coverings as appropriate apparel, is he indicating that this should be the default (v. 13)? Or, is it that women aren't required to wear head coverings, since their hair serves just as well (v. 15)?[1]

1. Ciampa and Rosner, *First Letter*, 503–22; Brock and Wannenwetsch, *Therapy*, 34–39; Bird, *Bourgeois Babes*, 22–25.

Taking the passage as a whole, it seems like Corinthian women were prophesying at church in ways that were somehow disrespectful in the congregation. Perhaps it was like taking off their wedding ring and presenting themselves as single at church. Perhaps it was a scandalous move in a culture that thought bounded hair was more modest. Perhaps it was something else entirely.

The good news is that we don't actually need to know the answers to all these questions to appreciate, hear, and follow Paul's main points. So, what *is* clear?

## The Things That Are Clear

Women are fully participating in the church gathering and speaking publicly before a mixed congregation.[2] Paul has no problem with this. He assumes this will be happening and affirms it. His point is not about whether women should be speaking and contributing in the main, mixed gathering, but *how*.

Paul does describe men (or husbands) as the "head" of women (or wives) in 1 Cor 11:3 ("the head of every man is Christ, and the head of every woman is man, and the head of Christ is God"). But does this mean that Paul is setting up some kind of cosmic hierarchy in 11:3, with woman at the bottom and God the Father at the top? Well, no. If he wanted to do that, he would have ordered his list that way (God à Christ à men à women). But instead, he uses these couplets: man/Christ, *then* woman/man, *then* Christ/God—not in the order you would expect if he were trying to place women at the bottom of the pecking order.[3] By ordering it this way, it's almost as if he wants to *prevent* readers from inferring there's some kind of cosmic, linear chain of command.[4] Instead, his argument

2. Some argue that although women are clearly prophesying here, they are nonetheless barred from weighing prophesy (see Smith, *God's Good Design*, 91–92). For an explanation of the social conventions of the time that likely influenced Paul's instructions, see Ciampa and Rosner. They conclude, "There is no clear support for any view that Paul was prohibiting women from speaking in tongues, prophesying, or taking part in the weighing of prophecies" (Ciampa and Rosner, *First Letter*, 723–24).

3. Bird, *Bourgeois Babes*, 22.

4. Only a few chapters earlier Paul has explained that "the wife does not have authority over her own body but yields it to her husband. In the same way, the husband does not have authority over his own body but yields it to his wife" (1 Cor 7:4). Given he has just taught *against* hierarchical authority in marriage in this earlier chapter, it would be very strange if hierarchical authority were his intention here in chapter 11. For more on the significance of 1 Cor 7 for marriage, see the next chapter of this book.

is about each one in the couplet bringing honour to the other. The next chapter of this book will unpack the idea of "head." What's important to notice is that the man or husband being described as "head":

- does not affect women's freedom to use whatever gifts they have;
- does not limit those to whom women may minister; it is assumed women minister to men and women alike;
- does not prevent women from ministering in public, at the church gathering.

In Corinthian culture, it was important for women to show honour to men in their lives. Paul's point is to *enable* ministry by women alongside men by ensuring appropriate conventions *while* doing so.

What we see in this passage is that the gifts women have and use are not determined by their relationships to men (as wives, mothers, sisters, or daughters). Their gifts and use are determined by the Holy Spirit alone. However, *how* they deploy their gifts matter, because they (and we) do not live as isolated, individual beings. We all live in relation to one another. What matters is that we exercise our gifts in a way that honours the relationships around us and is motivated by love.

And so, consistent with 1 Cor 12 and 13, Paul is saying yes, women use your gifts but do it in a way that shows love to the men around you. In this case, don't disrespect your husband or men in the congregation by what you do with your hair/head *when* you are publicly praying and prophesying.

This concern about showing respect to one another is related to Paul's other main, animating point throughout this passage: the interdependence of men and women (1 Cor 11:11).

To underscore this, Paul goes back to the story of creation. Women, remember, you come from man (since Eve was formed from Adam's side), so show men proper honour (1 Cor 11:8). But men, don't forget, you also come from women (since every person is born of a woman; i.e., their mother). Women, too, are deserving of honour (1 Cor 11:9). Show honour to one another in how you express your distinct gender. Paul is stressing the interdependence of men and women: *unity in the Spirit in our diversity* (1 Cor 12:12–13).

So ultimately, he concludes, "in the Lord woman is not independent of man, nor is man independent of woman" (1 Cor 11:11). In Christ, and in the Spirit, men and women are equal and interdependent. Paul does not erase gender difference. Gender matters. Neither does he prescribe or limit certain gifts to men and other gifts to women. Instead, he insists that when you exercise your gifts at church, you should do so in a way that shows honour and respect—and ultimately, love—to each other.

## 1 Corinthians 14:33–36

The following chapters continue to unpack Paul's central concerns: the circulation and celebration of gifts throughout the body (ch. 12) and the driving motivation of love (ch. 13). Then we get to chapter 14, which throws up another round of interpretive puzzles. We're not helped that it seems like Paul is quoting someone else, and that New Testament Greek doesn't have punctuation. That means we don't know where his words start, and his quoting others begins.

But there's one thing these verses *can't* mean. As in chapter 11, they can't mean that women are not to participate fully in the church gathering. Paul has literally just given detailed instructions on *how* women are to behave *when they are speaking publicly at church.* He assumes and affirms women's public ministry in the context of mixed gatherings.

Ironically, and tragically, 1 Cor 14 has been used to justify blanket bans against women speaking or teaching in church gatherings. Usually, the focus is on verses 34–36:

> Women should remain silent in the churches. They are not allowed to speak, but must be in submission, as the law says. If they want to inquire about something, they should ask their own husbands at home; for it is disgraceful for a woman to speak in the church. (1 Cor 14:34–36)

So what's going on here? Is Paul blatantly contradicting himself, here suggesting women shouldn't speak at all in the gathering, when in chapter 11 he was at pains to try to express how women should comport themselves *when* they are speaking?

As with chapter 11, let's focus on what is clear, and keep an eye out for Paul's main point. Here's where doing some biblical homework, especially around the original language, comes in handy.

The word often translated "silent" in verse 34 can be translated "quiet." It's already been used two times immediately before this verse. In both verse 28 and verse 30 Paul commands that anyone who does not have an interpreter, or anyone who is currently speaking when someone else also has something to say, should also be "silent." We've just seen earlier in chapter 14 that Corinthian church gatherings had problems with people shouting over the top of each other and speaking other languages without translation in ways that excluded people. In chapter 13 Paul has just described those who use their gifts without love as deafeningly loud gongs and symbols. It's a noisy racket at Corinth. His insistence on quietness seems consistent with the calls to use spiritual gifts in ways that are not self-serving but show love, respect, and honour. All this accords with Paul's main, concluding point: that there be good order (14:33, 40), so that everyone can benefit (14:26).[5]

Attention to the biblical languages can also help clarify Paul's instructions in verses 34–36. The word translated "speaking" in verses 34 and 36 can also mean something more like "chatter." One way of understanding the cultural dynamics in Corinth is this: women were often less educated than men. It may have been that when someone said something in the gathering that they didn't understand, women were more prone to turn to their neighbour to ask what was going on. Instead of doing this, Paul encourages them to wait to discuss with their (likely more educated) husbands in private.[6]

There remain other confusing elements of this passage. What does Paul mean by being in submission to the law, in verse 34? And what's the connotation of the word translated "shameful" or "improper" in verse 35?[7] But we don't need to resolve all these questions in order to determine what *is* clear. From the beginning and end of the passage in verses 26 and 39, it is evident that both men and women are instructed to bring something to share at the gathering, and to seek out the gift of prophecy.

## How Can We Apply These Principles About Gender and the Gifts of the Spirit in Our Culture Today?

We've taken a look at some of Paul's most perplexing passages. The debates they fuel show no sign of stopping. But we can still appreciate what is clear from these passages and in harmony with the rest of Scripture.

5. Ciampa, and Rosner, *First Letter*, 729.

6. Gorman, *1 Corinthians*, 373–74.

7. For a good overview of the interpretive positions on these two verses, see Sprinkle, *From Genesis to Junia*, 219–37.

Let's start by considering what conclusions are ruled out. What can we be sure that Paul is *not* saying from these passages in 1 Corinthians?

- Paul is not issuing a blanket prohibition against women speaking in a mixed gathering of believers. In chapter 11 he is deliberating on what women should or shouldn't have on their head *when* they are speaking. In chapter 14, he assumes that *everyone* brings a word to build up others in the gathering. His concern is that each part of the body distribute their gift for the building up of the whole (1 Cor 12:7). There is no doubt that women are an integral part of Christ's body and its circulation of gifts.
- Paul is not suggesting there are no-go zones of ministry for women. This would go against Paul's insistence in chapter 12 that every part of the body needs all the others, as well as his insistence in chapter 11 that men and women are interdependent.

What positive implications can we draw from these chapters of his letter to the church in Corinth?

1. Women's gifts, including those gifted as prophets and teachers (1 Cor 12:28), are not only for women, but for the whole church (1 Cor 12:7, 21). So, rather than create a parallel church of women-only spaces, we need to find more ways for men to benefit from the gifts the Spirit has given to women. This is not to say that gender-segregated spaces don't have their place, but they must complement—rather than replace—opportunities for women to minister in mixed contexts.
2. This passage is about showing respect, honour, and love to one another when it comes to gender. This means that *both* men and women's experiences and self-expression as men and women need to be honoured in our churches. We do not need to erase gender as we share our gifts, but should share our gifts in a way that honours others. This will mean sensitivity to how gender is expressed respectfully in different cultures and subcultures, without losing sight of the freedom that we experience in the gospel to serve in and for Christ's body.

The question today is, how should women and men share their gifts with the body in a way that builds up one another? This will have some cultural overlay that could be quite specific to a particular church and its context. What it certainly means, though, is that women's gendered experience should not constrain the sharing of their gifts with the whole body of Christ.

Complicated though they are, Paul's concern in these passages is that men and women are interdependent in the Spirit. This cannot happen if women are excluded from sharing their gifts with men. It also cannot happen if men and women pretend that there are no differences between us. Instead, by sharing our gifts, without hiding our gender, men and women showcase our interdependence, unity, and love in the Spirit.

## Bibliography

Bird, Michael. *Bourgeois Babes, Bossy Wives, and Bobby Haircuts: A Case for Gender Equality in Ministry*. Grand Rapids: Zondervan, 2012. Kindle.

Brock, Brian, and Bernd Wannenwetsch. *The Therapy of the Christian Body*. Vol. 2 of *A Theological Exposition of Paul's First Letter to the Corinthians*. Eugene, OR: Cascade, 2018.

Ciampa, Roy E., and Brian S. Rosner. *The First Letter to the Corinthians*. Pillar New Testament Commentary. Grand Rapids: Eerdmans, 2010.

Gorman, Michael J. *1 Corinthians: A Theological, Pastoral, and Missionary Commentary*. Grand Rapids: Eerdmans, 2025.

Smith, Claire. *God's Good Design: What the Bible Really Says About Men and Women*. 2nd ed. Newtown, Australia: Matthias Media, 2019. Kindle.

Sprinkle, Preston. *From Genesis to Junia: An Honest Search for What the Bible Really Says About Women in Leadership*. Colorado Springs: Cook, 2026.

# How the New Testament Turns Marriage on Its Head

Scott Goode

When I married my wife, Nat, many (many) years ago, our vows were not the same. I pledged to *cherish* her; she promised to *obey* me. These different promises reflect a particular understanding of the New Testament—one that assigns husbands and wives different roles. On this view, husbands are called to loving sacrificial leadership of their households, wives to voluntary submission to that leadership. Proponents of this view insist that men and women share equal dignity as divine image-bearers, yet they affirm a gendered authority structure—sometimes a hierarchy—within marriage. This understanding of marriage matters for a book about women's ministry because many infer from it that gender-based authority in the home provides theological warrant for differing roles for women and men in the church.

Those who support this understanding of marriage traditionally appeal to several New Testament texts. Most prominently, Eph 5:21–33 describes the husband as "head of the wife" and calls wives to "submit to their husbands in everything." This text underpins their concept of male leadership or *headship* in marriage. Other passages include Col 3:18–19; 1 Pet 3:1–7; Titus 2:3–5; 1 Cor 11:2–16; and 14:33–35. In light of their prominence, this chapter will focus primarily on two representative passages: Eph 5:21–33 and 1 Pet 3:1–7.

But before we get there, I want to draw your attention to another passage that rarely surfaces in discussions about headship in marriage. In 1 Cor 7:4 (NRSVUE) Paul writes,

> The wife does not have authority over her own body, but the husband does; likewise, the husband does not have authority over his own body, but the wife does.

Given that 1 Cor 7 offers the New Testament's most extensive discussion of marriage, and since this verse gives such a clear statement about authority within marriage, its near absence from discussions about headship is striking. I will begin by tracing Paul's argument to show how this often-overlooked passage presents a radical vision of equal partnership in marriage.

## 1 Corinthians 7:1–6: Reciprocal Authority and Mutual Responsibility in Marriage

Paul begins by acknowledging a previous letter from the Corinthians: "Now concerning the matters about which you wrote: 'It is good for a man not to touch a woman'" (7:1 NRSVUE). The verb "to touch" functions here as a sexual euphemism, and most modern translations render it accordingly: "It is good for a man not *to have sexual relations* with a woman" (NIV, italics added). This assumes that Paul is quoting the view of a group within Corinth who reject the legitimacy of sexual pleasure—even within marriage—in favour of a higher spiritual ideal. The difficulty with this interpretation is that there is little, if any, evidence that the problems in Corinth reflect these pleasure-denying tendencies. On the contrary, there is significant evidence that Paul is responding to sexual excesses (1 Cor 5:1–13; 6:9–20; 7:9, 36).

A closer analysis of the verb "to touch" in ancient literature shows that when the term refers to sexual activity, it carries a negative connotation—depicting men acting out of selfish sexual desire.[1] The Christian Standard Bible captures this sense well: "It is good for a man not to use a woman for sex" (1 Cor 7:1). This discovery is significant for what Paul writes next:

> But because sexual immorality [men using women for sex] is so common, each man should have sexual relations with his own wife, and each woman should have sexual relations with her own husband. (1 Cor 7:2)

1. Ciampa and Rosner, *First Corinthians*, 272–75.

Given Paul's commendation of singleness throughout the rest of chapter 7, he is not suggesting that everyone should marry, but rather that every married man—and likewise every married woman—should commit to an exclusive, sexually active relationship with their spouse. Paul's emphasis, however, goes further: it extends to the very *pattern* of sexual relations within marriage. In view of the sexual misuse of women by Corinthian men, as evidenced in the immediately previous section (1 Cor 6:12–20), Paul establishes a Christian ethic for marriage in which sexual relations are mutual. To be clear, he is not suggesting that marriage is the answer to sexual desire; such reasoning would fall into the very error Paul critiques—namely, the sexual use of another person for one's own gratification.[2] Rather, the contrast is between men using women for self-indulgent purposes and the reciprocal pattern of intimacy in marriage that is fitting for those who belong to Christ.

The next verses offer practical implications of such reciprocity while also expressing Paul's central claim about authority in marriage. The following outline using the NRSVUE—with my explanations in brackets—shows the logical flow of 1 Cor 7:1–6:

| | |
|---|---|
| Introduction (7:1–2) | Now concerning the matters about which you wrote: "It is good for a man not to touch [sexually use] a woman." But because of [such] cases of sexual immorality [men using women for sex], each man should have [sexual relations with] his own wife and each woman [should have sexual relations with] her own husband. |
| Sexual Implications (7:3) | The husband should give to his wife what is due to her and likewise the wife to her husband. |
| Central Marital Claim (7:4) | For the wife does not have authority over her own body, but the husband does; likewise, the husband does not have authority over his own body, but the wife does. |
| Sexual Concessions (7:5–6) | Do not deprive one another except perhaps by agreement for a set time, to devote yourselves to prayer, and then come together again, so that Satan may not tempt you because of your lack of self-control. This I say by way of concession, not of command. |

This outline highlights the way in which 1 Cor 7:4 functions as Paul's central claim about the character of marriage itself. Over and against men's sexual exploitation of women—which reflected, at least in

2. Paul's encouragement to marry rather than "burn with passion" (1 Cor 7:9) is likely addressed to an engaged couple, not a single person (see also 1 Cor 7:36–38).

part, ancient assumptions of female inferiority and subordination (see Gladwin's chapter in this book)—Paul's statement stands without parallel in the literature of the ancient world.[3] There is neither hierarchy nor a differentiation of roles. Rather, marriage is a reciprocal relationship in which each partner holds equal authority and serves the marriage with the same agency and responsibility.

These principles of shared authority and submission to one another are concretely expressed in the surrounding verses which outline a symmetrical pattern of sexual self-giving. Moreover, each spouse is granted equal agency, even where they might agree not to have sex. Paul addresses wives alongside their husbands as devoted to prayer and as vulnerable to sexual temptation. Decisions in Christian marriage, therefore, are to be negotiated and made by mutual agreement (1 Cor 7:5). These expectations anticipate how Paul addresses women throughout the rest of 1 Cor 7. In the various scenarios of singleness, marriage, separation, and widowhood, women are addressed as responsible agents who are called to recognise God's purpose for them. Indeed, in 1 Cor 7:14, wives—who, incidentally, are mentioned first—are depicted as agents of spiritual influence over their unbelieving husbands *in the same way* that believing husbands may influence their unbelieving wives. As mothers, they likewise carry the *same* spiritual influence over their children as fathers do.

In asserting these principles of shared authority and mutual submission, Paul is likely reflecting the *one-flesh* creation ideal described in Gen 2:24. Not only has he just quoted this text in 1 Cor 6:16, but he also refers to Jesus's affirmation of this creation principle in 1 Cor 7:10 (Matt 19:4–6; Mark 10:1–12), and he likely alludes to Gen 2–3 in verses between these references.[4] Perhaps, too, Paul is influenced by the portrayal of sexual love in the Song of Solomon in which a woman and her beloved freely participate in a relationship in which neither is more vulnerable nor more powerful: "My beloved is mine and I am his" (2:16).[5]

3. Fee, "Male and Female," 181.

4. For example, the nuptial analogy (1 Cor 6:17/Gen 2:24), the phrase "it is good for a man" (1 Cor 7:1/Gen 2:18), the verb "to touch" (1 Cor 7:1/Gen 3:3), and the temptation of Satan (1 Cor 7:5/Gen 3:1–5).

5. Wüst describes this ideal relationship and its consistency with 1 Cor 7:3–4. See Wüst, *Song of Solomon*, 53–54.

## Ephesians 5:21–33: Subverting Hierarchy Through Mutual Service and Unity

This one-flesh ideal also underlies Paul's teaching in Ephesians (Gen 2:24 is cited in Eph 5:31). At first glance, Eph 5:21–33 might not seem to reflect the mutuality of marriage observed in 1 Cor 7. Instead, it could appear to describe a relationship of order, authority, or even hierarchy, especially given the instructions for wives to submit to their husbands as head. However, careful attention to the literary context, together with an appreciation of the meaning and limits of the head-body metaphor within the flow of the argument, suggests that Paul's emphasis lies on the unity of marriage and the mutual service of spouses. Such an interpretation aligns closely with the teaching of 1 Cor 7:1–6.

Paul's specific instructions to the various relationships within the ancient household depend on the introductory statement in Eph 5:21: "Submit to one another out of reverence for Christ."[6] One way to read this verse is as a general heading introducing the forms of submission appropriate within the various relationships of the Christian household: wives to husbands (5:22–33), children to parents (6:1–4), and slaves to masters (6:5–9). Since there are no explicit reversals of the verb—for example, husbands are not told to submit to their wives—some argue that Eph 5:21 does not call for mutual submission, but rather for the proper submission of believers to those in authority over them.

However, even among those who interpret the passage in this way, some acknowledge that the idea of reciprocity gives a distinctively Christian shape to Paul's household code in Ephesians.[7] For example, Paul writes to masters, "Treat your slaves *in the same way*" (Eph 6:9, italics added). It is unclear which aspects of the preceding slave-master section (6:5–8) are in view, but at the very least the command means the cessation of threats and the recognition of a shared humanity grounded in the divine master to whom all belong and in whom there is no favouritism (6:9). The section addressed to children and parents likewise displays subtle hints of reciprocity. Just as children are to "obey your parents in the Lord" (Eph 6:1), so also fathers are to exercise their authority for the

6. The verb "be filled" (with the Spirit, Eph 5:18) is the imperative on which Paul's subsequent participle, "to submit" (Eph 5:21), depends. The absence of any verb in Eph 5:22 makes Paul's instructions to wives grammatically dependent upon what has come before.

7. Thielman, *Ephesians*, 373–74.

good of their children, who, it is implied, also belong to the Lord (6:4).[8] And lest we be tempted to think that Paul endorses the ancient view of the father as the primary authority over his children (see Gladwin's chapter of this book), we should note that Eph 6:4 represents Paul's attempt to regulate the *misuse* of paternal authority, and that this section of the code is framed by the call for children to obey and honour *both* parents equally (6:1–2).

Given these hints of reciprocity—even if they could not possibly be fully symmetrical in the relative circumstances—under the heading of "submit to one another" (Eph 5:21), we might ask what kind of reciprocity Paul envisions in marriage. Is there a principle of mutual submission, consistent with 1 Cor 7:1–6, that husbands and wives are called to practise?

Much ink has been spilt on the meaning of the word translated "head." In ancient literature, when used metaphorically, it could mean *source*, *leader in authority*, or *preeminent*. These meanings are not mutually exclusive. Along with many others, I take *preeminent* to best capture the social prominence husbands held in marriage—an assumed social status reflecting the obvious realities of the ancient world: marriage was organised around the husband's authority and honour, which wives were expected to uphold.[9]

Notably, Paul employs a *head-body* metaphor: "The husband is the head of the wife as Christ is the head of the church, his body" (Eph 5:23). In ancient literature, the head was seen as vital for the well-being of the body. In medical, political, and military examples, the head was considered the most powerful and competent part relative to the body, while the body's role was to serve, protect, sacrifice for, honour, and even love the head. The head even bore a duty of self-preservation![10] And so, while Paul's description of husbands as heads and his injunction for wives to submit would have initially resonated with prevailing social norms, his next command introduces a surprising twist: "Christ loved the church and gave himself up for her. . . . In this same way, husbands ought to love their wives as their own bodies" (Eph 5:25, 28). This call to sacrificial

8. Thielman, *Ephesians*, 401.

9. Many scholars prefer preeminence, including Thiselton, *First Corinthians*, 821; Barnett, *1 Corinthians*, §4; Campbell, *Ephesians*, 249. Complementarian scholars acknowledge that *prominence* and *authority* legitimately overlap in meaning; on this, see Grudem, "Meaning of κεφαλή," 199. My point of difference with Grudem, however, is my emphasis on the husband's prominent status and authority as conditioned by its ancient social setting.

10. Lee-Barnewall, *Neither Complementarian nor Egalitarian*, §8.

love toward a social subordinate, as Lee-Barnewall observes, represents a "reversal of status conventions":

> When Paul asks husbands, and not wives, to love and sacrifice, this reversal would be shocking in light of traditional status conventions because he tells the most honored part, the head, to perform the duties of the less honored member.[11]

The result of this role reversal, however, is not an inverted hierarchy, but a new oneness: "Husbands ought to love their wives as their own bodies" (5:28). Paul grounds this union in the one-flesh ideal of creation (Eph 5:31; Gen 2:24), which mirrors the communion of Christ and the church (Eph 5:32). Significantly, these theological foundations lead Paul to conclude, not with the language of submission and headship, but with that of respect and love (5:33). Notably, it is the more socially powerful husband who is now addressed first and the Greek mood of the verb used to address the wife is more suggestive ("may") compared to the one used for the husband ("must").[12] Moreover, these virtues of respect and love are elsewhere not exclusive to either partner or role within marriage (Titus 2:3–5; 1 Pet 3:7).

This way of understanding Eph 5:21–33 invites a thought experiment: what if Paul intended to encourage spouses into a relational pattern of mutual submission? Such a possibility would have been difficult to imagine in the ancient world. Legal and social norms reinforced a gendered hierarchy between wives and husbands, just as they did a status hierarchy between slaves and masters. In both cases, however, the revelation of Christ (3:8–12) reorientated reality in a way that invited those indwelt by his Spirit (5:18) to embody a new vision for living together, even if unable to fully express it within the constraints of the wider society. If this reading is correct, how, then, might Paul invite spouses to participate in a relationship of shared authority and mutual belonging consistent with that described in 1 Cor 7:1–6? Here lies the power of metaphor which Lynn Cohick explains "is designed to bring a new perspective to the reader":

> It would be almost impossible from a cultural standpoint for Paul's audience to make sense of a direct statement for husbands to submit to wives, for the social expectations would not have envisioned it. Moreover, the legal codes treated adult women as

11. Lee-Barnewall, *Neither Complementarian nor Egalitarian*, §8.
12. Walsh and Miller, "Translating Ephesians 5.33," 93–109.

> "minors," which would have made nonsense of Paul's request. Yet in terms of actual practices, Paul does in fact ask husbands to submit—in his command that they love their wives as Christ loved the church and gave himself up to death on the cross that the church might live. Such actions undermine the gender hierarchy by ceding honor to the wife as worthy of the husband's self-sacrifice.[13]

To summarise, the overarching call to "submit to one another" (Eph 5:21), together with the rhetorical effect of Paul's head-body metaphor, supports his emphasis on marital unity grounded in both creation and the Christ-church relationship. Although this ideal was constrained by the prevailing legal and social structures, the pattern of mutual service could take root in the mindset and relational dynamics of the Christian household, consistent with Paul's depiction of marital life in 1 Cor 7:1–6.

## 1 Peter 3:1–7: Coheirs of Salvation

While 1 Cor 7:1–6 and Eph 5:21–33 focus on life within the Christian household—emphasising mutual submission and unity—Peter places marriage on a more public stage. The home becomes a place of Christian witness amid tensions with, and even persecutions from, the surrounding culture. The instruction for wives to submit "in the same way" (1 Pet 3:1) situates these marital directions within the wider call to "submit yourselves for the Lord's sake to every human authority" (2:13). This includes submission to government (2:13–17) and to household masters (2:18–20), settings in which believers may suffer unjustly. In this context, Christ's own suffering serves as the model for believers to entrust themselves to "him who judges justly" (2:23).[14] This reference to Christ, woven into Peter's household code, suggests that his instructions to married believers also address situations that may be far less than ideal (3:1, 6). Indeed, the entire section is introduced by drawing attention to Christian witness in the face of hostility: "Live such good lives among the pagans that, though they accuse you of doing wrong, they may see your good deeds and glorify God on the day he visits us" (2:12; see also 2:15; 3:15–17; 4:12).

13. Cohick, *Ephesians*, 352–53.

14. As I explain further down, the encouragement to follow Christ's example is not grounds to stay in an abusive marriage.

Within this context, 1 Pet 3:1–7 presents the submission of wives as a posture that commends the gospel to a watching world—even to an unbelieving husband: "They may be won over without words by the behaviour of their wives" (3:1). Yet the situation is messy—even ironic—for the very existence of a mixed religious marriage would have been considered a failure of submission. As Plutarch explains, "A wife ought not to make friends of her own, but to enjoy her husband's friends in common with him. The gods are the first and most important friends. Wherefore it is becoming for a wife to worship and to know only the gods that her husband believes in."[15] In contrast, Peter expects Christian wives to express a degree of autonomy and maintain allegiance to Christ while embodying, as far as possible, ancient virtues of submission and associated ideals of the "inner self" (3:2–4).

To illustrate these ideals, Peter appeals to Sarah as a model of obedience (1 Pet 3:5–6), although scholars debate which occasions are in view.[16] Sarah refers to Abraham as "lord" only in Gen 18:12, and that in a moment of doubt over God's promise. Curiously, the Greek Old Testament never uses the verb "to obey" of Sarah toward Abraham; instead, it describes Abraham obeying Sarah (Gen 16:2; see also 16:5–6; 21:12). Even so, Sarah's submissive posture may be inferred from her departure with Abraham from Haran to Canaan (Gen 12:1–5), and from her willingness to comply with his requests even when they placed her in harm's way (12:13; 20:2). Perhaps such scenarios, where the Lord ultimately delivered her (12:17; 20:3), correspond to Peter's encouragement to wives to "do what is right and do not give way to fear" (1 Pet 3:6). Whatever the specific examples, Sarah's submission models courage in uncertainty and reflects the expected behaviour of wives within an ancient patriarchal culture. By following such an example, the women Peter addresses would commend Christian faith in their society in general—and to their husbands in particular.

It is important to note that this passage does not lend support to a modern scenario in which a wife might be encouraged to "bear up" under unjust treatment at the hands of her husband. Although Sarah is commended, Abraham's decisions that put her at risk are never endorsed in Genesis or by Peter. In fact, where submission to "unjust suffering" is addressed in the context of slavery (1 Pet 2:18–21), the emphasis lies

15. Plutarch, *Advice to Bride and Groom*, 140D.

16. Some scholars suggest that extra-biblical Jewish texts may also serve as background material (e.g., The Testament of Abraham).

on the injustice of such suffering and on the assurance that perpetrators will not escape God's judgment (2:12). Such hope motivated early Christian tradition to oppose, and where possible to overcome, entrenched forms of injustice, whether in the institution of slavery or within family contexts. Indeed, Peter—shaped by Jewish ethical tradition—would have firmly opposed the mistreatment of one's spouse, as becomes clear in the very next section in the way he addresses husbands.

Turning to husbands, he again situates his instructions ("in the same way," 1 Pet 3:7) within the wider call to show respect to everyone (2:17). Husbands are to "be considerate as you live with your wives, and treat them with respect as the weaker partner" (3:7). Such sympathy resonates with ancient ideals, although likely for reasons different from those of Peter. Whereas ancient sources might appeal to women's supposed moral or intellectual inferiority, Peter's treatment of women throughout the letter—and the example of Sarah's strength—makes such an interpretation doubtful. More likely, he refers to a woman's relative physical and social vulnerability: "the more vulnerable member."[17] He may even be continuing an allusion to Sarah's own comment about being "worn out" (Gen 18:12), past the age of childbearing, which is found in the same sentence where she calls Abraham "lord."[18] In any case, Peter's emphasis moves quickly from sympathy for relative vulnerability to recognition of an equal spiritual status: "Treat them . . . as heirs with you of the gracious gift of life" (1 Pet 3:7). A woman's perceived weakness in the ancient world was reason to maintain her subordinate status, but the movement in Peter's letter is toward her exalted standing. The single Greek word often translated "coheirs" (CSB) calls husbands—those with greater social power—to reimagine the marital relationship in light of their shared salvation (1:3–9). Here again Peter subverts ancient gender norms and grounds ideal marital relations not in cultural expectations but in the resurrection of Christ.

In 1 Peter, the literary context suggests that the submission of wives conforms to ancient ideals of public respect and with the missional aim of influencing an unbelieving husband. Peter does not ground this instruction in Gen 1–2, nor in the Christ-church typology, but he does appeal to Christ as a model of unjust suffering. An ideal relational pattern does not emerge until the end of the section, when husbands are summoned to

17. Keener, *1 Peter*, 245; Jobes, *1 Peter*, 209.

18. Bott, "Sarah," 243–59.

relate to their wives as coheirs of the salvation Christ provides. In a way analogous to Eph 5:21–33, those with social privilege are called to resist prevailing norms and reimagine patterns of relating in a way that reflects equal authority (1 Cor 7:4), mutual submission (Eph 5:21), and marital unity (Eph 5:28–33).

## Partners in Life and Ministry

Against the prevailing social norms of the ancient world, the New Testament reimagines marriage as a partnership in which each spouse shares authority, responsibility, and agency in their relationship. In the decades since Nat and I exchanged vows, this vision has increasingly shaped our life together. We have learned to communicate our needs honestly and assertively to each other. By each taking responsibility for ourselves, we have both ensured personal and spiritual growth while also sharing leadership in the faith formation of our children. We have built a friendship and partnership as equals, seeking to serve the well-being of each other, our family, and wider community.

Marriage requires navigating difference. Research suggests that only 31 percent of couples' problems are solvable. Given that this leaves 69 percent of marital problems as ongoing, couples require effective relationship skills to negotiate conflict, including positive start-up skills, the ability to repair interactions, self-sooth, accept influence, and compromise.[19] The idea that one partner holds ultimate authority or can cast a tiebreaking vote runs counter to both lived wisdom and the teaching of Scripture. Indeed, studies on flourishing marriages consistently point instead to mutual understanding, shared influence, cooperative decision-making, and an equal sharing of power and responsibility.[20]

Christian marriage, however, is not only a partnership in life but also a partnership in ministry. To be coheirs of salvation means that the service spouses offer one another is ultimately for Christ. Even if your spouse is not a believer, take heart—you convey spiritual influence throughout your household, whether as a wife and mother or as a husband and father. Being coheirs of salvation in the home also shapes how we understand ministry within the household of faith—the church. If Scripture addresses wives and husbands as equal partners in marriage, this provides theological support

19. Gottman, "Gottman Method Couples Therapy," 1–10.

20. Jonathan and Knudson-Martin, "Building Attunement," 95–111.

for the equal ministry of women and men in the church—a claim explored more fully in other chapters of this book.

## Bibliography


Barnett, Paul. *1 Corinthians: A Letter of Love*. Reading the Bible Today Series. Sydney: Aquila, 2022. Kindle.

Bott, Nicholas T. "Sarah as the 'Weaker Vessel': Genesis 18 and 20 in 1 Peter's Instructions to Husbands in 1 Pet 3:7." *Trinity Journal* 36 (2015) 243–59.

Campbell, Constantine R. *The Letter to the Ephesians*. Pillar New Testament Commentary. Grand Rapids: Eerdmans, 2023.

Ciampa, Roy E., and Brian S. Rosner. *The First Letter to the Corinthians*. Pillar New Testament Commentary. Grand Rapids: Eerdmans, 2010.

Cohick, Lynn H. *The Letter to the Ephesians*. New International Commentary on the New Testament. Grand Rapids: Eerdmans, 2020.

Fee, Gordon F. "Male and Female in the New Creation: Galatians 3:26–29." In *Discovering Biblical Equality: Complementarity Without Hierarchy*, edited by Ronald W. Pierce et al., 172–85. 2nd ed. Downers Grove, IL: IVP Academic, 2005.

Gottman, Julie Schwartz. "Introduction: An Abbreviated History and Overview of Gottman Method Couples Therapy." In *The Marriage Clinic Casebook*, edited by Julie Schwartz Gottman, 1–10. New York: Norton, 2004.

Grudem, Wayne. "The Meaning of κεφαλή ('Head'): An Evaluation of New Evidence, Real and Alleged." In *Biblical Foundations for Manhood and Womanhood*, edited by Wayne Grudem, 145–202. Foundations for the Family Series. Wheaton, IL: Crossway, 2002.

Jobes, Karen H. *1 Peter*. Baker Exegetical Commentary on the New Testament. Grand Rapids: Baker Academic, 2005.

Jonathan, Naveen, and Carmen Knudson-Martin. "Building Attunement and Gender Equality in Heterosexual Relationships." *Journal of Couple & Relationship Therapy* 11 (2012) 95–111.

Keener, Craig S. *1 Peter: A Commentary*. Grand Rapids: Baker Academic, 2021.

Lee-Barnewall, Michelle. *Neither Complementarian nor Egalitarian: A Kingdom Corrective to the Evangelical Gender Debate*. Grand Rapids: Baker Academic, 2016. Kindle.

Plutarch. *Moralia*. Translated by Frank Cole Babbitt. Vol. 2. Loeb Classical Library 222. Cambridge: Harvard University Press, 1928.

Thielman, Frank. *Ephesians*. Baker Exegetical Commentary on the New Testament. Grand Rapids: Baker Academic, 2010.

Thiselton, Anthony C. *The First Epistle to the Corinthians*. New International Greek Testament Commentary. Grand Rapids: Eerdmans, 2000.

Walsh, Julie, and Jeffrey D. Miller. "Translating Ephesians 5.33." *Bible Translator* 74 (2023) 93–109.

Wüst, Kamina. *Song of Solomon*. Matthias Bible Guides. Sydney: Matthias Media, 2024.

# Leadership, Teaching, and Women in 1 Timothy, 2 Timothy, and Titus

Michael F. Bird

Is 1 Tim 2:11–15 the biblical door slamming in the face of women who believe that they are called to preach, teach, and lead in the church? Or else, as Christopher Hutson notes, "this verse is the slender column that supports the entire stained-glass ceiling above which women are not allowed to rise in many churches."[1] I imagine many people have rushed to this chapter because for them this text is the number-one issue they have questions about, or else perhaps they want to see if their opinions on this contested subject are validated here.

You might be surprised to know that I have changed my mind on the meaning of this passage. I once believed that this text was a defensive wall erected to keep women, feminists, and liberals from accommodating church leadership to worldly values. I changed my mind, not by a capitulation to culture, but from immersing myself in the world of the early church, and reading passages like 1 Tim 2:11–15 (and others) with fresh eyes. Such is what I want to do in this chapter, which will be admittedly longer than other chapters in this volume, but this is because of the somewhat technical nature of the issues and problems discussed. In the end, I hope to show that in God's design, women have a place and valued roles at all levels of leadership in the church and its ministries.

Women and church leadership matters because leadership matters. Leaders are important to any organisation as they provide direction, structure, and set the cultural tone. However, a cursory glance across Paul's letters

1. Hutson, *Timothy and Titus*, 75.

and the book of Acts suggests that the precise leadership offices, functions, and responsibilities within the early church do not appear to be entirely clear or even.[2] Plus, we have to navigate the subject of Christian leadership and gender rules in marriage and the church; a topic upon which much ink has been spilt.

The letters of 1 Timothy, 2 Timothy, and Titus together make up the Pastoral Epistles (PE) and are the part of the New Testament that has the most to say about church officers and leadership. They set out the qualifications for overseers (1 Tim 3:1–7), elders (Titus 1:5–16), deacons (1 Tim 3:8–13), general instructions about the character and tasks of a church leader (1 Tim 4:6–16; 2 Tim 2:14–26; 4:1–5; Titus 2:1–10), and of course a particularly notorious and contested restriction on women from some kind of teaching role (1 Tim 2:11–14). If we are to uphold the New Testament, and the PE in particular, as authoritative for understanding the qualities and qualifications for a Christian leader, then these letters must be taken seriously for what they teach about what that leadership and teaching authority look like in practice.

This chapter will briefly sketch out the qualities of a Christian leader according to the PE. I'll also assess whether women are prohibited from the leadership roles and teaching ministries of the church. To do this, first I'll look at the general attributes and abilities required of church leaders. Second, I'll examine 1 Tim 2:11–14 and analyse its precise prohibition on women teaching in the churches. This will hopefully yield a picture of what makes a good Christian leader and how women can fit into such a leadership role.

In a nutshell, while 1 Tim 2:11–15 makes a prohibition that restricts the women *in Ephesus* from a particular kind of teaching—motivated by a variety of localised reasons—the text does not establish a masculine moat around the teaching and leadership offices of the church.

## The Marks of a Christian Leader in the Pastoral Epistles

The PE are not a leadership manual as if they aim to describe *7 Habits of Highly Effective Pastors* or *The Indisputable Laws of Christian Leadership*, to echo the names of bestselling leadership guides. Yet, as Paul writes to Timothy and Titus, instructing them on how to pastor, protect, discipline,

2. For example, Giles, *Patterns of Ministry*; Giles, "Church Order, Government," 219–26.

and nurture the assemblies under their care, Paul *does* make a number of exhortations about the character and conduct of Christian leaders.

Christians leaders specified as overseers and deacons are to have a moral character. They must have integrity, pursue holiness, be hospitable, be above reproach, be faithful to their spouses (if married), and be self-controlled (1 Tim 3:1–13; Titus 1:5–9). The reference to wives does not require an overseer to be a man any more than it requires them to be married. They are to be effective managers of their own households—though in practice it was often mothers, wives, and daughters who did the heavy lifting in that role (1 Tim 3:4–5; Titus 1:6). In addition, Christian leaders are custodians of the faith and have the responsibility of teaching doctrine and responsibly handling Scripture (1 Tim 1:3–4; 2 Tim 2:15) with the added task of ensuring that their churches remain faithful to Christian teaching as handed down from the leaders of the early church (1 Tim 6:20–21; 2 Tim 1:13–14). Paul emphasises, too, the importance of mentoring and raising up the next generation of leaders, who are encouraged to train and equip others for ministry (2 Tim 2:2). Finally, Christian leaders need fortitude and resilience, they should be able to endure hardships and remain steadfast in their faith, serving as examples to their congregations (2 Tim 2:3–4). I hasten to note that these qualities are not restricted to a single gender—i.e., men—but the PE are not without controversy concerning the access of women to the offices of teaching and leading in the church.

## Reading 1 Timothy 2:11–15 in the Shadow of the Artemis Cult

The prohibition on women teaching in 1 Tim 2:12 is anchored in the particular circumstances in Ephesus associated mostly with the towering religious and sociocultural influence of the Artemis cult on Ephesus and its people, including upon new converts.[3] It makes sense then to look into the relevance of the Artemis cult—the economic, social, religious, and political hub of Ephesus—in relation to Paul's letter to a ministry apprentice living in Ephesus.

3. See Strelan, *Paul, Artemis*; Hoag, *Wealth in Ancient Ephesus*; Immendörfer, *Ephesis and Artemis*; Hooker, "Artemis of Ephesus," 37–46; Ellis, "Apostle Paul in Ephesus," 22–34; Glahn, *Nobody's Mother*.

Some scholars reject this move on the grounds that Paul does not explicitly mention Artemis. They claim that bringing Artemis to the analysis becomes a convenient way to circumvent Paul's clear prohibition, which is anchored in creation and not social context. For instance, Tom Schreiner asserts that, "There is no clear evidence in Paul's letters that the Artemis cult played a role. Paul does not mention the cult, nor is there any specific notion in the text that shows the influence of the cult."[4] I acknowledge the weight of the objection, but I think such an objection can be addressed for three reasons.

1. In Luke's account of Paul's ministry in Ephesus in Acts 19, the cult of Artemis was a massive factor. Devotion to Artemis impacted the events of Paul's ministry in Ephesus, climaxing in a vicious mob that gathered for the purpose of lynching Paul. The significant number of converts who abandoned paganism to follow Jesus was detrimental to the business of idol-makers who made their living from iconic devotion to Artemis and who accused Paul of "dishonoring the great goddess Artemis" (Acts 19:27). So, in 1 Timothy as in Acts 19, Paul addresses the consequences of the Artemis cult without having to explicitly state the edifice's presence because the Artemis cult cast a looming shadow upon everything in Ephesus.
2. One cannot interpret Paul's letters in a vacuum nor flatten out the distinctives of the Ephesian context by saying Ephesus was simply the same as every other Greco-Roman city. While some things might be true everywhere, nowhere is like everywhere, every place has its own atmosphere and complexities. Paul's remarks in 1 Tim 2:8–15 are not necessarily deployable or need to be duplicated in every house church situation any more than his defence of his apostleship needed to be rehearsed in every church he had established (1 Cor 9:1–27).
3. New Testament scholar Michael Immendörfer wrote a whole thesis on the Artemis cult as the background to the letter to the Ephesians.[5] He found similar language in Paul's letter to the Ephesians and inscriptions and coins about Artemis. Immendörfer thinks Paul's letter to the Ephesians may have even been written for converts from the Artemis cult. If Immendörfer is even partially right,

4. Schreiner, "Response to Linda Belleville," 108. Similarly, Baugh, "Foreign World," 25–64.

5. Immendörfer, *Ephesis and Artemis.*

> then why not think that Artemis provides the background to 1 Timothy? After all, 1 Timothy is addressed to Timothy in Ephesus and his situation as a pastoral leader there.

I do have a couple of important caveats at this point about the use and misuse of appeals to background to explain (away) Paul's prohibition in 1 Tim 2:12.

First, the connection to Artemis does not change the fact that Paul does make a prohibition about a woman teaching a man (however we understand the who, what, and why). A real restriction is made with argumentation to back it up and it was urgent and important at the time to do so. What I am trying to press is that correctly grasping the context of Ephesus, dominated as it was by the Artemis cult, explains the circumstances behind the prohibition, puts the prohibition about a woman teaching into a concrete situation, accounts for its departure from the teachings of the rest of Paul's letters, and ensures that we do not apply the prohibition in ways for which it was not intended. In other words, the *where* and *why* of the prohibition in 1 Tim 2:12 are important for *how* we apply it today!

Second, many scholars unfortunately appeal to an incorrect view of the Artemis cult. The Artemis cult was not a hyper-feminist cult, nor was it a fertility religion, and neither was it a cult run by females only.[6] The Artemis cult had long had male officiates called *kyretes* who were involved in its rites, operation, and leadership. Women did play a prominent role and Artemis was particularly popular with women because she was the goddess of midwifery, childbirth, and virginity.

A basic biography of the Artemis cult runs as follows:[7]

- The cult of Artemis existed since the fourth century BC to the third century AD.
- In the Artemis myth, Artemis was the virgin daughter of Zeus and Leto. After seeing her mother Leto go through a painful nine-day labour for her brother Apollo, she asked Zeus for permission to remain an eternal virgin and to roam about helping women in childbirth. A woman would pray to Artemis in childbirth, "Goddess, give me a good birth or a quick death."

6. A point emphasised by Glahn, *Nobody's Mother*.
7. See Mussies, "Artemis," 91–97; Higgins, *Seven Wonders*.

- Ephesus was the temple warden of the goddess Artemis. The Artemesion, a massive temple complex, was to Ephesus what Disneyland is to Anaheim in LA. The Artemesion was one of the largest buildings in Mediterranean world, even larger than the Athenian Parthenon, and was one of the seven wonders of the ancient world.
- The Artemesion was the centre of religious, social, economic, and political life in Ephesus. Artemis provided the sacred reality into which the residents of the city lived as the goddess was the patron and protector of the city. This is why it was easy to whip up a mob who could chant for two hours, "Great is Artemis of the Ephesians" (Acts 19:34). Devotion to the goddess was the measure of patriotism as much as piety in first century Ephesus.

How does the Artemis cult help us make sense of 1 Tim 2:8–15 in first-century Ephesus? Let's set our bearings with a primer on the text and then go through verse by verse to see how.

## A Primer on 1 Timothy 2:8–15: Paul's Concern About Bad Teaching

This brings us to 1 Tim 2:8–15, a passage fraught with debate about gender roles, church authority, and who can lead and teach in the church. Some detect here a prohibition for all time against women teaching and leading in churches, while others identify a specific episode that only restricts women from certain roles because they remain mired in the worldview of Ephesus (the city where Timothy was conducting his ministry) and need to be further instructed. Paul's first letter to Timothy begins with Paul's greeting to Timothy and then, in 1 Tim 1:3–11, he goes into a warning about false teaching. The letter also ends with another warning about false teaching in 1 Tim 6:2–10. So, exhortations about the dangers of false teaching tops and tails the letter, meaning that *orthodox teaching and worship are really the major issues of concern, not gender hierarchy* per se.

What was this false teaching that Paul worried was taking hold in Ephesus? For my mind, I think the false teaching described here is a type of proto-Gnostic view that had begun to emerge in Jewish circles and was gaining attention and adherence in the Ephesian churches.[8] This

8. Gnosticism is a complex and contested phenomenon. In sum, Gnosticism

proto-Gnosticism is typified by a belief that the god of creation was a wicked god, who made the world in all its horrors and material chaos, and that salvation comes from a different God, the God of Jesus, the God Jesus acts on behalf of. What indicates this are four things:

1. The false teaching is based on interpretation of the Old Testament, and Gnostics engaged in spiritual interpretations of the book of Genesis.
2. The false teaching is characterised by myths, endless genealogies, and speculations. Later Gnostics also had a big interest in speculative cosmology about the divine fullness, a cosmic being known as Sophia, the Demiurge or "world-maker," and similar things.
3. At the very end of the letter, Paul warns about "what is falsely called knowledge" (1 Tim 6:20), which is reminiscent of how the church father Irenaeus later referred to Gnosticism.
4. I conclude that the false teaching in Ephesus that Paul warns about is similar to a scheme that the Jewish Christian author Hegesippus spoke about, according to Eusebius, which had Gnostic qualities.[9]

This heresy might not be the presenting issue in 1 Tim 2, but it does show that Paul is sensitive to anything that detracts from "the faith" that Timothy has received and is called to defend (1 Tim 1:2; 3:9, 13; 4:1, 6; 5:8; 6:10, 12, 21).

What is most likely is that in Ephesus, similar to the situation in Corinth where gender roles were also causing controversy (see the chapter by Rademaker and Erickson in this volume), so, too, here in 1 Tim 2, Paul is urging Timothy to address a local situation in Ephesus. The backstory is that some wives were disturbing households and house churches by badgering their husbands with erroneous ideas. They were perhaps under the

---

replaces the biblical story with a story of conflict among cosmic beings. In the story, one ignorant and malevolent cosmic being called the Demiurge makes the world and becomes the God of Israel. However, this cosmic being wants to see pre-existent souls trapped in their bodies—their souls can only be released by attaining secret knowledge of their origins, and Jesus comes as a revealer to help people escape the body, the world, and the Demiurge, and return to their cosmic mother ship called the *pleroma*. In sum, it sets up the God of the Old Testament against the God of the New Testament. It is some developing view of this heresy that I think is behind some of the things Paul opposes in Ephesus.

9. Eusebius, *Historia ecclesiastica*, 4.19.

influence of some false teachings related to myths and ascetic practices, and these same women had yet to fully disengage themselves from their inherited religious culture in Ephesus, principally the cult of Artemis. Such occasion is why they needed to be better instructed.

This means that the prohibition on a woman (or wife, the Greek can mean either) teaching and usurping authority over a man in 1 Tim 2 is local and specific rather than for all times and places. The setting is clearly public worship based on the prior literary context. The male-female relationships here pertain to marriage since the pairing of male/female is most appropriate for marriage relationships, frictions of power and authority cut the sharpest in marriage, and (like 1 Cor 11) the relationship between husbands and wives *during public worship* was a continuing point of contention. Furthermore, the prohibition is to do specifically with what is happening in Ephesus. The smoking gun is 1 Tim 2:15, which is a clear allusion to the Artemis cult with the mention of "saved through childbearing" because Artemis was the goddess of childbirth. So note the specific situation: frictions in marriage relationships, exhibited during public worship, touching upon gender, authority, and teaching, caused by factors unique to Ephesus and the Artemis cult.

If the prohibition about women leading and teaching was for all times and places, then the rest of the Old Testament and New Testament does not make any sense because women clearly did lead, teach, and prophesy. The price of maintaining a universal application of the prohibition in 1 Tim 2:12—where women can never lead or teach men in the church, in mixed assemblies, or at Bible study—is an unceasing festival of tortured exegesis because you have to engage in acrobatic interpretive moves to explain away the leadership and/or teaching roles attributed to Deborah (Judg 4–5), Huldah (2 Kgs 22:14; 2 Chr 34:22), female prophets in the early church (Acts 21:9; 1 Cor 11:5), Priscilla (Acts 18:6; Rom 16:3; 2 Tim 4:19), Phoebe (Rom 16:1–2), Nympha (Col 4:15), Junia (Rom 16:7), plus evidence from non-Christian sources and from early Christian art about women serving in the church. In other words, restricting ourselves to a universal interpretation of 1 Tim 2:12 means we must then neglect or downplay a multitude of passages throughout both the Old and New Testaments.

Rather than detecting in 1 Tim 2:8–15 a broad-brush prohibition against all women teaching any men everywhere in all circumstances, we do better to see women in Paul's circle operating as benefactors, delegates, apostles, prophets, coworkers, house church leaders, and fellow prisoners for the gospel. As such, 1 Tim 2:11–15 is local and contextual as it "speaks directly to the problem in Ephesus, where we have some high-status, well-to-do women, likely with some education, who are trying to assume the mantle of teaching before they have learned the apostolic message properly, and in all likelihood after they have already been misled by false teachers."[10]

## 1 Timothy 2:8–15—A Very Short Commentary on What Paul Prohibits and Encourages

When it comes to Paul's comments about women in Ephesus, we first find a prohibition about women wearing "elaborate hairstyles, gold, pearls, or expensive clothes" (v. 9).

Such an exhortation against women wearing flamboyant displays of wealth, apparel, and cosmetics can be found in many Biblical passages. The problem of overly decorated apparel was particularly acute in Ephesus where participants of the Artemis cult habitually dressed in extravagant fashion. For example, an ancient romance novel called *Ephesiaca*, set in Ephesus, tells us in detail what a procession in the temple of Artemis looked like.

> A local festival for Artemis was underway, and from the city to her shrine, a distance of seven stades, all the local girls had to march sumptuously adorned.
>
> Heading the line of girls was Anthia, daughter of Megamedes and Euippe, locals. Anthia's beauty was marvelous . . .
>
> Her hair was blonde, mostly loose, only little of it braided, and moving as the breezes took it. Her eyes were vivacious, bright like a beauty's but forbidding like a chaste girl's; her clothing was a belted purple tunic, knee-length and falling loose over the arms, and over it a fawnskin with a quiver attached, arrows [. . .],[11] javelins in hand, dogs following behind.
>
> Often when seeing her at the shrine, the Ephesians worshiped her as Artemis, so also at the sight of her on this occasion the crowd cheered; the opinions of the spectators were various, some in their astonishment declaring that she was the goddess herself was someone else fashioned by the goddess, but all of them

10. Witherington, *Socio-Rhetorical Commentary*, 231. See also Gupta, *Tell Her Story*, 163–81.

11. Ellipsis in original.

> prayed, bowed down, and congratulated her parents, and the universal cry among all the spectators was "Anthia the beautiful!"[12]

Given such fetching attire worn by women during processions for Artemis, Paul is not merely calling for modest dress in verse 9 to the effect that women shouldn't show off their ostentatious bling. Rather, he means, "Do not dress like one of the priestesses and participants in the Artemis cult."

Continuing the same line of thought, Paul also adds, "They [the women in the Ephesian churches] should make themselves attractive by doing good, which is appropriate for women who claim to honour God" (v. 10). In effect, you honour God the Father, not by fashion but by faithful action, not by dress but by deeds. Again, this is good advice to women living in Ephesus who are urged toward a new pattern of devotion and piety.

Paul then moves to the topic women's education and submission: "A wife [woman] is to learn quietly with full submission" (v. 11). Even the most conservative of commentators acknowledge that women need to be taught and are worth teaching. The quietness/silence is not absolute but is for their period of instruction. It is in terms of their training in the faith that quietness and submission are required. Applied to the local context of Ephesus, a wife, or woman, reared on the Artemis cult, needs to be a good disciple and learn from her Jesus-following teachers.

When a person converts from paganism to Christianity, they do not get the total package of theology in one hit as if the Nicene Creed and Westminster Confession get instantaneously downloaded into their brain. New converts often engage in an immediate transfer of allegiances and know some of the basic theological facts of Christianity, but often they start out with a kind of default syncretism, whereby they mix and merge former beliefs with new beliefs, until they defrag their mind and heart from paganism and become more consistent and thorough going in their Christian beliefs and practice. These women, immersed in the "theology" and "culture" of the Artemis cult needed to be taught, and they should submit to the instructions of their male teachers. Paul Trebilco and Simon Rae put it this way: "The call then is not for total verbal silence from women, but for them to exhibit a peaceful and gentle attitude" in their learning.[13]

This brings us now to the centre of debate—namely, how to understand the prohibition about a woman (or wife) exercising authority (and/

12. Xenophon, *Ephesiaca*, 2.2, 5–7.

13. Trebilco et al., *1 Timothy*, 58.

or control) over a man (or husband): "I don't allow a wife [woman] to teach or to control her husband [or to exercise authority over a man]. Instead, she should be a quiet listener" (v. 12). This is the point at which many commentators believe a glass ceiling has been created and beyond which women may not pass.

As we proceed further, we must look at four particular issues:

1. What type of authority is exercised?
2. Is "holding authority" and "teaching" the same activity?
3. Claims about the order of creation and the gullibility of women.
4. What is the meaning of "saved through childbearing"?

## What Type of Authority?

What authority is exercised comes down to the meaning of the Greek word *authenteō*. Is it a positive or neutral word for "to exercise authority," or does it have a negative connotation, meaning something like "domineer" or "dictate"? Even if we put Ephesus and Artemis to the side, this word's range of meaning and its usage shows that the prohibition Paul makes about "authority" is not straightforward. Consequently, the meaning of the word *authenteō* in 1 Tim 2:12 is notoriously debated. Here is a summary of my findings about it:

- There are lies, there are damnable lies, and then there are biblical word studies. No word has a singular, enduring meaning because words change in meaning over time. All words have a range of meanings, connotations, and usages.
- The word *authenteō* is used only once in the New Testament, so we have no further example for the use of this word from within the Bible.
- If Paul wanted a more neutral term for "authority" then maybe he would have used *exousia* as he does in 1 Cor 11:10. It makes sense to think that Paul uses a different word in 1 Tim 2:12 because he wants to make a different point.
- In context of 1 Tim 2:12, *authenteō* is the opposite of "remain quiet." What is the opposite of remain quiet? Maybe something like bossy and boisterous!

- The old King James Version—which is hardly a revisionist feminist translation—rendered *authenteō* as "usurp authority over the man," which is negative. Wycliffe's translation from the 1300s was "neither to have lordship on the husband" and also sounds negative in its translation of *authenteō*.
- The closely related word *authentēs* can be used in relation to murder—which is as negative as it comes.

People look for other examples of the word *authenteō* in all sorts of places, from astrology to zoology, but the best parallels are the documents that seem to have a similar usage in a similar context, like a household or house church.

There is a passage in John Chrysostom's homilies on Colossians where he says that husbands "should not be despotic or domineer [*authentei*] the wife."[14] Perhaps the closest analogy for Paul's usage of *authenteō* in 1 Tim 2:12 is found in Pseudo-Hippolytus's fragments, where we read this:

> The wife will give up her own husband to death, and the husband will bring his own wife to judgment like a criminal. *Masters will lord it over their slaves savagely*, and slaves will assume an unruly demeanour toward their masters.[15]

Hippolytus warns that in the last days masters will *authenteō* their slaves very severely. Much like 1 Tim 2:12, Hippolytus assumes a household context where this *authenteō* is going down, and it is very bad for slaves!

In sum, while there are varied usages of *authenteō*, it appears that it is not a neutral word about the mere possession of authority, but refers to an intensified sense of authority, to have absolute authority, to usurp authority, to domineer or dominate with authority, and even abuse authority.

We do well to remember that the Artemisian cult was a context of intense rivalry. Here, women sought positions of status and honour by rising through the positions of authority in the cult of Artemis. To have rank in the Artemis cult was to have social status in Ephesus.

It is possible that people, including women, tried to *authenteō* their way to ascendency in the Artemis cult and other local cults. So imagine a TV

14. Chrysostom, *Homilia Colossians*, 27–31.

15. Pseudo-Hippolytus, *Consummatione Mundi*, 7.

show on *Artemisian Succession* or *The Real Priestesses of Ephesus* where women are fighting to become the #1 priestess in Ephesus. Yes, this is not a feminist cult or women-only cult, men are involved in it, but if that same spirit of rivalry in the Artemis cult and that same habit of bossing about inferiors is played out in the home or in the church, how might Paul correct it? Probably the way he does in 1 Tim 2:11–15!

## Authority and Teaching or Authoritative Teaching?

Why does Paul focus on teaching here? Most likely because Paul wanted to make sure teachers were qualified to do so and understood God's teachings. But is holding authority and teaching one and the same activity? I think the two words are grouped together quite deliberately to make one activity. That makes sense because across 1 Tim 2, Paul pairs various items and actions together, usually as synonyms:

| | |
|---|---|
| v. 1 | kings and everyone who is in authority |
| v. 1 | a quiet and peaceful life |
| v. 1 | godliness and dignity |
| v. 4 | all people to be saved and to come to a knowledge of the truth |
| v. 5 | one God and one mediator |
| v. 7 | a preacher and apostle |
| v. 7 | I'm telling the truth and I'm not lying |
| v. 7 | in faith and truth |

It is likely then that *authenteō* and *didaskō* (to teach) are two words combined into a single idea, or else that usurping authority is extended into the type of teaching performed, a single domineering way of teaching.

Given the negative connotations of *authenteō* and its pairing with *didaskō*, plus the emphasis on false teachings across 1 Timothy, I take the clause as meaning that a wife should not attempt to "dominate her husband with dubious doctrines." The closest analogy is Rev 2:20, which admonishes the church of Thyatira because they allow the false prophetess Jezebel "to teach and to mislead my servants," clearly two negative things fused together.

Otherwise, what a wife should do is the opposite of domineering her husband with horrible heresy. Instead, she should listen and learn.

I think that means detox from idolatry and polytheism, learn to discern good from bad teachings, and get wisely discipled.

## Creation and Deception

As if we did not have enough controversial verses to mull over, Paul next declares, "For Adam was formed first, then Eve. And Adam was not deceived, but the woman was deceived and transgressed" (vv. 13–14). Paul seems to infer from Gen 1–3 that Adam's authority comes from his being created first, while Eve is associated with deception. Yet does it follow that men are by nature fit to lead and women by nature are disqualified from leadership?

I do not want to be one of those scholars who try to problematise a straightforward reading of a text and replace it with an obscure and idiosyncratic interpretation, but I do not think Paul's appeal to the order of Adam and Eve's creation and to Eve's deception is straightforward.

Remember, Paul can tell the Corinthians that, "Does not even nature itself teach you that if a man has long hair it is a disgrace to him, but that if a woman has long hair, it is her glory? For her hair is given to her as a covering" (1 Cor 11:14–15). What is natural to Paul here seems to be determined by cultural gender norms of hair length and head dress. Even appeals to the order in which Adam and Eve were created are not necessarily about creation but reflect cultural norms buttressed with an understanding of how people perceive the natural world. Paul offers an argument that reasons from the creation story to undergird a *social* sense of custom and decorum about the relationships between men and women in a contentious situation.[16]

Are women really more gullible than men? The testimony of Biblical history, Paul's ministry, and human experience tells against the notion that Eve, like all women, is particularly susceptible to deception, while Adam, like all men, is especially immune to deception. Paul, when writing to the Corinthians, worries that the *entire* Corinthian assembly, men and women, might be deceived as Eve was deceived by the serpent (2 Cor 11:2–4). The danger of deception is a human problem, not a woman problem. If women had a natural proclivity to deception, then that would be a flaw in God's design of women. Paul treats Eve's deception as a historical fact, not a general feature of womanhood, so it is wrong to infer that men

16. Wedgeworth, "Good and Proper," 88–97.

can be leaders because they are supposedly discerning, while women are disqualified from leadership because they are purportedly gullible. Eve's deception simply illustrates what might happen if the women in Ephesus fail to learn quietly and in submission to their teachers.[17]

## Saved Through Childbearing

The section ends with Paul's enigmatic exhortation about women experiencing salvation through childbirth: "But she [a wife] will be saved through childbearing, if they continue in faith, love, and holiness, with good sense" (v. 15). I think it unlikely that Paul is saying that no Christian mother will die in childbirth if she (a) submits to male authority or (b) pursues the Christian faith in a way approved by male authorities in the church. I also think it unlikely that Paul is referring to Mary as the mother who births Jesus. Nor could it mean that women will only experience salvation if they embrace motherhood and female submission.

Childbirth was one of the most dangerous things a woman could do.[18] Artemis was the goddess of hunting, virginity, and childbirth. Her worshippers prayed to her as "saviour" asking for either a good birth or a quick death. This would have been important for women converting to Christianity, who would have wondered who *now* would protect them in childbirth if they abandoned the worship of Artemis. Paul answers that question by implying, in effect, that, "Artemis is not your saviour, Jesus is! Jesus is with you in life and death."

## So Where Does That Leave Us?

While 1 Tim 2:11–15 has been taken to mandate a restriction of women from holding teaching authority, such as the office of pastor or elder, Paul is mainly responding to a local situation in Ephesus caused by women who are still immersed—socially, religiously, and culturally—in the Artemis cult. He prohibits them from domineering with dubious ideas, telling them instead to grow in the faith through submission to sound instruction in the faith.

Once upon a time, I thought that 1 Tim 2:11–15 was the biblical door slamming in the face of women who believed they were called to

17. See Westfall, *Paul and Gender*, 108–18.

18. See Cohick, *Women in the World*, 135–40; Weissenrieder, "What Does," 313-36.

preach, teach, and lead in the church. What changed my mind was not compromising the authority of Scripture, not interpretive gymnastics to get around Scripture, but a deep dive into Scripture itself. Beginning with Rom 16 and facing up to the ministries of Phoebe (16:1–2), Priscilla (16:3), and Junia (16:7), I had to change my mind based on what Scripture said about women participating in the mission and ministry of the church. Putting 1 Tim 2:11–15 under a microscope exposed the pathogens giving us ill-fitted interpretations of this passage; whether it was appeals to an ancient fertility cult in Ephesus, or an assumption that women were by nature stupid and servile, they was wrong. Instead, by locating this text in its ancient context and tracing the line of argument, I realised that Paul's prohibition here was for a specific situation, not universal and generally applicable. For such reasons I embrace the ministry of women at all levels of the church.

## Bibliography

Baugh, S. M. "A Foreign World: Ephesus in the First Century." In *Women in the Church: An Interpretation and Application of 1 Timothy 2:9–15*, edited by Andreas Köstenberger and Thomas Schreiner, 27–79. 3rd ed. Wheaton, IL: Crossway, 2016.

Chrysostom, John. *Homilia Colossians*. Translated by J. H. MacMahon. In vol. 5 of *The Ante-Nicene Fathers*, edited by Alexander Roberts et al. Buffalo: Christian Literature, 1886.

Cohick, Lynn H. *Women in the World of the Earliest Christians: Illuminating Ancient Ways of Life*. Grand Rapids: Baker, 2009.

Ellis, James W. "Apostle Paul in Ephesus: Christianity's Clash with the Cult of Artemis." *European Journal of Theology and Philosophy* 3 (2023) 22–34.

Giles, Kevin N. "Church Order, Government." In *Dictionary of the Later New Testament & Its Developments*, edited by Ralph P. Martin and Peter H. Davids, 219–26. Downers Grove, IL: InterVarsity, 1997.

———. *Patterns of Ministry Among the First Christians*. Melbourne: Collins-Dove, 1989.

Glahn, Sandra. *Nobody's Mother: Artemis of the Ephesians in Antiquity and the New Testament*. Downers Grove, IL: InterVarsity, 2023.

Gupta, Nijay K. *Tell Her Story: How Women Led, Taught, and Ministered in the Early Church*. Downers Grove, IL: InterVarsity, 2023.

Higgins, Michael Denis. *The Seven Wonders of the Ancient World: Science, Engineering, and Technology*. New York: Oxford University Press, 2023.

Hoag, Gary G. *Wealth in Ancient Ephesus and the First Letter to Timothy: Fresh Insights from Ephesiaca by Xenophon of Ephesus*. Bulletin for Biblical Research Supplement 11. University Park, PA: University of Pennsylvania State Press, 2015.

Hooker, M. D. "Artemis of Ephesus." *Journal of Theological Studies* 64 (2013) 37–46.

Hutson, Christopher R. *First and Second Timothy and Titus*. Paideia. Grand Rapids: Baker Academic, 2019.

Immendörfer, Michael. *Ephesians and Artemis: The Cult of the Great Goddess of Ephesus as the Epistle's Context.* Wissenschaftliche Untersuchungen zum Neuen Testament 2. Reihe (WUNT II) 436. Tübingen: Mohr Siebeck, 2017.

Mussies, Gerard. "Artemis." In *Dictionary of Deities and Demons in the Bible*, edited by Karel van der Toorn et al., 91–97. Leiden: Brill, 1998.

Pseudo-Hippolytus. *Conummatione Mundi.* Translated by S. D. F. Salmond. In *The Ante-Nicene Fathers*, edited by Alexander Roberts and James Donaldson, 5:242–54. New York: Christian Literature, 1886.

Schreiner, Thomas R. "A Response to Linda Belleville." In *Two Views on Women in Ministry*, edited by James R. Beck, 105–9. Rev. ed. Counterpoints. Grand Rapids: Zondervan, 2009.

Strelan, Rick. *Paul, Artemis, and the Jews in Ephesus.* Beihefte zur Zeitschrift für die neutestamentliche Wissenschaft 80. Berlin: De Gruyter, 1996.

Trebilco, Paul, et al. *1 Timothy: A Pastoral and Contextual Commentary.* Asia Bible Commentary Series. Carlisle: Langham Global Library, 2023.

Wedgeworth, Steven. "Good and Proper: Paul's Use of Nature, Custom, and Decorum in Pastoral Theology." *Eikon* 2 (2020) 88–97.

Weissenrieder, Annette. "What Does σωθήσεθαι [sic] δὲ διὰ τῆς τεκνογονίας 'To Be Saved by Childbearing' Mean (1 Timothy 2:15)? Insights from Ancient Medical and Philosophical Texts." *Early Christianity* 5 (2014) 313-36.

Westfall, Cynthia Long. *Paul and Gender: Reclaiming the Apostle's Vision for Men and Women in Christ.* Grand Rapids: Baker, 2016.

Witherington, Ben, III. *A Socio-Rhetorical Commentary on Titus, 1–2 Timothy and 1–3 John.* Vol. 1 of *Letters and Homilies for Hellenized Christians.* Downers Grove, IL: InterVarsity, 2006.

Xenophon of Ephesus. *The Story of Anthia and Habrocomes.* Translated by Jeffrey Henderson. Loeb Classical Library 69. Cambridge: Harvard University Press, 2009.

# Rank or Reciprocity? Hierarchy or Gift?

## *The Trinity, Authority, and Gender Relations in the Church*

Jacqueline Service

In the early centuries of the church there was a priest who sought to defend the supremacy of God the Father. On his reading of Scripture and theological reasoning, it appeared to him that God the Father was eternally God, with all the characteristics, nature, and functions of God. Then there was Jesus—functionally and essentially not quite God, a little less. Drawing on a cluster of Bible texts, such as "my Father is greater than I" (John 14:28), the priest concluded that Jesus was a subordinate being to God the Father.[1]

Other Christians, however, sensed that something important was being missed. Certain texts were emphasised in ways that failed to account for Scripture's full witness. Moreover, serious theological implications followed. How could Jesus save humanity if he wasn't fully God? How could he judge or forgive sin without the same authority as God the Father? Only *God* could judge, save, and forgive.

These believers understood that if Jesus did not share the Father's authority and nature, he was not God at all. To say that Jesus differed in nature, character, authority, or will, even slightly, denied him the *fullness* of divinity. In a biblical worldview, only two categories existed—God or *not*-God. Knowing what was at stake, the church judged this teaching as incompatible with the gospel, declaring, "Those who say: 'He is of

1. Athanasius answers this heresy in his work *Four Discourses Against the Arians*, 1.58.

another "substance" or "essence"' [i.e., not fully God] . . . are condemned by the holy catholic and apostolic Church."[2]

Now that is, in broad terms, the story of Arius and the church's rejection of his teaching at the Council of Nicaea in AD 325. The document arising from that Council, the Nicene Creed, was expanded further in AD 381 at the Council of Constantinople to likewise affirm the full divinity of the Holy Spirit. This Creed remains a basic confession of faith among churches across the world. You've likely recited or read it yourself.

One of the Creed's defining features is the confession that Jesus is "God from God, Light from Light, true God from true God . . . of one being with the Father."[3] These phrases, though simple, deliver profound theological truths. Let's note two—the easily overlooked word *from* signals that there is a real relation between the Father and Son, while the repetition of *God*, *Light*, and *true God*, insists on the full equality and unity of their authority.

We will return to these truths shortly. I want you to note, though, that while the content of this ancient creed may feel distant, the way we understand authority and relations within God's life continues to shape how we think about authority and relations within the church.

## What Does the Trinity Have to Do with Men and Women?

So, you might be wondering why Arius appears in a book about women. In recent decades, similar echoes of interpreting the relations between the Father and Son through a hierarchical lens have surfaced in evangelical debates about the respective roles and authority of men and women in the church. Significantly, some argue that Jesus is subordinate in authority to the Father, not only during his earthly life, but eternally within the life of the Trinity.[4]

Unlike Arius, however, today's advocates of this view explicitly affirm the Nicene Creed and insist that Jesus is not inferior to the Father. They agree that God is One. At the same time, however, the view proposes that what differentiates the Father and the Son are differences in authority. Instead of asserting an absolute and unqualified equality between the

2. Catholic here means "universal" church and is not referring to the Roman Catholic Church; see Anglicans, "Nicene Creed."

3. Anglicans, "Nicene Creed."

4. Ware, *Father, Son, Holy Spirit*, 97–98; Grudem, *Systematic Theology*, 249–51.

Father and Son, Jesus is understood as equal *but* functionally subordinate. The Son is understood to share fully the Father's nature, but not his authority; accordingly, the Father is described as sending, commanding, and leading, while the Son is described as obeying and submitting.[5] Jesus and the Father are said to be equal in essence yet ordered asymmetrically through differing roles and functions. This approach is known as eternal functional subordination (EFS) and is presented, in part, to distinguish the Father from the Son. Critics, however, worry that differences in Trinitarian authority equate to differences in God's being, introducing hierarchy into God's life.[6]

The core of this perspective—equal but functionally subordinate—is what I would describe as a classic example of the motte-and-bailey fallacy. A *motte* was a defensible castle on a hill, while the *bailey* was the more vulnerable courtyard below. In argumentation, a controversial idea (the bailey) is advanced, but when challenged, retreat is made to a safer one (the motte). Here, the acceptable claim—*Jesus is equal with the Father*—shields the more difficult claim—*Jesus is eternally subordinate*. But, as I will argue, these two conclusions prove difficult to reconcile. If Jesus is equal with the Father, he is not eternally and uniquely subordinate; if he is eternally and uniquely subordinate, he is not fully God. And, if he is not fully God, the gospel unravels.

One key reason a hierarchical view of the Trinity gained contemporary momentum is that it seemingly provided a theological analogy for church life. The relations between men and women were said to be likewise patterned on the relations between the Father and Son: women are equal to men as image-bearers of God (Gen 1:27) *but functionally subordinate*. Women were therefore said to have differing and subordinate roles, functions, and authority due to a relational ordering of male and female that echoes the supposed ordering of the eternal divine relations.

While this understanding has been roundly challenged and rejected by scholars, including by evangelical theologians, the idea nevertheless persists in some church circles.[7] In what follows, I will briefly discuss how the orthodox doctrine of the Trinity offers a richer and more relationally full account of God's life than some of the hierarchical interpretations you may have encountered.

Two questions will guide this chapter:

5. Grudem, *Systematic Theology*, 250.

6. Holmes, "Classical Trinitarianism," 259, 270–71.

7. Bird and Harrower, *Trinity Without Hierarchy*; Barrett, *Simply Trinity*, 213–59.

1. Is the claim that the Son is eternally subordinate to the Father compatible with Trinitarian teaching?
2. Can the Trinity be used to justify hierarchy between men and women in the church?

## Is Eternal Subordination of the Son Compatible with Trinitarian Teaching?

It is not uncommon for Christians to view the Trinity as an unintelligible relic or as a mystery best avoided. Many may affirm that God is one nature in three persons—the Father, the Son, and the Holy Spirit. They affirm that God is Trinity and Jesus is God. Yet, the details of how this is so are hazy at best. At worst, some imagine God as a hierarchy: the Father as *God*-God, the more authoritative one, while Jesus and the Holy Spirit are slightly less—*kind-of*-God but maybe not *God*-God.

Trinitarian teaching, however, concerns *the* central confession of who the Christian God is and is therefore something we ought to pursue with care. It is here we encounter the wonder of God's very being as a unity of relational love; where the triune persons share a unique unity of everything divine—will, characteristics, and authority. What is revealed is the incomprehensible mutuality of self-giving and other-centred love—a love that is vastly different from human relationships, commonly characterised by self-interested hierarchies and personal competition. The Trinity is not an idea that mirrors human structures but an encounter that calls them into question.

It's a difficult thing to comprehend how God can simultaneously be one in three and three in one. Nothing like it exists in our created order. But this truth is vital to understand as it bears directly on claims that God's life is ordered by an eternal hierarchy of authority and submission. One helpful way to approach this mystery is to hold together three intertwined truths of Trinitarian teaching:

1. God's oneness cannot be divided.
2. God's threeness cannot be merged.
3. The only difference among the Father, Son, and Holy Spirit is how they are *related* to one another, not levels of authority.

Let's unpack this.

## The Truths of the Trinity: Unity, Distinction, and Equality

"God's oneness cannot be divided" means that the Father, Son, and Holy Spirit, while *distinct* from one another, are never separate, nor can they fail to share the same qualities (including authority). In fact, God's unity is so complete that an act of one divine person is inseparably an act of all three. The Nicene Creed's phrase—"Light from Light"—helps us here.

Light has three distinct elements—the source, the beam, and the illumination—yet they are simultaneously one. You cannot remove one and still have light. Each depends on, and completes, the other. The source of the light may be ordered "first," yet it has no expression without the beam or the illumination. Importantly, light is not a one-way hierarchy: its existence arises through *reciprocal mutuality*—like a shared movement of gift and receipt.

This analogy belongs to the created realm, so it's necessarily imperfect. But consider what happens when we speak of God's eternity and equality. Let's say that the Father is the *eternal* source, the Spirit the *eternal* beam, and the Son the *eternal* illumination. The unseen Father is made known through the Son and the Spirit. In fact, the Father makes his self-revelation to the world dependent on the Son and Spirit. This means that the Son and Spirit share the same life-giving authority as the Father, and that the Father *receives* his Fatherhood dependently through them.[8] What we see in the Trinity is a mutuality akin to personal gifting and receiving in love. The Son is the Son because of the eternal gift and receipt of the Father's being; so, too, the Father *is* the Father because of the gift and receipt of the Son and Spirit. On this account, earthly concepts of one-way hierarchy, authority, and submission prove theologically inadequate for describing the triune God.

To *receive* is to yield, to submit or give way to some other thing. When you stop at a stop sign, you yield to its authority, you submit or obey it—in a manner of speaking you *receive* the stop sign. Or consider a tree that bends to the breeze, it gives itself to the authority of the wind as it receives it.[9] In this sense, the Father might even be said to "submit" to receiving his being as Father in relation to the Son and Spirit, and vice versa. Now, by *submit* I do not mean the kind of obedience we see when one person is placed over another. I mean the eternal giving and receiving within God's own life—a shared life of love rather than a chain of command. Applying this concept

8. Pannenberg, *Systematic Theology*, 322–24.

9. Milbank, "Can a Gift," 120.

to the Father, however, can feel unsettling—but why? Perhaps because we imagine submission in primarily worldly terms—as representing a lower status in a chain of command—and we envision "Fatherly" authority apart from humble and vulnerable expression. If we are serious about upholding Trinitarian teaching that God's oneness cannot be divided, this must entail a genuine mutuality of nature among the three divine persons—including the nature of authority.

In saying that "God's oneness cannot be divided," we must immediately clarify that this does not mean that "God's threeness is merged." Returning to our light analogy, we can discern that whilst the light is one, its three aspects remain genuinely distinct. The distinct three (source, beam, illumination) do not dissolve into simple undifferentiated oneness. There is *distinction* in the unity. We can recognise, even though we might not be able to categorise, each distinct element. This is even more so with the personal relations of the Trinity. Real distinctions exist among the three. Yet, what distinguishes the Father, Son, and Holy Spirit is *not* differing levels of authority or functions, but rather what theologians refer to as the "relations of origin."

I'll spare you the technical detail, but broadly the relations of origin mean that the Father, Son, and Holy Spirit are related not by rank or authority but in a way that holds unity and distinction together. In Western theology it is expressed this way: the Father is eternally *unbegotten*, the Son is eternally *begotten*, and the Holy Spirit eternally *proceeds* from the Father and the Son. This language speaks of relation, not rank. It essentially says that the Father is *not* the Son, the Son is *not* the Father, the Spirit is *not* the Son, and so on. The terms describe real distinction and real relational unity, but—and this is vital—it is not based on hierarchy. As Letham says, "All that the Father is, the Son is, except for being Father. Nothing could be further removed from subordinationism."[10]

The relations of origin protect two truths at once: each divine person is fully God, and yet each is not the same person. So, while in Scripture we see distinct actions—the Father sends the Son, the Son is incarnate, and the Holy Spirit is poured out—these acts are inseparably the work of all three.[11] As such, there is no differing authority, nature, or will. Attempting to distinguish the Father, Son, and Holy Spirit based on authority and submission risks turning God's oneness into an illusion.

10. Letham, "Athanasius," 138.

11. Thompson, "Trinity to the Cross," 22–23. Thompson treats the cross as an act of profound Trinitarian unity.

For this reason, many theologians conclude that classical Trinitarian theology does not sit comfortably with the idea that the Son is eternally subordinate to the Father in function or authority. Such accounts diverge from long-standing creedal categories toward models of command and obedience more familiar to human experience than the wonder of God's shared life.

## The Bible's Portrait of the Trinity: Relations of Self-Giving Love

So, how do we reconcile the Father, Son, and Holy Spirit as eternally unified and coequal when the Bible seems to depict Jesus as submitting to the Father? What do we do with passages such as, "The Son can do nothing of his own accord, but only what he sees the Father doing" (John 5:19)?

It's worth pointing out that there are many biblical interactions between the Father and Son that cannot be reduced to relations of authority and submission. In fact, many passages strongly infer shared authority and mutual giving. The apostle Paul describes the Father *handing over* his kingdom—which includes rule and authority—to the Son (1 Cor 15:24). Jesus directs the Father—"Father, glorify your name"—and the Father affirmatively responds (John 12:28). Jesus announces the nature of his co-authority with the Father—"The Father judges no one but has given all judgment to the Son" (John 5:22) and "All that the Father has is mine" (John 16:15).

The New Testament is rich with portraits of giving and receiving among the Father, Son, and Holy Spirit. At Jesus's baptism, as he gives himself to the waters, the Father delights in him—"This is my Son whom I love" (Matt 3:16–17)—while the Spirit descends in unified affirmation. Here, we glimpse *mutual* delight in united purpose. We see also that the Holy Spirit "glorifies the Son" (John 16:14), bears witness to Jesus (John 15:26), and enables confession of Jesus as Lord (1 Cor 12:3). Jesus likewise glorifies the Father (John 17:4), praises him (Luke 10:21), and serves his will (John 6:38). And what of the Father? Jesus describes their intimate mutuality: "All I have is yours, and all you have is mine" (John 17:10). We likewise read that the Father glorifies the Son (John 8:50; Luke 10:22) and exalts him (Phil 2:9; Heb 2:8).[12] Taken together, Scripture depicts the Father, Son, and Holy Spirit *existing* in a shared life of giving and

12. Service, *Triune Well-Being*, xiii.

receiving that enriches rather than ranks. This movement shapes God's life: a life marked by generosity and humble other-centredness, where no divine person ever seeks their own glory but the blessing of one another.[13]

Does the Son glorify and obey the Father? Yes. But this is not evidence of mere subordination or eternal hierarchy, it is but one expression of the mutual self-giving love that characterises triune life.

## The Shape of Divine Authority

As we've been exploring, there is much in Scripture and theology that give weight to perceiving the relationships among the Trinity as a unified life of mutuality, not relations characterised primarily as authority and submission. Yet even if we were to frame the divine relations (and by extension, the relations between men and women) in those terms, we would need to allow Scripture itself to define the substance of authority and submission. Jesus himself understood authority and submission quite differently from typical human inclinations, saying:

> You know that the rulers of the Gentiles lord it over them, and their high officials exercise authority over them. Not so with you. Instead, whoever wants to become great among you must be your servant, and whoever wants to be first must be your slave—just as the Son of Man did not come to be served, but to serve, and to give his life as a ransom for many. (Matt 20:25–28)

Here, Jesus radically redefines authority by reference to his own actions. Authority is revealed in servanthood and vulnerability. Using Jesus's own definition, his "submission" to the Father appears, in fact, to be the expression of divine *authority*. Certainly, the apostle Paul connects divine authority with vulnerable self-giving, identifying the cross as the *power* of God (1 Cor 1:18).

Let's push this a little further. We've said that Jesus is fully divine (Col 2:9; Heb 1:3) and that each triune person shares the same divine nature. On this logic, we should expect, then, to see evidence of the same contours of such "authority" in the Father and the Spirit. Recall Jesus's words: "Anyone who has seen me has seen the Father" (John 14:9). In other words, look at Jesus and you see what the unseen Father is like. This means that the characteristics of the Father are visible in Jesus, and Jesus's characteristics are consistent with the Father's. Athanasius, an

13. Service, *Triune Well-Being*, 154.

early defender of orthodox Trinitarian theology makes this point, saying all the attributes of the Father, including authority are evidenced in the Son: "The Father is eternal, immortal, powerful, light, King, Sovereign, God, Lord, Creator, and Maker. These attributes must be in the Image [that is, the Son], to make it true that he 'that has seen' the Son 'has seen the Father John 14:9.'"[14] But so, too, upholding the one divine nature, we must consider that the self-giving and servant-hearted authority that characterises the life of Jesus must likewise characterise the Father.

Sometimes, however, I think we imagine the Father quite differently: as self-sufficient (he doesn't need anyone else) or primarily one who commands, directs, wills, commissions, chooses, and decrees. Yet, when we envision the Father in this narrow way, we risk emptying him of characteristics that, like Jesus, display humble receptivity, self-sacrifice, servanthood, vulnerable love, and utter self-giving. In so doing, divine authority looks markedly different in the Father and the Son. When the Father's characteristics have little in common with the Son who says, "Anyone who has seen me has seen the Father," something is very wrong with our understanding of the unity of the one God.

## God and the Redemption of Relationships

So, we arrive at our final question: can the Trinity be used to justify hierarchy between men and women in the church? The short answer is no. Let me offer a few final thoughts.

I think I've pretty much pressed the point that subordinationist arguments diverge from faithful Trinitarian theology. So, while some may continue to defend a subordination of women to men in the church, such a case *cannot* be grounded in the doctrine of the Trinity without serious implications. Like the early church, we must be careful of teachings or popular piety that unintentionally diminish Jesus as "the *fullness* of divinity" (Col 2:9, italics added)—in authority, being, or act—or that undermine his shared nature with Father. Likewise, we should be wary of accounts that diminish the Father's self-giving nature. The Father, who eternally gives and receives in triune love, is no untouchable commander, but the One whose very nature is demonstrated in Christ's humble self-giving (Heb 1:2).

14. Athanasius, *Four Discourses Against the Arians*, 1.21.

Likewise, any theology that attempts to draw a straight line from God's inner life to human social arrangements must reckon with the profound differences between Creator and creature.[15] While there is an affinity that allows for imitation, there is also a vast dissimilarity. God is not simply a scaled-up version of humanity. God is uncreated, eternal, and perfect; humanity is created, finite, and sinful. Two big leaps are needed to sustain an idea that the Trinity should be an archetype for gendered relations—a hierarchy in the eternal relations of God, and a direct imitation from God to humans—both leaps, however, fall biblically and theologically short.

When we diminish Jesus's full divinity, obscure the Father's humble authority, blur the vast differences between the triune God and humanity, or project human hierarchies onto God, we distort our understanding of God's character, ways of working, and redemptive purposes. Inevitably, we also distort how the church orders its own life together. The temptation is that we let worldly models of relating shape the church rather than God-shaped ones. Yet, those called by God have been called into communion with the triune God to be transformed—to be holy, other-centred, not considering ourselves better than others, but giving each to the other in service—for the glory of God. Here, male and female acknowledge distinction, not to "lord it over" (Matt 20:25) one another, but as our given reality by which we live out a redeemed relationality worthy of the *one* body of Christ (1 Cor 12:4–27).

## Bibliography

Anglicans Online. "The Nicene Creed." Last updated May 23, 2017. https://anglicansonline.org/basics/nicene.html.

Athanasius. *Four Discourses Against the Arians.* Translated by John Henry Newman and Archibald Robertson. In *The Nicene and Post-Nicene Fathers*, 2nd ser., edited by Philip Schaff and Henry Wace, 4:306–47. 1891. Repr., Grand Rapids: Eerdmans, 1980.

Barrett, Matthew. *Simply Trinity: The Unmanipulated Father, Son, and Spirit.* Grand Rapids: Baker, 2021.

Bird, Michael F., and Scott Harrower, eds. *Trinity Without Hierarchy: Reclaiming Nicene Orthodoxy in Evangelical Theology.* Grand Rapids: Kregel, 2019.

Grudem, Wayne A. *Systematic Theology: An Introduction to Biblical Doctrine.* Grand Rapids: Zondervan, 1994.

15. Volf, "Being As God Is," 5.

Holmes, Stephen. "Classical Trinitarianism and Eternal Functional Subordination." In *Trinity Without Hierarchy: Reclaiming Nicene Orthodoxy in Evangelical Theology*, edited by Michael F. Bird and Scott Harrower, 259–71. Grand Rapids: Kregel, 2019.

Letham, Robert. "Athanasius." In *The Holy Trinity in Scripture, History, Theology, and Worship*, 127–45. Phillipsburg, NJ: P&R, 2004.

Milbank, John. "Can a Gift Be Given? Prolegomena to a Future Trinitarian Metaphysic." *Modern Theology* 11 (1995) 119–37.

Pannenberg, Wolfhart. *Systematic Theology*. Vol. 1, translated by Geoffrey W. Bromiley. Grand Rapids: Eerdmans, 1991.

Service, Jacqueline. *Triune Well-Being: The Kenotic-Enrichment of the Eternal Trinity*. Lanham, MD: Fortress Academic, 2024.

Thompson, Mark. "From the Trinity to the Cross." *Reformed Theological Review* 63 (2004) 1–23.

Volf, Miroslav. "Being As God Is." In *God's Life in Trinity*, edited by Miroslav Volf and Michael Welker, 3–18. Minneapolis: Fortress, 2006.

Ware, Bruce A. *Father, Son, and Holy Spirit: Relationships, Roles, and Relevance*. Wheaton, IL: Crossway, 2005.

Part 2

# Stories from on the Ground

# Unpacking the Backpack

## *A Story of Women's Ordination in Australia*

Laura Rademaker

Whenever we read the Bible, we come to it wearing a backpack. The stuff in your backpack comes from your parents, your family of origin, and your childhood. It also comes from your parent's parents, your home country, and city. They all had their own backpacks, and they handed some of their contents down to you.

You are wearing the backpack of history.

Before you even open your Bible, your backpack is there. It's not that the backpack controls how you interpret the Bible. It's much more subtle than that. Our backpacks are big and awkward, so they make some positions feel uncomfortable, but others might feel more normal and natural. Your backpack might make you more likely to lean one way or the other. It might set a more comfortable direction or even hide things that others see clearly. Whether you know what's in it or not, the backpack is there.

You can't take your backpack off. Nor should you—having this backpack is part of being human. But you can start to understand what's in it. When we become more aware of it, we can feel where it weighs on us more heavily. We can also start to see that other people have their own backpacks, and we might even learn from theirs.

I became a historian, in part, because I wanted to be a better Bible reader. I wanted to know what was in my backpack.

Some of what's in your backpack comes from the pastors who have most shaped you. There were events in their lives and mentors who taught them, and all of this went into what they handed on to you.

Evangelicals in Melbourne Anglican churches would know that women serve as senior pastors, even bishops, and that evangelicals—reading the very same Bible—disagree on this issue. But in Sydney, Anglicans have never seen a woman senior minister. Younger Sydney Anglicans may not know that other evangelicals do things differently. Is this a question of faithfulness to the supposed "plain reading" of Scripture? Is one city more godly than the other? Hardly. You see, your "normal" comes from your context.

Why is there one "normal" in Sydney and another in Melbourne? If you want to understand why your church or denomination holds a particular position, why it codified some things but left other questions open, the best place to find the answer is by looking in backpacks: history.

I'm going to focus on the Anglicans first because that's my backpack. But it's also because this story has had an enormous influence on evangelical culture in Australia. Even if you're not from Sydney or have nothing to do with Anglicanism, if you're an evangelical Christian in Australia, odds are that this story has had some impact on your church or people close to you. Now let's unpack a little of what's in Australian evangelicals' backpacks when it comes to women's ministry leadership.

## The Missionary's Question

It was the mid-1980s. A respected theologian at the Sydney Anglican theological college, Moore College, reached the end of a public lecture in which he told his audience why he believed women should not lead churches.

An older woman raised her hand. She was so tiny most of the crowd couldn't see her. But they knew the voice.

"Tell me, reverend, when I was a missionary, I led churches and preached to men. Was that sin?"

"Well," he faltered, "I suppose it was a shame there were no men to take up the task."

Undeterred, she pressed him: "That was not my question. Was it sin?"

He couldn't answer.[1]

The woman was Mary Andrews. She had been a missionary with the Church Missionary Society (CMS) in China during the Second World War and was in China when the first woman in the worldwide Anglican

1. This story was shared with me by Geoff Broughton, who was in the room at the time.

Communion was ordained in Hong Kong in 1944, Florence Li Tim-Oi. When the Communists came to power, Andrews was harassed and even interrogated, eventually evacuating in 1951.

On her return to Australia, Andrews served as principal of Deaconess House in Sydney from 1951 to 1975, training women for mission and ministry. But in this role, she also preached regularly to congregations of men and women. She wasn't what you think of as a typical 1970s feminist. But her experience as a missionary had made her into an avid supporter of women's ministries at all levels.

I don't think Mary Andrews knew Florence Li Tim-Oi, but she would have known that Tim-Oi's ordination came off the back of the ordination of CMS women missionaries as deacons in Fukien beginning in 1922. Mary Andrews herself served as a deacon in China. When Lucy Vincent, another CMS missionary, was ordained as a deacon in the diocese of South China in 1931, Archdeacon Mok publicly called for Chinese women to follow her. And they did, not only as deacons, but eventually as priests; Florence Li Tim-Oi was in the room that day.[2] In China, Mary Andrews preached, led services, baptised, and married people—the lot. She also saw Chinese women preaching and leading churches. She wanted this for Australia. But when she came back, she was bitterly disappointed. "In Australia, instead of making progress as far as women's ministry was concerned, it was going backwards."[3]

For many evangelicals, the growing calls to expand women's ministries came, not from second-wave feminists, but from the mission field. Since the nineteenth century, most missionaries have been women. They saw the fruits of what can happen when women are enabled to teach (including teaching men), and they wanted to bring this home to Australia. These women did plenty of Bible teaching in churches when home on furlough, even if it wasn't always called a sermon. There were also the women who stayed home but worked hard raising the funds, sitting on committees, writing newsletters, hosting prayer gatherings, raising awareness for missional causes at home and abroad. It started to make less and less sense to them that formal leadership in churches could be reserved to men. And they noticed women in the Bible doing the kind of work they also did. Some denominations in Australia (Salvation Army, Congregationalists) started ordaining women in the late nineteenth and

2. Murray, "Role of Women," 87–88.

3. Andrews, "Interviewed by Ritch."

early twentieth century. For the Anglican church, the debate began in the early twentieth, reaching its climax in 1992.

## A Broader Evangelicalism

Many would be surprised to learn that in 1984 a Sydney diocesan committee, tasked with investigating women's ordination, concluded that Anglican dioceses *should* be able to ordain women as priests, and that the majority of the committee supported ordaining women as priests, even there in Sydney.[4] In 1988 it was still possible for leading Sydney Anglican conservatives to acknowledge that the debate around women's ordination was not only between liberals and evangelicals but was also a debate *among* evangelicals. As the editor of a new conservative magazine, *The Briefing*, wrote, for evangelicals, it was not the authority of the Bible that was at issue—they all agreed on that—but differences of interpretation. As a solution to the women's ordination question, he suggested rethinking hierarchical leadership entirely according to what he saw in the New Testament. This would in turn open more ministries to women, allowing evangelicals to unite around what ministries women can do, rather than dividing over whether women should remain excluded from the role of senior minister.[5]

The same month those ideas went to print, on the other side of the world another group of conservative evangelicals published their views on gender, leadership, and ministry, this time using a theological category of male headship. The *Danvers Statement* on biblical manhood and womanhood was published in Chicago, November 1988, and intended to be the final word on what the Bible taught about gender.

> Adam's headship in marriage was established by God before the Fall, and was not a result of sin. . . . Governing and teaching roles within the church are restricted to men.[6]

It did not take long for conservatives in Sydney to embrace what became known as complementarianism. In 1990, Kristen Birkett and Joanne Dowe published an article in *The Briefing* with strong echoes of

4. Some suggested women should be able to be ordained as priests but be excluded from the role of rector (i.e., senior minister); see Anglican Diocese of Sydney, *Report Concerning Ordination*.

5. Payne, "Evangelical Double Standard," 1–4.

6. Council, *Danvers Statement*, affirmations 3 and 6.

the *Danvers Statement*. Men "have the position of headship in marriage and in the church," and wives are commanded "to submit."[7]

This idea hadn't come out of nowhere for Australians. Moore College principal, Broughton Knox, had been thinking about "headship and subordination" (as he called it) since the late 1970s.[8] The conservative position put forward in the 1984 report did use the phrase "headship and submission," but preferred the term "subordination" over "submission" and also argued that "women do not bear the image of God to the same extent as men."[9] This was not the complementarianism of the *Danvers Statement*. Lecturer John Woodhouse was articulating a kind of evolving complementarianism in 1985, describing a "hierarchy of responsibility" between men and women, whose relationship was not "symmetric."[10] But after the *Danvers Statement*, conservatives had a theological system and language—the corresponding ideas of "headship" and "submission"—and a name—"complementarianism"—for their position.[11] The previous overtly hierarchical language of "subjection" and "subordination"—on the grounds of some kind of spiritual or intellectual inadequacy in women—was replaced with the softer language of "submission." Women were affirmed as equals to men, but they were not to act as men's equals due to the "order" between them.

Now at this point you might be surprised that complementarianism developed so recently. Isn't it the "traditional" view? Far from it. The position held by most theologians throughout church history was that women can't lead churches because they are mentally or spiritually defective. Women are supposedly lacking in rationality and easily tempted, so it was fitting for men to rule.[12]

There were always people who objected to this low view of women and women who ministered despite it. Until the Fourth Lateran Council in 1215, it was still possible for women to be set aside—"ordained"—for church leadership. But even after that, there were always women who

7. Birkett and Dowe, "God and Women," 3–7.

8. Knox, "Minority Report," 3. See also Cameron, *Enigmatic Life*.

9. Anglican Diocese of Sydney, *Report Concerning Ordination*, 5.

10. Woodhouse, "Ordination of Women," 13; Moore Theological College, "Ordination of Women."

11. John Stott had also paired "headship" with "submission" in 1984 in *Issues Facing Christians Today*, 246.

12. See Williams, *How God Sees Women*.

were accepted in leadership and who taught men.[13] It was a kind of unresolved contradiction of church history. Take Martin Luther and his wife Katharina von Bora. Martin believed God made women incapable of leadership; men are "commanded . . . to govern and have the rule over women. . . . God did not create [women] for ruling, and therefore they never rule successfully."[14] Meanwhile, Katharina's gifting was obvious to him. He called her "theologian," "doctor," and "preacher." She ruled the Luther household, and contemporaries wondered if, given her confidence and learnedness, she ruled Martin too.[15]

Acceptance that women and men are equally able and called by the Spirit to lead churches took off in the nineteenth century in churches like the Salvation Army, Congregationalists, and Methodists. The view that women and men are intellectual and spiritual equals, but that leadership in church and home is nonetheless reserved for men, is a more recent biblical interpretation. It is a product of the late twentieth century.

Complementarianism became the position of an influential conservative strand of the Sydney diocese. But it was not the stance of the diocese as a whole, which, even as late as 1991, considered women's leadership in ministry a debatable matter. A prominent female evangelist in Sydney could speak openly about her love of preaching to mixed congregations without expecting or attracting any controversy.[16] It was unremarkable. A report commissioned by the 1991 Sydney Synod presented two evangelical views: one for, the other against women's ordination as priests. It noted both views were "firmly and unashamedly evangelical," both "affirm Scripture as the living Word of God," and both "submit to Scriptural authority." What they disagreed about was *not* the authority of the Bible but simply the "interpretation and application" of the Bible.[17]

By that point, the debate around women's ordination had reached an impasse at the national Anglican General Synod. In 1989, a bill to permit women's ordination as priests had, for a third time, failed to achieve the required two thirds majority. So, two days before Christmas 1991, the bishop of Canberra and Goulburn, Owen Dowling, announced he would be ordaining eleven women in February anyway. That is, without

13. Barr, *Becoming the Pastor's Wife*, 49–67.

14. Luther, *Luther's Works*, 15:130.

15. Stjerna, *Women and the Reformation*, 60–63.

16. This was evangelist Robyn Claydon in "Gospel, Women and Word."

17. Anglican Diocese of Sydney, *10/91 Ordination of Women*, 1–2.

the authorisation of the General Synod. He did this in direct defiance of the archbishop of Sydney, to whom he had vowed obedience.[18]

It was all over the news. The media hailed Dowling as a hero for women's rights.[19] Dowling compared himself to Martin Luther: "Here I stand, I can do no other!"[20]

## The Explosions of 1992

That January, conservative Sydneysider Phillip Jensen held an urgent meeting with the Anglican primate Keith Rayner in Melbourne. Rector of St. Matthias church in Sydney, Jensen had already founded the Ministry Training Strategy (MTS), Matthias Media, and *The Briefing*. He had transformed the Katoomba Christian Conventions as its chair and established the Campus Bible Study and Mid-Year Conference at the University of New South Wales. He meant action.

The meeting did not go well. According to Jensen's allies, Rayner essentially told him to settle down. Instead, Jensen came home from Melbourne to form yet another organisation, the Reformed Evangelical Protestant Association: REPA. Jensen wanted "revolution." His deputies were "colonels." More than opposing women's ordination, REPA wanted a full-scale upheaval of Sydney Anglican culture such that mission and evangelism were prioritised always, everywhere.[21]

It was a REPA colonel who decided to take Dowling to court in January 1992. Outraged by Dowling's decision to act without the General Synod, Bruce Ballantyne-Jones recruited two plaintiffs who applied for a court injunction to stop the ordinations.

The pro-women's ordination camp was incensed. Christians taking each other to court seemed to them a clear violation of 1 Cor 6. So much for biblical authority, they thought. But it was not only the pro-ordination camp who expressed concern. Peter O'Brien, then vice principal of Moore College, reminded his readers of the need for "godly wisdom" if considering taking fellow Christians to court.[22]

18. Downie, "Canberra Bishop Against Primate."
19. Liosatos, "Broadcaster Applauds Bishop Dowling."
20. Dowling quoted in Mason, "Challenging Church Law," 77.
21. Ballantyne-Jones, "Changes in Policy," 189–91.
22. O'Brien, "Courting Disaster?"

The injunction was granted on appeal. The planned ordinations were blocked by the court, a move that was deeply painful for the women involved.[23] Meanwhile, on the other side of the country, Archbishop Carnley of Perth ordained ten women. As an archbishop, there was no legal mechanism to stop him (but they did try).

Then, just after dark one Sunday evening in April, Dowling met a young man with tattoos and no shirt in a public park in Bendigo and (allegedly) offered him money for sex. The man turned out to be a cop. Dowling was charged with soliciting.[24] We'll never know exactly what happened that night. For the purposes of this story, though, what matters is that it was a very public scandal. Emotions ran hot.

It's hard to think of a more explosive way to discredit the cause of women's ordination. There would be no more appealing to 1 Cor 6 in defence of Dowling. For many conservatives here was the proof, it seemed, that the pro-women camp loved to be praised in public, but were not prepared to live lives of holy obedience. Proof, it seemed, that they had no respect for the law, either of God or of the nation.

Lest any conservatives wondered if Dowling were just a bad apple, he was followed by a string of powerful men in their own scandals. These men had ardently supported women's ordination, presenting themselves as on the side of justice, but revealing themselves, at least in the eyes of conservatives, to be morally bankrupt.

Dowling resigned as bishop (for his health), was warmly farewelled, and took up a new role as rector in a Tasmanian parish the following year. The charge was dropped after an unusual intervention from the Director of Public Prosecutions, who decided it was "not in the public interest" to pursue the case.[25]

Meanwhile, at morning teas across Sydney churches, whenever conversation "drifted towards the O-debate" (women's ordination had become so divisive it was now mentioned in coded language), "there was always someone who said . . . 'and you know what the next thing'll be? Gay clergy.'"[26] It wasn't about what the Bible taught about women

23. Downie, "Grief and Joy."

24. Downie, "Devastated Bishop"; Downie, "Bishop to Face Court"; Downie, "Bishop to Fight Charge."

25. Uhlmann, "Bishop Freed," 1; "Curious Aspects," 8; Downie, "Dismissal Too Late," 8.

26. Payne, "Is Homosexuality Next?," 13.

anymore. Women had come to represent the thin end of the wedge in an ugly culture war for the Anglican church.

The fuse was lit.

The REPA movement ripped through Sydney. A month after Dowling's arrest, it had exploded to 551 members. By September 1992, the majority of Sydney clergy had signed up.[27] Some complained that REPA had begun asserting that their view on women was actually the only view of "all Bible believing Christians."[28] The *Danvers Statement*—less than four years old—now supposedly represented the "normal" and "common reading" of the Bible, anything else was "revisionism." Those who disagreed allegedly did so out of "a desire to avoid the meaning and implication of Scripture."[29] There was no other faithful option for evangelicals, it was claimed.[30] There was much about REPA to commend. But it was also extremely effective at mobilising Sydney against the ordination of women.

In July 1992, the NSW Supreme Court ruled that secular courts could not intervene in internal Anglican church matters, unless property was involved. Dowling had won. In November 1992, with a two-vote margin, the General Synod passed a motion to allow Anglican dioceses to ordain women as priests. Most dioceses did. But Sydney did not.

REPA fizzled out after a couple of years. But that is only because its revolution was successful. It changed the terms of engagement in Sydney, and not only in Sydney, but through its networks all over Australia. Many of that generation went on to become university campus staff workers themselves. Others planted independent evangelical churches. They trained a new generation of gospel workers through the MTS apprentice scheme, equipping them with Matthias Media resources and sending them to complementarian conferences. Their new theology, complementarianism, became the norm, if not compulsory. At Moore College, for instance, complementarianism is now listed as one of its core "values" alongside other things like "Christian faith" and "integrity." These organisations have been phenomenally successful, their ministries have raised a new generation of leaders working, not only in Sydney, but across Australia and even the globe.

After REPA, everyone knew that if you felt called to work in Sydney, or in its associated organisations, you kept your mouth shut about women.

27. Ballantyne-Jones, "Changes in Policy," 189.

28. Browne, "Bad REPA," 3.

29. Jensen and Payne, "Revision Tests," 2, 8.

30. Payne, "When Is an Evangelical?," 9–10.

None of this was inevitable. Only a generation ago, it was acceptable, even normal to acknowledge that fellow evangelicals had valid differences on questions of women's leadership. Whether women would be ordained as priests was an open question.

A lot of people were very hurt in 1992. And it was women who bore the brunt and have carried the heaviest burden from the actions, mostly, of men. The camps are entrenched and many, even now, are still angry. Yes, women were ordained in Anglican churches across most of Australia, beginning in 1992, but not all events of that year were a win for women, or a win for God's church.

The backpack is heavy. The sheer weight has meant that few Australian church leaders today have wanted to look afresh at what the Bible says on women's ministry, especially if this might mean they have to leave their tribe. Better not to go there.

But if we are to read the Bible openly and honestly, we need to recognise that whatever our view, we come with a story weighing on our backs. Perhaps it's still possible to take that messy history and turn it into something beautiful.

## Bibliography

Andrews, Mary. "Interviewed by Diana Ritch." December 14, 1987. National Library of Australia Oral History Collection. https://nla.gov.au/nla.obj-216012298/listen.

Anglican Diocese of Sydney. *10/91 Ordination of Women to the Priesthood*. 1993. https://docs.sydneyanglicans.net/s/sfsites/c/sfc/servlet.shepherd/document/download/069OlooooGYlgfIAD.

———. *Report Concerning the Ordination of Women to the Priesthood Pursuant to Synod Resolution 7/83*. 1984.

Ballantyne-Jones, Bruce. "Changes in Policy and Practices in the Anglican Diocese of Sydney, 1966–2013: The Political Factor." PhD diss., Macquarie University, 2013.

Barr, Beth Allison. *Becoming the Pastor's Wife: How Marriage Replaced Ordination as a Woman's Path to Ministry*. Grand Rapids: Brazos, 2025.

Birkett, Kirsten, and Joanne Dowe. "God and Women." *Briefing* (September 1990) 3–7.

Browne, J. "Bad REPA." *Southern Cross* (August 1992) 3.

Cameron, Marcia. *An Enigmatic Life: David Broughton Knox*. Melbourne: Acorn, 2006.

Council of Biblical Manhood and Womanhood. *The Danvers Statement*. Wheaton, IL: CBMW, 1988. https://cbmw.org/about/the-danvers-statement/.

"Curious Aspects of Soliciting Case." Editorial, *Canberra Times*, August 26, 1992, 8.

Downie, Graham."Bishop to Face Court for Soliciting for Prostitution." *Canberra Times*, April 11, 1992, 1.

———. "Bishop to Fight Police Charge." *Canberra Times*, April 12, 1992, 1.

———. "Canberra Bishop Goes Against Primate, Will Ordain Women." *Canberra Times*, December 24, 1991, 1.

———. "Devastated Bishop Denies Allegations of Impropriety." *Canberra Times*, April 9, 1992, 1.

———. "Dismissal Too Late to Save a Reputation." *Canberra Times*, August 27, 1992, 8.

———. "Grief and Joy at Goulburn: Church in 'Double Bind' on Women Priests." *Canberra Times*, February 3, 1992, 1.

"The Gospel, Women and the Word." *Southern Cross* (April 1991) 10.

Jensen, Phillip, and Tony Payne. "Revision Tests." *Briefing* (October 1992) 2–8.

Knox, B. D. "Minority Report on the Ordination of Women to the Priesthood." *Australian Church Record*, April 28, 1977, 3.

Liosatos, Tonia. "Broadcaster Applauds Bishop Dowling." *Canberra Times*, January 10, 1992, 3.

Luther, Martin. *Luther's Works: The American Edition*. Edited by Jaroslav Pelikan, translated by Martin Bertram. 55 vols. St. Louis: Concordia, 1955–1986.

Mason, Keith. "Challenging Church Law: 'Phillimore's Rule.'" In *Preachers, Prophets & Heretics: Anglican Women's Ministry*, edited by Elaine Lindsay and Janet Scarfe, 77–94. Sydney: UNSW Press, 2012.

Moore Theological College. "Ordination of Women: Dr. Scholler and Dr. John Woodhouse." March 1985. Vimeo, November 21, 2019. https://vimeo.com/374814787.

Murray, Jocelyn. "The Role of Women in the Church Missionary Society, 1799–1917." In *The Church Mission Society and World Christianity, 1799–1999*, edited by Kevin Ward and Brian Stanley, 66–90. Abingdon: Routledge, 2019.

O'Brien, Peter. "Courting Disaster? 1 Corinthians 6 and Christians Going to Court." *Southern Cross* (April 1992) 25.

Payne, Tony. "The Evangelical Double Standard." *Briefing* (November 1988) 1–4.

———. "Is Homosexuality Next?" *Briefing* (September 1992) 13.

———. "When Is an Evangelical?" *Briefing* (October 1992) 9–10.

Stjerna, Kirsi. *Women and the Reformation*. Malden, MA: Blackwell, 2009.

Stott, John. *Issues Facing Christians Today*. Basingstoke: Marshall Morgan & Scott, 1984.

Uhlmann, Chris. "Bishop Freed of 'Trivial' Charge." *Canberra Times*, August 26, 1992, 1.

Williams, Terran. *How God Sees Women: The End of Patriarchy*. Independently published, 2022.

Woodhouse, John. "The Ordination of Women: Are the Barriers Biblical?" *Southern Cross* (June 1985) 13.

# A Bigger Picture

## *How Scripture on Women Taught Me to Better See Women*

Andrew Cameron

I'd like to tell a story about some things I've seen, in relation to the ministry of women, in my own small window onto Australian Anglicanism.

I was not always an Anglican. I grew up in a Christian household, but one that churched at a place I found profoundly unhelpful. Everything I heard there was contradictory, shallow, and uninteresting. I don't know if I'd still be a Christian without a local Anglican minister who showed me how the Bible had a story and made deep sense of my condition and of Christ's work. Reading the Bible in the order it presented itself was such a relief, against the cherry-picking and harvesting of it I had seen elsewhere.

Like every human movement, Anglicanism has dozens of smaller organisations, subgroupings, and networks. So after more twists and turns, I found myself in a Bible study group under one of these Anglican subgroups, and led by a woman. She took us through the book of Hebrews. It blew my mind. I still remember much of what I learnt from her.

But not long after, the same organisation had a policy turnaround on whether women should lead mixed-gender groups. Her role was altered so that when it came to adults, she would only now meet with and lead women. I was too young (around twenty) to realise that a cataclysm was erupting within several Christian denominations on what women could and could not do. Her experience, and change of role, was a part of this upheaval.

I had no further encounters with all that while I did a few other things—got a science degree, worked in an old folks home, a housing office, a bank, at the railway—all the while going to church in a lower-middle class outer suburb that did not think much about the cataclysm. I was dimly aware that roles for women were changing throughout society, but I didn't pay much attention. My mum and dad were pretty traditional, although they had no explicit theory or views on it all. I did what most young blokes do: work, get married, and hang out with young people who had different concerns.

Yet I was hoping to become a Christian minister, because the way the Bible led us to Jesus Christ was so amazing to me. When I landed in theological college, I dropped straight back into that cataclysm, debating what women should and shouldn't do, during exactly the most convulsive four years (1989–92) the Australian Anglican church had experienced on the matter of what ministries the church would recognise for women.

Any theological college—actually, any human group at all—works pretty hard to induct you into a set of views. You don't realise it when you are in your twenties, but the institution exists to "form" you around various convictions in order to pass them on to another generation.

Much of this formation, induction, and positioning is right and proper. Perhaps most importantly, this college worked quite hard at something they called "biblical theology": an understanding that the whole Bible comes together into a coherent whole, an emerging story arc that transcends time and space and culture, all overseen by a God whose character is consistent, enduring, and trustworthy. All the diverse authors of the Bible contributed something to humanity that, under God, comes together to give we tiny humans the Godhead's own angle on reality. That truly still takes my breath away, to be invited to participate in something so majestic and yet so kind.

Something important follows from this approach. I find less need to be reactive or suspicious toward parts of the Bible that go against my grain, because there is a larger story within which it can make sense. Maybe an original author was reacting to something in an ancient context that needs to be taken into account. Or, some later development in Scripture resolves a tension or question that arose earlier. Something about God becomes clearer as Scripture unfolds. Maybe my own cultural formation is to blame for my reactivity.

At theological college, we all took a close interest in an ever-expanding eruption surrounding women's ministry and ordination. There were wildcat ordinations of women as priests; court cases; people crying and placarding in Anglican governance meetings; anguished discussions; papers, speeches, articles, books; and many, *many* heated arguments.

It is hard to convey the animosity of those days. But, in summary, a majority (depending on how you count it) of Australian Anglican representatives agreed that women could be ordained as priests (or presbyters), enabling them to serve as senior ministers of a local church, and as bishops. Hence women could now perform all the roles available to men. However, several major patches in Australian Anglican-land disagreed, and still do. In those places, women are ordained as deacons, and they serve as assistant ministers, chaplains, and in other roles.

Those who thought the offices of priest and bishop were only for men were broadly of two kinds. The first, from what gets called the "Catholic wing" of the Anglican church, went roughly like this: Christ was a man; a priest in some ways stands in Christ's place; so a priest should also be a man. (I hope I am not misrepresenting.)

My "mob," the evangelicals, did not like that argument at all (for reasons—too many to recount here—to do with the word *priest*). However, my mob had a key text of Scripture that weighed heavily upon us. The apostle Paul says, "I do not permit a woman to teach or to assume authority over a man; she must be quiet" (1 Tim 2:11). Hence, no senior church leadership for women, nor any preaching to mixed congregations of adults.

So weirdly, these two wings of Australian Anglicanism, who often opposed each other, were now playing on the same team to say women may be ordained as deacons but not as priests or bishops. Opposed to those two wings was a coalition of people for whom it was legitimate for a woman to be ordained to all three of those offices. There were a variety of arguments in favour, some biblically and theologically grounded and some not. At the time, the spurious arguments most caught my attention, thus hardening my resolve to oppose change.

Another biblical text came up in this discussion. To the highly chaotic and class-stratified church of Corinth, Paul says, "Women should be silent" and "if there is anything they desire to know, let them ask their husbands at home" (1 Cor 14:34–35). The comment continues a long chapter addressing all sorts of yelling and chaos in the church. To me, clearly it says to the women in this mix: don't add to this ruckus, please. No yelling above it all "What's happening!?" or whatever. Previously, Paul had expected that women will "pray and prophesy" in this same church

(11:2). So I do not believe we have warrant to absolutise 14:34–35 across all situations. Context indicates that it pertains to one kind of situation.

That text does touch upon something else, however, that matters hugely. Another area of dispute and discussion concerns Paul's and Peter's teachings on the relationship between a woman and a man in marriage. It gets tangled here, because some argue that the teachings on how men and women in marriage are to relate applies also to how men and women in a church should relate. I neither believe nor argue that. But I still think this area matters, for reasons that will become clear.

In brief, the apostle Paul (1 Cor 11:2–16; Eph 5:22–33; Col 3:18–19) and the apostle Peter (1 Pet 3:1–7) argue for a kind of pattern in a marriage where a man's generally greater physical strength will be deployed always to love and serve a wife and children and where women willingly cooperate with that. I say "cooperate" when the operative word is often translated "submit." In 2 Cor 8:13, Paul uses this same word to picture people whose joyful generosity wells up from their "confession of the gospel of Christ," in a context where he's issued no commands. That's why I think the word primarily indicates joyful cooperation or "team-play." I wish translators would use a better English word for this Greek word than "submit." It's more subtle than that.

You can spin "authority" and "submit" as a hierarchy, like a king to a subject. Indeed, the "submit" word *does* get used that way in Rom 13:1, concerning the impersonal relation with whoever governs us (although even that context may envisage a posture of cooperative response). But what if a couple inhabits it like this: I, a man, have a power of strength given *primarily* to do good to another; I, a woman, have a capacity to cooperate with those efforts. Because, we're in this together. Paul also insists that "in the Lord woman is not independent of man or man independent of woman. For just as woman came from man, so man comes through woman" (1 Cor 11:11–12). Elsewhere, "the wife does not have authority over her own body, but the husband does; likewise the husband does not have authority over his own body, but the wife does" (1 Cor 7:4). Peter will say to men of their wives, they are "heirs with you of the gracious gift of life" (1 Pet 3:7). These statements elegantly destroy any notion of one being greater and the other lesser.

In this discussion, I don't identify as either egalitarian or complementarian, since the meaning of these modern terms shifts and slides in ways I don't agree with. What seems more interesting and important to me is how these passages give a man and a woman an envelope of operations on how to be married well. They're not philosophy, or anthropological theory, or a text written for a course in gender studies. They give brief, summary advice, probably in response to common patterns of behaviour each apostle has seen. Each passage corrects common vices that men might be into and that women might be into, but we're left to imagine what those might be. Nor do they go into specifics of who does what within the household or outside it. "Work that out together," they seem to say; "but husbands, just use your power to *love and serve*, and women, *work with him* as far you can."

I've gone into this area because I now think 1 Tim 2:11–15 concerns a (generic) married couple. I'll explain why, and why it matters, below. I neither believe nor argue that the teaching on marriage governs how men and women in churches are to generally relate.[1] But I watched as my circles sought to live out the view that this text *does* describe how Christian men and women are generally to relate. I'll convey my impressions as far as I can remember them.

In public interactions between men and women—colleagues with colleagues, students with students—I did not personally witness any Christian man using these texts to justify dismissive or abusive behaviour toward women. Among the married couples I knew, relationships generally seemed strong; if there were difficulties, they did not obviously arise from male entitlement as grounded in these texts. More widely, in the conservative churches I knew and in the theological college I studied in and then worked for, I only recall seeing civility and careful consideration directed from men toward women.

It could be argued that at this time, I did not have eyes to see what was "really" going on. For example, the studied civility I saw from men toward women can mask a marginalizing or sidelining of women's agency (a kind of "pedestaling"). The social nuances, and my blind spots, could be examined at length. Even so, I don't recall witnessing anything overtly bad.

However, over time I did become aware of a pattern that filled me with unease, a pattern that emerged over twelve years of teaching students in this context. Men were in general quite at ease to state a point, and to robustly push forward their point, to a degree that sometimes required quite robust pushback from me. That was not the case with all the thoughtful, insightful women studying there. Each conversation for them was dogged by timidity, self-doubt, and a cascade of qualifications. I

1. Also, that notion completely sidelines Scripture's teaching on singleness. See further Treweek, *Meaning of Singleness*, and Treweek, *Single Ever After*.

would find myself saying, "No, that's a good thought," and "It's okay, keep going," and noticing the need for constant encouragement to think and speak. Obviously enough, if you are surrounded by conversations about when it was inappropriate to "teach" a man, much second-guessing follows for a woman about whether her opinion or insight or contribution gets to have serious traction. Too many conversations I had with women, especially those whom I taught, were laced with second-guessing and anxious self-justification about whether it was appropriate to be having this or that thought, saying this or that thing, or putting her position with any force.

Once, I walked in when a woman was teaching the Bible to other women, and she visibly faltered, concerned that my presence meant she was now "teaching" a man. I felt sad for her and that something had gone severely wrong for a biblical statement to operate as totalised law in this way. I felt sad that her mind was also now overburdened with this extra demand on "reading the room," distracting her from her primary and by far most important task.

After witnessing what seemed clear and chronic distress in several women, I thought: the position and practice my group holds had better be right, or else I should not participate. When I raised my concerns with men in charge, they couldn't really see what I was getting at. But these patterns caused me to question how my circle's position on 1 Tim 2 was being deployed within our group's culture. Also, and more worryingly, the domain of what was considered to be a women "teaching" a man grew and grew. More and more contexts would delimit what women could say or do. Complementarian clauses began appearing in organisational statements of faith, which seemed to me way more than could be warranted.

Nor could I make sense of several facets of how the text itself was explained and of what was left unexplained in it. My attempts to discuss it were not warmly received—an odd behaviour for a group that sought to be biblically based. I don't recall being belligerent or agenda-driven in these attempts. It was more that the position had been settled, a received consensus with no prospect of change, and conversation on it was unwelcome.

That mood may even be defensible when the point at issue is something elemental to the Christian faith. For those I knew at that time, a point elemental to the Christian faith *was* at stake. The Bible speaks clearly; it often says things we do not want to hear; so to question the "clear" teaching of 1 Tim 2:11–12 can be seen as a form of spiritual rebellion.

I had concerns, though, about whether the supposed clarity of the text was dominated by my circle's spin on it. (Things always seem "clearer" when everyone around you becomes inducted into the same view.) Only much later have I become aware of scholarship around the likely backdrop of this letter, related elsewhere in this book. But at this stage of my thinking, even with only the markers internally available within the text of 1 Timothy, I had unresolved questions.

The letter does address how churches should be set up and run. But not every verse of it; and after 1:3–4, the only overt indicator that we're considering how to run an early church occurs in 3:1. The section 2:8–15 bears striking resemblance to 1 Pet 3:1–7 where Peter outlines Christlike behaviour for wives. In doing so, women are freed from enslavement to physical beauty and encouraged to pursue the beauty of a "gentle and quiet spirit"—not silence, note, but a peaceful posture, a release from anxiety, flowing from trust in God's kindness.

In 1 Tim 2:13–14, we find the arc of Gen 2–3 highly compressed into two verses. The ancient account concerns the plight of the first married couple, ending, for women, in the tragedy of painful childbirth for women, and in the clearly *illicit* "rule" of the husband over the wife. Conversely though, 1 Tim 2:15 lands on childbirth optimistically. A woman (singular) is "saved through childbearing" if "they" (plural) remain or continue in "faith and love and holiness, with modesty."

At one level, all this could sound a bit cryptic. When I asked one senior leader why a passage about church order lands on childbirth, he literally shrugged (in a seminar where he sought to expound the accepted view of 1 Tim 2:11–12. I found his avoidance of verse 15, in that context, extraordinarily negligent). Others propose that the text alludes to Mary's birthing of the Christ. But very obviously, particularly in the ancient world, childbirth sits squarely within the domain of marriage, not of who runs churches.

Mike Bird's chapter in this book suggests a plausible background in first-century Ephesus that may explain this attention to childbirth. However, even if we did not have this knowledge and only had the text before us, what might it suggest? Could the passage reassure married Christian women that the tragedy of the first marriage can be redeemed? I can well imagine a Christian woman from a Greek background, having just become familiar with the story of the fall in Gen 3—amplified by the pagan conceits of first-century Ephesus—being terrified of the curse upon childbirth. Could the passage simply reassure her that the darkness of childbirth is mitigated when "they"—the couple—live together with faith, love, and holiness; with the man putting aside his anger for prayer; and with the woman no longer needing to fixate upon her beauty?

There are other tantalizing aspects to the passage, such as the significance of the word for "authority" that is not used elsewhere in the New Testament. It likely connotes and prohibits a domineering stance, which would cohere with Christ's and the apostles' insistence that we don't dominate or "lord it over" each other, under any circumstance. It also coheres with the general sense of a marriage marked by love and cooperation, not dominance and competition.

However, a much bigger puzzle puzzled me.

You may recall how I had been gripped, transformed even, by that biblical theology that watches for broad Scriptural trends emerging across millennia. A corollary to it becomes that "Scripture interprets Scripture": we expect some parts of the Bible to assist us in making sense of others. You can take that too far, muting the voice of one biblical author with that of another. But on the whole, since God oversees the emergence of Scripture, we should expect to see resonances the original authors both did and did not intend, and greater clarity and richness build through the great story arc of the Bible.

This approach has delivered profoundly helpful accounts of the way Christians receive Old Testament wisdom, prophecy, and law; what we are to make of the character of God throughout the Bible; the nature of Christ's humanity, divinity, and saving work; how Christians are not narrowly nationalistic, but joyfully internationalist in terms of God's people and God's mission; and much more.

Yet, on the question of women's ministries, and on this issue alone, my tribe had doubled down onto *one* key text as a control text, using it as absolute master of all other parts of Scripture. The received account of 1 Tim 2:11–12 operated as "divine command deontology," to use a technical term: a statement with the force of divine authority that brooked no special pleading, exception, or dispute. All other Scriptures were then harmonised with it in ways that seemed quite forced. This from the Christian network who had taught me how *not* to harvest and deploy individual verses in that way.

But throughout Scripture, we see a sustained account of women as capable, able agents whose voices and actions significantly enable the human good. To be sure, women are not idealised. They remain flawed human beings. Many male individuals are heinous in the Bible, and also a few females, although they are the outliers. Also, women are in general clearly navigating distorted human cultures that include rampant polygamy, fertility-religious sex-trafficking, neglect and abuse by husbands, and all the other gender-distorted horrors of humanity resulting from the fall. (Just because a behaviour is described without comment in the Old Testament, it does not follow that we're expected to approve it. Old Testament authors do not loudly "virtue signal" in the way we expect today, which frees them subtly to subvert practices taken for granted in their time.)

But even given all that, we see a succession of women portrayed as people of influence and agency. I don't want only to focus here on women who teach men in Scripture. I think that misses the point, which is to highlight the way women in general are regarded among several biblical authors. Here are just a few examples. I think of Abigail (1 Sam 25:2–42), whose husband is called "fool," and who turns around a dangerous situation with generosity, quick action, and great social skills. I think also of Deborah, whom God raised up as one of several judges over Israel (Judg 4–5). The striking portrayal of a Shunammite women (2 Kgs 4:8–37; 8:1–6) shows a woman with a depth of character and love, who made a profound impression on the prophet Elisha. The canny plotting of Rahab (Josh 2:1–21; 6:17–25), which frankly disturbs modern Christians, is straightforwardly applauded by New Testament authors (Heb 11:31; Jas 2:25). I remain stunned by the respect Jesus accords to the Syrophoenician woman (Matt 15:21–28; Mark 7:24–30), when in his only trip to a foreign land, he went out of his way to meet her, hear her, and affirm her bold speaking.

The high point, of course, of Jesus's general honour toward women becomes their first witnessing his resurrection, several then becoming its first heralds to the apostles (Luke 24:10). Priscilla became prominent in the early church (Acts 18–19; Rom 16:3–4; 1 Cor 16:19; 2 Tim 4:19), as did Junia, "notable among the apostles" (Rom 16:6). It is special pleading to sidestep how obviously they were teachers and leaders (driven solely, I suspect, by the need to harmonise with that "control text," outlined above).

And then, of course, there are the Proverbs of Solomon. Many women are mentioned in the book of Proverbs; not all are great (Prov 6:24–26; 7:5–27; 14:1; 21:9). But the several mothers in Proverbs are culture-builders. A mother even teaches her son, a king, how to rule well (Prov 31:1–9). The very personification of God's wisdom is feminine. She cries out wisdom at a crossroads, at a gate, to businessmen, and to kings

(Prov 8), and invites all in as an impressive, hospitable matriarch (Prov 9:1–6). I have a further theory that the "wife of noble character" (Prov 31:10–31) operates poetically as a collage of many real-world women, doing all the things that embody wisdom. This rapid-fire coda to the book brings home all the best aspects of wisdom exemplified by this idealised woman, who seems clearly to be a composite of many impressive *actual* women.

There are some bad actors and insensitive characters too (e.g., Potiphar's wife; Jezebel; Delilah). Women are not idealised. However, the vast weight of these portrayals show a respect for women, their agency, and their influence, and with no finely parsed delimitation of when women were teaching or influencing men.

In sum, it struck me as strange that I was not hearing a biblical theology of women themselves. In other words, against this incredible backdrop, it was plain odd that Paul would make a flat, universalised assertion against women verbally guiding and generally influencing men.

As I was having these realisations, I serendipitously came upon a little-known scholarly work that turned on the lights.[2] When Dr. B. Ward Powers addresses 1 Tim 2:11–15, he notes that the Greek words often translated as "man" and "woman" do double-duty in that language for "husband" and "wife."[3] He lays out the parallel with 1 Pet 3, and the relation of the reference to childbearing to Gen 3. He outlines how a church setting has incorrectly been inserted into this text.

His work explained and confirmed my hunches, and I concluded I no longer had warrant to view 1 Tim 2:11–12 as a main "control text." I now think the text has habitually been misread. Misread over many generations, to be sure; and an interesting question would be to untangle the how and why of its reception history. I now also believe that the burden of proof lies with anyone who posits a husband-wife pattern applies to male-female relations in general. One would need to work hard to make that case, and I would contest it on several grounds. Given this

2. Powers, *Ministry of Women*.

3. In this passage, the Greek words used for "man" and "woman" that could also mean "husband" and "wife," do not take a definite article (i.e., there's no "the"). Elsewhere in the New Testament, the *presence* of a definite article often specifies that "husband" or "wife" is meant, rather than the more general "man" or "woman." So, the absence of "the" in Greek here is used to argue against Powers's position and that this passage itself cannot be about marriage. But I've tracked it through the New Testament, and this definite article thing is by no means hard and fast. So I don't believe this objection can be a relevant consideration.

conclusion, and the weight of a biblical theology of the importance of the agency and wisdom of women, I now regard it as right and proper to encourage, train, and form appropriately gifted Christian women for all the ministries of the church.

Of course, no one has a right to be ordained. Women have the same testing and discernment of their gifting and character that any man should have, before stepping into their ministries. The recognition of anyone's gifting for ministry is the task of a church, not a project of an individual's will, ambition, or sense of entitlement.

I try hard now to take seriously the many godly, faithful, and capable women I encounter. I listen harder and discern their wisdom, even if they are burdened by internal self-censoring and misplaced concerns of overstepping. It matters to me to encourage and train those women for whom it is realistic and proper that they engage in teaching and leadership. I see it as part of my task to assist in those journeys as I am able.

## Bibliography

Powers, B. Ward. *The Ministry of Women in the Church: Which Way Forward? The Case for the "Middle Ground" Interpretation of the New Testament*. Adelaide: SPKA, 1996.

Treweek, Danielle. *The Meaning of Singleness: Retrieving an Eschatological Vision for the Contemporary Church*. Downers Grove, IL: InterVarsity, 2023.

———. *Single Ever After: A Biblical Vision for the Significance of Singleness*. Charlotte: Good Book, 2025.

# Chinese Bible Woman Meets Australian Christianity

Grace Lung

The young female pastor got up to speak. The university students shot glances at each other. One guy whispered, "Do we just shut our ears? Do we walk out?" but we were frozen. A woman preaching represented everything we were taught to resist—"liberal," "secular," "feminist." Real believers were "biblical," and the Bible, we thought, clearly excluded women preaching to men.

Chinese female pastors in Australia, like the woman who preached that day, are caught in the in-between. Within the Chinese church, there are traditionalists, those who expect Confucian and Taoist quiet, dutiful womanhood. At the same time, there are those who recognise women as leaders who built and sustain the modern church in China. Now, in an Australian context, these women can become collateral damage. They are stuck in between in the complementarian and egalitarian battleground of Western Christianity (see Erica Mandi Manga's chapter for an explanation of these two camps). Nevertheless, they have sought to be faithful, finding effective, creative ways to minister the gospel from the in-between spaces.

I was one of those second-generation Chinese Christians. I avoided the Chinese side of my church whenever I could. Every time I was with the older generation of Chinese Christians, I was anxious to please, but my Chinese language wasn't fluent enough. I felt like a disappointment.

Instead, I found Western Christianity was a refuge. I learned to look with scorn at my Chinese community's so-called inferior theology and traditions. But I could not reconcile the undertone that I felt suggesting that the entire history of the Chinese church, a church that has long been led by women, was misguided. I started questioning my assumptions and talking to the "other side." I was surprised at what I found.

In this chapter I share stories from the Bible, from history, and from other women that led me to where I am today. First, I will walk you through the cultural and religious context of Chinese Christianity and its transmission through the Chinese-heritage church in Australia. I interviewed Chinese Australian church leaders, and I'll share what they told me about their experiences. Then we will look at how Chinese history and culture have interacted with Australian evangelicalism's battleground on questions of gender. We will see the examples of Old Testament women who, while relatively powerless, served faithfully. I will end with a path forward toward healing and integration for female leaders with Chinese heritage.

## Chinese Cultural and Historical Context

### The Confucian and Taoist Tradition

While traditional Chinese culture is patriarchal, Chinese women have demonstrated remarkable faithfulness and activity in society and in the church.

Within Confucian relationships, there is relational order. Because of this order, mothers tend to have more honour than childless wives or single women. Mothers rule the family and domestic realm, often exercising managerial authority over husbands.[1] Single women, by contrast, face prejudice. Labelled "leftover women," they are seen as those who have failed expected norms of femininity, of subordination and sacrifice in the family.[2] China's other major worldview is Taoism. Within Taoist thought, women are more prominent and powerful, seen as indispensable and the complementary yin to men, who are yang. However, yin women embody "stillness and receptivity."[3]

There are exceptions where women fall outside these traditions but are still revered. The fierce, warrior-like archetypal women, such as Mulan, display strength and "masculine style" attributes. They are praised only because they serve the collective: nation, or family. Once achieved, they return to the domestic realm.

1. Chan, "Confucianism and Gender," 408–22.
2. Gui, "'Leftover Women,'" 1957.
3. Nadeau, *Asian Religions*, 66.

Even though Chinese people would hardly identify as Confucian or Taoist, the worldviews are woven into everyday life, including the present-day migrant church. Often, Chinese female pastors are expected to conform to Confucian norms. One Chinese Australian female pastor explained it this way:[4]

> *When a young pastor was being ordained, the team decided that all pastors should share the responsibilities for the event. . . . The Senior Minister then specifically asked me to lead the women to serve in the kitchen on the day.*

Also, because church is seen as family, family roles become part of the leadership. Often leaders' wives have power in the church even though they hold no formal title. Their influence is seen as an extension of their husbands over the church family. One pastor shared:

> *The elder's wife confronted me in the courtyard. She held a Bible . . . she asked me to read 1 Corinthians 14:34–35. She wanted to emphasise to me "it is shameful for women to speak in church."*

For Chinese female pastors, their title is not necessarily authoritative, as commonly understood in the West. They may find themselves marginalised, in favour of the male pastors' or elders' wives. But under the Confucian patriarchal system, pastors' wives do not have it easy either. Their unpaid labour can be oppressive when perfection is often expected.[5]

But there are two concurrent streams at work when it comes to women in the Chinese church. One, as I've just described, comes from cultural norms and prioritises women's roles as wives and mothers. But the other stream—that of the Bible Women—came out of Chinese history. I'll tell this story in the next section.

## The History of the Chinese Bible Women

What happens when Confucian womanhood meets Protestant missions? Since male missionaries were culturally inappropriate to evangelise Chinese women, British women (including Australians) were enlisted to the

4. Personal experiences were shared in confidential correspondence with the author in November and December of 2025 and names are withheld by mutual agreement.

5. Lin and Wang, "Clergy Wives," 1–2, 965.

cause.[6] By the 1910s, over 60 percent of Protestant missionaries in China were women, most of them single.

Despite the Chinese cultural practice of only educating males at the time, the missionaries used education and medical training to lift the status of Chinese women. It was also strategic to train Chinese women to evangelise their own.

However, this did not occur without criticism from those emphasising a Confucian or Taoist tradition. To counter allegations that Western education would take Chinese women outside the sacred family unit, female missionaries also emphasised the duties of the Christian wife and mother. However, their converts caught more than they were taught. This education empowered a generation of educated Chinese "Bible Women" to move beyond the home sphere to teach God's word both within and outside their households.

This move was accelerated by the Second World War due to wartime necessity and post-war scarcity. Male leaders were often killed or absent. Surviving women kept the church afloat. Florence Li Tim Oi is one notable example.[7] In all reports she was a humble deaconess, "a priest in all but name." When she was ordained as a priest so that she could administer the sacraments, it was in the context of wartime necessity. She was later asked to resign from the priesthood after much opposition within the wider Anglican church. In rural areas, women such as Dora Yu and Mary Stone (Shi Meiyu) led massive revivals as they served the sick and preached the gospel. They became significant leaders in the first half of the twentieth century.[8]

Women were also enlisted in China's nation building. During national milestones such as the May Fourth Movement (1919) and Mao's socialist reconstruction and Cultural Revolution (1950s onward), traditional Confucian views were questioned. Women were needed in the workforce, agricultural labour, and in public life. With the abolition of Christian denominations and the establishment of the Chinese Communist Party's sanctioned church, the "Three-Self Patriotic Movement," the expanding roles for women in Chinese society were also reflected in churches. Women made up a significant majority, and female pastors

6. Australian missionaries to China in the nineteenth century also included Chinese Australian Christians.

7. Wong and Chiu, *Christian Women*, 111–12.

8. Chow, "Remarkable Story."

became the norm.[9] But this was not simply the influence of Communism. Even in democratic, British-occupied Hong Kong, most denominations recognised female leadership and ordained women.[10]

So although British missionaries had taught Chinese women to serve in the home, many Chinese women looked to the agency and faithful Bible teaching of these female missionaries.[11] The Chinese women followed their example, in an era that required their active contribution. Two streams emerged, one where women were often expected to provide administration, care, and kitchen duties; gendered expectations didn't disappear. But at the same time, women could also hold official titles and preach the gospel. They did so faithfully. In doing so, they made a significant contribution to the explosion of Christianity in China.

## Chinese Australian Women in Australia

China's instability in the early twentieth century brought waves of Chinese migrants to Southeast Asia and the Pacific Islands. They brought their faith with them. After the White Australia policy ended, many more Chinese migrated to Australia because of regional conflicts, poverty, education, and skilled migrants. They founded Chinese-language churches, which developed into English ministries for their children. By 2019, there were 239 Chinese-heritage churches across Australia.[12]

What happens when Chinese sociocultural-religious systems are transported to Australia?

In Australia, Chinese female leaders not only endure Confucian patriarchal structures, but they also experience racial inequality. In one study, 45 percent of the Asian Australian women experienced racism in their ministry contexts. Of these, 20 percent stated that their experience was "constant or significant." In addition, 44.5 percent experienced negative stereotypes of women with 25 percent of these reporting their experience was "constant or significant."[13] Hill reported that these included "a sexualised and fetishised view of Asian women . . . an expectation that Asian women are good at administration, finances, and

9. Chow, "Remarkable Story."

10. Yau, "Path of Biblical Equality," 49.

11. Chung, *Chinese Women*, 102–4.

12. Tsoi and Chia, *Chinese Church in Context*, 18.

13. Hill, *Sunburnt Country*, 27.

bookkeeping . . . an idea that Asian women are caring, soft, nurturing, docile, sexually available, submissive, and domestic."[14] These stereotypes came from *both* Asian patriarchal and Western contexts.

They also face Western individualism, which encourages Chinese women to be an authentic individual, "stop saying sorry," and fight for her rights. This may be uncomfortable for those more accustomed to Chinese collectivism.

However, the same study found that 88.89 percent of Asian Australian female leaders believe their gender is a strength. These women have "the ability to work across cultures, the ability to not be perceived as a threat (the way a white male might be), and the ability to identify with and relate to the most vulnerable people in a society . . . [they] talked about being perceived as intelligent, caring, reliable, diligent, thoughtful, and competent."[15]

Their situation is complex. Like Chinese Bible Women, these women form the backbone of many migrant churches. But the older generation tends to accept their exclusion from church senior leadership. One pastor relayed her own conversations with several older women:

> *[These older Chinese women] were biblically trained, . . . articulate, spiritually mature, and deeply capable. Yet they consistently declined leadership roles because they believed such positions "belonged to men." Interestingly, these same women openly lamented the gender inequality within the church and wished for a healthier model for the next generation.*

The tensions they experience reflect the two streams of gender norms in the Chinese church: the Confucian and Taoist ways of being, on the one hand, and the experience of the ministry of Bible Women, on the other.

Amongst each other, they could privately lament. This practice is referred to in Chinese as "吃苦"—i.e., swallowing sorrow. In *More Than Serving Tea*, Tracey Gee writes, "In the Asian worldview, suffering is simply an assumed part of the way the world is. . . . Americans [and most Australians too!] ask God to take the suffering away; when people in other parts of the world suffer, they ask God for strength to endure it well."[16]

Would the next generation have a healthier model?

14. Hill, *Sunburnt Country*, 27–28.

15. Hill, *Sunburnt Country*, 37–38.

16. Toyama and Gee, *More Than Serving Tea*, 71.

## The Chinese Heritage Church and Australian Complementarianism

In Australia, Chinese churches commonly create English congregations for the second generation to worship. They seek locally trained pastors who are Chinese Australians, or culturally competent Anglo-Australians, to oversee these congregations. Hence, the second generation tend to experience spiritual formation outside the Chinese-heritage church through these leaders.

This formation included a strong Western complementarian view of women in Scripture through some university campus ministries and some major Bible colleges. The atmosphere was combative: the leaders of the complementarian movement believed the gospel was at stake. The "Other" were the "liberals," "secular feminists," who did not believe the Bible. One key emphasis within this movement was that the ministry of the word is authoritative and that women should not exercise this authority over men.

The resulting impact in Chinese-heritage churches has been significant.

First, the emphasis on women's roles as a barometer of faithfulness to the Bible gave rise to a general tension and suspicion between the younger English congregations and older Chinese congregations. The English side observed that women were being employed as pastors on the Chinese side, and that these women also preached the word. It was hard for the younger generation to see the Chinese congregation as anything but the unbiblical Other. But their parents were hardly the liberal, secular feminists they had been warned about!

The older Chinese congregations, meanwhile, were initially unaware of this stance. In one instance, back when I still had doubts about the older generation, I was encouraged to preach at the Cantonese service. When sharing that my hesitation to preach at mixed congregations was due to my theological position, I found the key leaders had not even heard of the terms *complementarian* and *egalitarian*, much less the debates. Another pastor reflects:

> *Chinese Congregation members who were aware of the issue ranged from bewilderment to condescension. Some were surprised and confused that the English Congregation held such a "traditional point of view."*

For us who had grown up in the Australian evangelical world, it was hard to see how the complementarian and egalitarian framing and battles were actually an expression of the West's preoccupation with orthodoxy ("right belief") and their resulting historical and cultural debates.

Once aware of each other's differences, the two generations sometimes responded with anger and verbal abuse. In one church, a devoted female member was barred from leading a Bible study group on her own. Once the parent discovered this, they were infuriated. The English congregation appeared unreasonable, given that there was a need for leaders. The pastors prepared a position paper proposing a "one church, two systems" model. But a Chinese faction proposed that the English congregation should leave. As the conflict intensified and hurt increased, the English congregation eventually left (and at least four pastors). Disconnected from their ancestral communities, their spiritual formation continues in Western spaces. This caused a deep rift in families, both biological and spiritual.

But these Western spaces had their own challenges. Complementarian female leaders sometimes policed each other. When I experienced difficulty in marriage or ministry leadership, I was questioned whether I had been submissive enough, and whether I was intimate with my husband. Finding someone who could speak with cultural nuance and pastoral sensitivity was difficult without feeling pushed back into Confucian norms or into Western evangelicalism's lens on women's role and place.

The theological battles of white Australian Christianity were based in arguments that had nothing to do with my culture or history. So when Western theological binaries of complementarian and egalitarian are applied uncritically to Chinese-heritage churches in Australia like mine, our communities became collateral damage to battles not our own.

## Negotiating the Matrix

Chinese Australian women in paid Christian ministry sit at the intersection of multiple complex categories. Our work is at once:

- Generationally challenging: the second generation is expected to submit and obey elders due to their age.
- Culturally challenging (East): traditional ideals of women can limit women into caring roles while pragmatism is needed for migrant survival.

- Culturally challenging (West): we are caught between feminism and patriarchy as a racialised Other.
- Theologically challenging: we are caught between complementarian vs. egalitarian.

Any combination of these views can exist within the same church. Each side claims to have the "biblical position." We feel caught in between, pushed to the margins.

How do we cope?

Anxiously seeking to please, only showing one side of myself in one context and another in the other is one coping mechanism. With complementarians, I am submissive and differential. With egalitarians, I speak up. But this can be exhausting. It requires a frequent denial of oneself, unable to integrate each identity into a coherent whole. Another coping mechanism is to tread carefully:

> *English congregations did not allow women to preach, whereas the Chinese congregations did. I could only preach in English in Teens' services and Women's events. I needed to tread carefully so that I do not cause any issues. Otherwise, I may jeopardise my preaching ministry.*

While senior church leaders discuss and debate the role of women, the women themselves are often quiet. Whether it's fear from stepping outside cultural norms, feeling pressure to conform to the stereotype of the "demure Asian woman," or wanting to avoid "usurping a man's authority," women are often *invisible.*

However, invisibility does not mean passivity. Where earlier generations previously may have "swallowed sorrow" or tried to please everyone, I present this generation an alternate option.

## In-Betweenness

Because societal, cultural, generational, and theological factors can marginalise Chinese Australian women, I suggest that the question of "Whose side am I on?" is less important to the question "Where am I located?" So, a more helpful concept to frame Chinese Australian female leader's experience is *in-betweenness.* Theologian Sang Hyun Lee calls this the theology of "liminality." It is "the positive, creative nature of the in-between-ness in marginality. . . . Freed from structure, persons in liminality are also available to a genuine communion with others."[17] This is often how God's yes to women is revealed. Lee elaborates that Jesus himself is an in-between person who used human weakness to display divine glory. Jesus understands and is often ministering to those in the margins of Roman and Jewish society.[18]

This creative in-betweenness in marginality can also be seen in the Old Testament. Relatively powerless female figures can do God's work through subversive or shrewd methods. We see it in Scripture through the lives of Esther, Ruth, and Bathsheba.

## Esther

As a woman in King Xerxes harem, Esther had little power. She was an object, and for most of the story, she simply followed Mordecai's direction. However, when her people's lives were threatened, she used a series of banquets to save them. Hertig writes that she was both bold and tender. She was innocent as a dove and as shrewd as a serpent.[19]

## Ruth

Like Ruth, many Chinese Australian women are treated as a foreigner or identified as someone's wife, daughter-in-law. Although these are marginal categories, Ruth used multiple identities (foreigner, family, refugee, God-fearer) to navigate challenges for herself and Naomi. Instead of pushing away one part of herself, she owned them all and used them for her and God's purposes.[20]

## Bathsheba

Some women reclaim their agency and voice for the sake of others. Bathsheba began as a victim, taken from Uriah for David. But later in 1 Kgs 1, she used her position and voice like a lioness to advocate for herself and Solomon's future.[21]

17. Lee, *From a Liminal Place*, 4–6.
18. Lee, *From a Liminal Place*, 61.
19. Hertig, "Subversive Banquets,"25.
20. Gin, "Ruth," 65–67.
21. Sun, "Bathsheba Transformed," 36–37.

And so, with in-betweenness, we are not alone. In Luke 1:39–45 we see a picture of support and solidarity when the teenager Mary seeks out Elisabeth the elder, and Elisabeth celebrates with Mary. In Chinese churches, language, culture, and theology can feel like barriers that silo female first- and second-generation leaders. While I was preparing this chapter I heard my older sisters in Christ share their stories; I felt moved. They were not secular feminists trying to usurp a man's authority, they were actually marginalised too. But they sought to trust God whilst being effective in their ministries. We were not alone in private lament but faithfully trusting God in solidarity with each other.

## God's Work in the In-Between Spaces

Like Bible Women and migrant female pastors who served in in-between spaces, I also see God working in my own story through experiences of marginalisation.

The margins are inherently uncomfortable, neither here nor there. It is mentally and psychologically costly, facing pressure and invalidation on so many fronts, never feeling enough: not traditionally Chinese enough, not Western enough, not "biblical" enough, not "woke" enough. Not old enough, not male enough, not feminine enough. In an unfamiliar gathering, I'm not sure which me was welcome.

Today, I feel less anxious. As I meditate on Jesus Christ, and on the witness of these women in the margins, I have learnt to embrace this uncomfortable space. Marginality can be dehumanising, but the in-between spaces are where God creatively works. The creative in-between can be mysterious, we don't know how the Holy Spirit will work. But I have learnt to keep listening and discerning; to trust and follow the open doors. Despite the hardships, I have seen his incredible work through me when I feel the most marginal as a Chinese Australian woman. The truth that *I am enough in Jesus* strengthens me to endure and follow him. And I am not alone, as I find community with other female leaders, and with God, here, in the margins. I hope these stories offer the next generation pathways for healing and integration.

This in-between reframing also helps me to see my mission to the numerous marginal others. The minorities, vulnerable, needy—those most open to Jesus. By owning where I am located, I find many others like me, ready to receive the healing, belonging, and dignity that Jesus gives.

God forms female leaders who are both past and present, East and West, with silence and voice. He transforms those of us in the margins to do his incredible creative work.

## Bibliography


Chan, Sin Yee. "Confucianism and Gender." In *The Oxford Handbook of Confucianism*, edited by Jennifer Oldstone-Moore, 408–22. Oxford: Oxford University Press, 2023.

Chow, Alexander. "The Remarkable Story of China's 'Bible Women.'" Christianity Today, March 16, 2018. https://www.christianitytoday.com/history/2018/march/christian-china-bible-women.html.

Chung, Mary Keng Mun. *Chinese Women in Christian Ministry: An Intercultural Study*. Asian Thought and Culture 48. Washington, DC: Lang, 2005.

Gin, Deborah Hearn. "Ruth: Identity and Leadership from Multivocal Spaces." In *Mirrored Reflections: Reframing Biblical Characters*, edited by Young Lee Hertig and Chloe T. Sun, 57–71. Eugene, OR: Wipf & Stock, 2010.

Gui, Tianhan. "'Leftover Women' or Single by Choice: Gender Role Negotiation of Single Professional Women in Contemporary China." *Journal of Family Issues* 41 (2020) 1956–78.

Hertig, Young Lee. "Subversive Banquets of Vashti and Esther." In *Mirrored Reflections: Reframing Biblical Characters*, edited by edited by Young Lee Hertig and Chloe T. Sun, 15–29. Eugene, OR: Wipf & Stock, 2010.

Hill, Graham Joseph. *Sunburnt Country, Sweeping Pains: The Experiences of Asian Australian Women in Ministry and Mission*. Faith and Justice in These Lands Now Called Australia. Eugene, OR: Wipf and Stock, 2022.

Lee, Sang Hyun. *From a Liminal Place: An Asian American Theology*. Minneapolis: Fortress, 2010.

Lin, Ching-Ying, and Kenneth T. Wang. "Clergy Wives and Well-Being: The Impact of Perceived Congregational Perfectionism and Protective Factors." *Religions* 15 (2024) 965.

Nadeau, Randall L. *Asian Religions: A Cultural Perspective*. West Sussex: Wiley, 2014.

Sun, Chloe T. "Bathsheba Transformed: From Silence to Voice." In *Mirrored Reflections: Reframing Biblical Characters*, edited by Young Lee Hertig and Chloe T. Sun, 30–42. Eugene, OR: Wipf & Stock, 2010.

Toyama, Nikki A., and Tracey Gee, eds. *More Than Serving Tea: Asian American Women on Expectations, Relationships, Leadership and Faith*. Downers Grove, IL: InterVarsity, 2006.

Tsoi, Grace Kwan Sik, and Philip P. Chia, eds. *Chinese Church in Context: Voices from Downunder*. Australian University of Theology Publications. Eugene, OR: Wipf and Stock, 2025.

Wong, Wai Ching Angela, and Patricia P. K. Chiu, eds. *Christian Women in Chinese Society: The Anglican Story*. Hong Kong: Hong Kong University Press, 2018.

Yau, Cecilia. "China—The Path of Biblical Equality for the Chinese Women." In *Global Voices on Biblical Equality: Women and Men Ministering Together in the Church*, edited by Aída Besançon Spencer et al., 36–51. House of Prisca and Aquila Series. Eugene, OR: Wipf and Stock, 2008.

# God Chooses the Least Expected

Vanessa Bennett

God has the habit of choosing the least expected person at various times throughout the Bible.

My own story is one of God choosing an unlikely leader in his church.

I grew up in what could be coined a "C & E family." I was born and duly christened in the Church of England (i.e., "C of E"), what is now known as the Anglican Church of Australia. I grew up on the northern beaches of Sydney where our family would attend church most Christmases and occasionally at Easter. Hence the expression "C & E," Christmas and Easter family.

When I was in year 5, my younger sister and I were taken to the local Anglican Church to attend Sunday School while our parents spent the mornings doing other things. From a young age I had a heightened sense of hypocrisy. If they didn't attend church, why should my sister and I? I argued my case to them, but to no avail.

The next time it came to getting in the car to be dropped off at church, I was determined not to go. So, I ran off. After some effort by my parents, my visiting grandparents, and a neighbour to catch me, I was put in the car with my sister and taken, rather late, to Sunday School. That effort must have been enough to bring an end to our Sunday School attendance, much to my relief.

Some weeks later, I received a card from the Sunday School saying how much they missed me and that they hoped I'd be back soon. I was incensed. They didn't know me. How could they miss me?

I don't know where the anger came from, but I vividly remember standing in the kitchen, tearing that card to pieces, and throwing it in the bin. At that moment I swore to have nothing to do with the church again. The End. I wanted nothing to do with church or God.

But God had other ideas.

When I went to high school, my two closest friends were both Christians. They challenged me to look into the person of Jesus. I began reading the New Testament, Christian books in the school library, and even the Anglican Book of Common Prayer to learn how to communicate with God, if he was there.

At the same time, my grandfather was dying of cancer. Being particularly close to him I also wanted to know if there was life after death.

As I explored the evidence for Christ and his resurrection, I became convinced that he was who he claimed to be. He was the Son of God who loved me so much that he died for my salvation and rose to eternal life. Through him I am forgiven, cleansed, and given new life.

At that moment I experienced a profound sense of being called, not just to follow Jesus as my saviour, but to serve him in ministry even though I didn't have the words for it at the time. As Lord of All, who had given his all for me, he deserved my all, my whole life in service of him. It is a call that has remained with me ever since.

I joined the local Anglican Church, St. Mark's Avalon Beach, and got involved in the youth group and helping out with the evening service. I also began leading the Christian group at high school.

After the evening service one week, when I was in year 12 at school, I was asked what I planned to do after school. I was standing in the rear of the church with a small group of young adults enjoying some food and drink. The rector was clearing away a few things near the front of the church. I pointed to the rector and answered, "What he's doing." This was 1982.

The group I was in started laughing. I was left feeling confused and somewhat humiliated as the group dispersed to talk with others. What I didn't know at that time was that women could not be ordained leaders in the Anglican Church. As I stood alone feeling dejected, a wise retired minister came up alongside me. He had overheard the conversation and seen its impact on me. Despite knowing the Anglican Church's position on women's leadership, this older minister encouraged me to keep pursuing God's call, trusting God to open the way. That retired minister was

Carl Hammond, son of former Moore Theological College principal T. C. Hammond.

Carl could have come up and explained the church's position and then tried to steer me toward some other more "suitable" means of service. But he didn't. He positively encouraged me to follow God wherever he led, trusting that the Lord would guide, provide, and open the way. Carl kept the future open to the sovereign work of God.

Carl's words have remained with me as a constant encouragement and have proven true. God has been faithful in opening unexpected doors and leading me on an unexpected journey.

After finishing high school, I completed a science degree with a diploma of education before teaching mathematics and geography at an Anglican school. During this time, I was given opportunities to preach and lead services at my church. I then began studying theology part time at night at Morling Baptist College while continuing to teach at school and serve at church.

Once I completed my first theology degree, I was appointed as a part-time lay assistant minister at St. Andrew's Anglican Church, Wahroonga, on Sydney's North Shore. That role involved leading and preaching at various church services and overseeing pastoral care across the parish.

While in that role, the archdeacon for women, Di Nicholios, visited me and encouraged me to seek ordination as a deacon. I was accepted as a Sydney Anglican candidate and began studying for a master of arts in theology at Moore Theological College. I was also required to complete a couple of undergraduate subjects to supplement my degree from Morling Baptist College.

Not everyone I studied with was supportive of women studying for ordained ministry. There were some who challenged me about what I was doing, even questioning my marriage because it was me, not my husband, studying for ordained ministry. After all, they argued, I should be submitting to his headship at home and church. My response was to tell them I was doing what my husband was encouraging me to do, to which they didn't have an answer. My husband, Paul, has always been my greatest support.

Another great support was my senior minister, Terry Dein. He was an advocate for me at Moore College when it came to negotiating what subjects I needed to complete for ordination. He also provided me with opportunities to preach and to exercise leadership in a number of contexts.

As I studied the Bible and was challenged by others about the role of women in the church, I became more and more convinced that God does indeed say yes to women as leaders in his church.

On the eighth of February, 2003, I was ordained a deacon in St. Andrew's Cathedral, Sydney.

I continued serving on the ministry team at Wahroonga. In the eight years I served with Terry and the team at Wahroonga (a team of three men and two women), we worked well together, supporting and encouraging each other, using our various gifts, and seeing people's lives transformed. Men and women partnering together in the service of Christ enabled us to minister to more people across a diversity of ages, gender, and social backgrounds than any of us would have done on our own.

With a change in leadership at Wahroonga, there was a shift in attitude toward women in leadership in the church. It became clear that I needed to find another ministry position. So, in 2005, I accepted the role of chaplain at Meriden Anglican School for Girls. As chaplain, I was also a member of the school executive leadership team. The role of the chaplain on the leadership team communicated the centrality of faith in the Anglican tradition in the life of the school.

With my appointment, the principal encouraged me to see the school as my parish and to lead it as I saw appropriate. I was the first female chaplain appointed in the school, and it was a wonderful opportunity for a woman to model the Christian faith in a girls' school. It enabled me to combine my teaching and ministry experience in an environment where the students were keen to ask questions and explore aspects of life and faith.

It was such an encouragement to see the number of students in voluntary lunchtime Christian groups growing year after year with the support of a youth worker in the chaplaincy team. There were also opportunities to engage with parents and Old Girls. One parent even asked me if she could come to chapel because her daughter loved it so much and kept coming home with questions. She wanted to hear what her daughter was hearing in chapel so she could better engage with her in faith conversations.

Meriden had a connection with St. Anne's Anglican Church, Strathfield, so I became involved in that parish. This included leading and preaching at various services.

During my time in Sydney, I was greatly encouraged as I witnessed the transformation of people's lives in Christ while I was involved in church and school ministry.

However, over time I had seen a shift in the acceptance of women in leadership and preaching positions across the Anglican Diocese of Sydney. As ministers who were supportive of women in these roles began retiring, the number of parishes offering women such opportunities declined.

I also encountered hostility from some clergy who were opposed to women in ordained ministry and leadership. That hostility ranged from being accused of not being a Bible-believing Christian because I didn't understand the Bible the way they did on this issue, to being completely ignored when attending ministry conferences. One leader went as far as advising me that, given the shift in attitude in the diocese and my training and experience in ministry, there was no longer any place for me there. The hostility I faced became the catalyst for needing to move on. As damaging as some of those experiences were, God used those difficult times to open other unexpected doors, providing ministry opportunities while bringing healing and growing my trust in him.

One unexpected door opened when the Bishop of the Diocese of Canberra and Goulburn, Stuart Robinson, contacted me and asked if I would be willing to be ordained as a priest (known as *presbyters* in Sydney) which would allow me to serve as a senior minister in his diocese. Following the interview processes, I was ordained priest in Goulburn Cathedral on the morning of the twenty-seventh of November, 2010. A number of us then travelled the short distance to the Parish of West Goulburn where I was inducted as rector (or senior minister) in the afternoon. This position also came with the role of chaplain at Goulburn Base Hospital.

What had been laughed at all those years ago had come to fruition. God had indeed opened the way, as Carl had promised. What had not been possible, had become possible. I felt awe and wonder for all Christ had done, along with a sense of responsibility for all that lay before me as I stepped up to serve God and his people in this new capacity.

Being the first female rector of the Parish of West Goulburn, there were some people, male and female, who were unsure about the appointment of a woman. Overwhelmingly, Paul and I were warmly welcomed and supported by the parish. For me it was a matter of just getting on with the ministry to which God had brought me, serving the parishioners, hospital patients and staff, and members of the community as I shared the love and good news of Jesus with them. As people got to know me, heard me preach, experienced my leadership and pastoral support, any initial concerns quickly evaporated. It was encouraging to see the parish growing during my time there.

Having settled into the community and being keen to stay there, another unexpected turn occurred well into my fifth year there. Within three days, Wednesday to Friday, in one week, four bishops rang me about possibilities in seven different parishes across four dioceses. I rang Paul at work to ask, "Do you think God is trying to tell us something?"

After a whirlwind of flights, interviews, phone calls, and much prayer with Paul, I was inducted as vicar (another name for a senior-minister role in the Anglican system) of the Parish of St. Thomas, Moonee Ponds, in Melbourne.

Being the first female vicar of the parish, yet again, meant that a few parishioners were unsure about the appointment of a woman. I did what I did before, just got on with the ministry before me.

I was also open to conversations with those who had different theological positions to mine. The common point we all shared was that each of us, as Christian brothers and sisters, loved the Lord Jesus Christ, and were keen to grow in our knowledge, love, and service of him. We agreed on the key foundational truths of our Christian faith, as summarised in the traditional creeds of the church. When it came to issues such as the role of women in the church, among other issues, we could agree to disagree while remaining brothers and sisters in Christ worshipping alongside each other. Over time, concerns about a female vicar once again evaporated.

Christ's church has the opportunity to model respectful conversations on points of difference in a world that seems to be becoming more fractured and angry. Our desire to love Christ, to worship him, to grow in our knowledge and service of him, and to share the life he offers through his death and resurrection, is far more unifying than our points of difference, especially on the role of women in the church.

In February 2020, I was given another opportunity to put this into practice when I was appointed as archdeacon for Essendon, while remaining vicar at Moonee Ponds. This role meant supporting the ministry of fifteen Anglican churches in the Essendon region.

These churches had various worship styles, theologies, ethnicities, and cultural circumstances. The support we could provide each other as church leaders in our meetings together was of far more value than our differences. We were all keen to serve the Lord and see his kingdom grow in our part of Melbourne.

Being archdeacon for Essendon provided the opportunity to work alongside Bishop Genieve Blackwell as she led intentional conversations between small groups of representatives from a few parishes at a time. These conversations explored how the Anglican Church in the inner north of Melbourne could be more effective in its mission looking ten years forward into the future. From these conversations, one parish released property for a church plant, while another two parishes from divergent styles of worship decided to merge. Both new ventures are now flourishing ministries.

Working alongside Bishop Genieve I was able to observe various challenges bishops face. She is well suited and gifted for meeting those challenges. It was not a role I had any desire to do. Then, out of the blue in February 2024, I received a phone call from Mark Short, bishop of the Diocese of Canberra and Goulburn, asking me if I would be interested in the role of Assistant Bishop in that diocese.

My initial response was shock and a hesitancy. Before making any assumptions about the role, I thought I should, at least, ask what the role would entail. When I was told it involved overseeing the training, mentoring, and professional development of ordained and non-ordained leaders, among other bishop responsibilities, I saw how that tapped into my education background and my passion to see people learn and grow in their knowledge and service of the Lord.

This threw me into a quandary.

I love local church ministry. I am passionate about seeing people come to know Christ, and grow in their knowledge, love, and service of him. Coming out of the COVID-19 lockdowns in Melbourne, the Parish of St. Thomas, Moonee Ponds, had turned a corner and was growing numerically as well as spiritually. There was a renewed energy as new people became involved in the life of the parish. The church community was in a good place moving forward. I was keen to stay and be part of this ongoing growth and renewal the Lord was bringing.

On the other hand, there was this opportunity to be involved in the training and formation of future and current church leaders in a diocese I had come from. Paul and I prayerfully sought the Lord's guidance.

This was a difficult decision to make. The comfortable decision would be to stay with the parish. But following Jesus isn't a call to comfort. Nor is it about feeling adequate for the role. Accepting Bishop Mark's invitation would involve stepping out of my comfort zone and trusting the Lord for his provision and equipping.

As Paul and I prayed about it and sought the wisdom of a couple of close friends, my personal hesitancy was more than countered by the others' endorsement. The words of Carl Hammond again rang in my mind: "Follow the call of the Lord and he will open the way." That young girl who swore she'd have nothing to do with the church could never have imagined what had now transpired. I said yes to Bishop Mark's invitation and what God had in store for my next stage of ministry.

On the twenty-fourth of August, 2024, I was consecrated bishop at St. Saviour's Cathedral, Goulburn, the same place where I had been ordained as priest.

One of the first roles I was given as the new assistant bishop in the Diocese of Canberra and Goulburn was to chair a Women in Leadership Commission. The commission was set up to address the disparity between male and female leadership in the diocese. This disparity was highlighted in a report by a women-in-ministry working group to the synod, the governing body of the diocese, in September 2024.

God says yes to women, but church structures, unconscious and cultural biases, and some attitudes create more hurdles and barriers for women than men. This is not only a concern for our diocese or denomination.[1]

My hope is that the Women in Leadership Commission can help bring about changes in our diocese that will encourage women to step up and use their God-given gifts of leadership in the church, that they may reach people who might not otherwise be reached for Christ. I am aware that other dioceses are also looking to address this issue of disparity.

I've often reflected on the quote, "You can't be what you can't see," attributed to American activist Marian Wright Edelman. The concept highlights the need for women to see other women in leadership to encourage them to consider the possibility for themselves. Role models are important.

In the early stages of my journey, there were no female role models in church leadership. The role models I had were male clergy. The support of male clergy has been essential in encouraging me to step up in ministry. I am thankful for the opportunities I was given in those early

1. Sandeman, "Big Gap."

years to try my hand at various ministries, which included preaching and leading, and to study God's word and theology. Today, the voice of men speaking up for and supporting women in leadership, and giving them ministry opportunities, is just as vital as having female role models.

As I look back, I am amazed at what the Lord has done in transforming a young girl who wanted nothing to do with him, and leading her on a journey around and over barriers and challenges, and through unexpected openings to the place she is today as a bishop in the church of God. The Lord can indeed use the least expected as leaders in his church today. What might God be putting before you?

The Lord continues to guide and equip, as I continue to learn and grow. There is much I still need to learn. There is much still to be done in service of his kingdom and in encouraging women to say yes to God's yes to them.

## Bibliography

Sandeman, John. "The Big Gap in Women's Leadership on Local Churches Is Not Only Explained by Male-Leaders-Only Networks." The Other Cheek.Com, September 21, 2025. https://theothercheek.com.au/the-big-gap-in-womens-leadership-on-local-churches-is-not-only-explained-by-male-leaders-only-networks.

# Backward in Heels

## *The Experiences of an Australian Evangelical Ordained Woman*

MEGAN POWELL DU TOIT

WHEN I MEET PEOPLE who only know me through my public voice, they are often surprised by my physical appearance. I am small, five-foot nothing, blonde, with a baby face that has often meant I am taken for younger by many years. My voice is soprano. A public leadership role was never where I imagined myself to be.

I was born premature, the girl of girl/boy twins. I was also born with a vision disability—exotropia—the opposite of crossed eyes where both my eyes would drift outward, out of alignment. After three surgeries this was cosmetically corrected by ten years old. I had spent all my primary school years with a visible and socially isolating difference. I was understandably very shy. In high school, I refused requests to join the debating team, both hating public speaking and conflict.

I entered university planning to become an actor, a job in which I could hide within other roles. But then I had a life-changing experience. At eighteen I experienced a call to become a pastor. The daughter of a Baptist pastor and academic, this was not a welcome call. My first response was to suggest to God instead my much more confident—and male—twin. Yet I could not shake the sense of a call to pastoral ministry. Indeed, I found myself in tears at church, feeling the tension between singing about my willingness to give my life to Christ while withholding myself from this call. Eventually, I reached out to others I respected and asked what they thought of me in pastoral ministry. To my surprise, I found that they encouraged me to explore this call. My father counselled me to go get some secular work experience first, which I gladly did. However, after two years in the secular workforce I felt a renewed sense of urgency. I was reluctant to give up my fledgling career in publishing so soon, but I did and went to theological college. However, I did so hoping that God would find me pastoral roles in which I wouldn't have to preach much, if at all; I remained terrified of public speaking. Little could I have foreseen where ministry would take me.

My experience of ministry since has been both of more and different opportunities than I expected, but also of greater difficulties than I imagined. Sometimes it is a kindness that we don't know all of God's plans. It has felt often like dancing backward in heels, to echo a famous quote about dance duo Fred Astaire and Ginger Rogers.[1] This could be said of ordained women in Australian evangelicalism as well. Amid obstacles and opposition, we have often had to meet higher standards and be more resilient than our male counterparts. Yet despite the difficulties, we rejoice in serving the kingdom of God. This has been my story, and I am going to tell you my story as it intertwines with the larger story of Australian evangelical women.

A caveat before I begin: my story is an uncomfortable one for many, and it is difficult for me to tell. I will of necessity, like Paul in 2 Cor 11:16—12:10, tell aspects of my story which sound either boastful or overly negative. Please bear with me, as I am attempting to show the reality for women who seek to serve God, in the hope that we will be able to enable more women to serve, to the glory of God.

## Women's Ordination in Australian Evangelicalism

Let's set the scene of Australian evangelicalism. Australian evangelicals are a significant group within Australian Protestantism. The most recent statistics on church attendance in Australia reveal the five largest Protestant denominations are Australian Christian Churches (ACC, previously Assemblies of God), Baptist, Anglican, Uniting, and Presbyterian.[2] ACC is Pentecostal, and fits into a broader evangelical categorisation. The Baptist and Presbyterian churches in Australia are almost all evangelical, while the Anglican and Uniting churches are mixed.

1. Thaves, *Frank and Ernest*.
2. Powell et al., *Church Pulse Check*, 14–16.

In the two largest of these denominations, women can be ordained and hold senior leadership roles. The ACC have allowed women to do so since their inception in 1937.[3] I was accredited in the Baptist Association of NSW and ACT in 2003, which meant I could be ordained by a local church. The first women were accredited and then ordained in the association as recently as 1999, while I was studying for ministry. The first Australian Baptist woman ordained was Marita Munro in 1978 and as of 2024, all state associations within Australian Baptist Ministries ordain women. Many of our sisters in other evangelical churches in Australia are unable to be ordained due to denominational rules.

For some women, therefore, the barriers are overt. For others, the barriers are more subtle, due to attitudes and systemic issues. Moreover, there are no simple lines to be drawn between the different barriers, with theology intimately connected to its contexts.

I have had some people say to me that women seek ordination in order to gain power. Other women have told me they have also had this said to them. But my own experience, and that of others, has shown that even when ordination is allowed, women do not have an easy time. It is difficult for me to accept that women enter ministry leadership for power and status. Instead, in evangelical contexts in Australia, a woman entering ministry often takes up a heavy cross. Yet though all disciples are called to carry their crosses (Matt 16:24), we aren't called to add to each other's load. Rather, we are to carry each other's burdens (Gal 6:2).

## The Problems of the Pioneer

When I first heard that call from God, women were not yet allowed to be ordained within my denomination. I knew therefore that answering this call would be difficult, though I didn't understand then the extent of the difficulty. When I applied to theological college, the supportive faculty member interviewing me felt it necessary to warn me that I would find it difficult to find employment as a pastor, so that I knew what I was up for before I invested my time and money. I left a promising career in publishing for uncertain prospects, but what else could I do? I was determined to obey God's call on my life to serve Christ whatever the cost.

When I went for ordination, I was the first female student to do so in the Baptist Association of NSW and ACT. The first women to apply had

3. Grey, "Torn Stockings and Enculturation."

been from the backlog of women who had already trained but had previously been barred from ordination before this was changed in 1997. I was also the first woman who was married to a man who was not a pastor himself. As the student with the highest grades in my year, I was encouraged to go first. The idea was that I'd have the best chance, paving the way for other women. I was asked many questions as part of the process. Two of them stayed with me.

The first was directed at my husband, asking whether he planned to do morning teas. This revealed the way that women in ministry upend understandings of gender roles, with a discomfort about a man potentially taking on the service roles given to ministry wives (see David Ray's chapter for an experience of a ministry husband). As it turns out, my husband has been on many a morning or afternoon tea roster, and this has been a blessing to the church. One wonders how the questioner thought about Jesus washing the feet of the disciples.

The second question was directed at me. I had done well academically, and both faculty and denominational staff thought this would be in my favour. But now it was viewed with suspicion: this man asked how I planned to deal with failure, inferring I was unprepared for the rigours of ministry. Indeed, another man I trained with suggested that I would find it difficult to find a job because I was too intelligent. He suggested that no male senior pastor would want to have a smarter female associate.

It has been my experience that academic achievement and pastoral giftedness have stood in the way at times. In one instance, I applied for a family and children's ministry role at a church but was knocked back, as they thought I should instead be applying for senior pastor roles. At that stage among Baptists in Sydney, female senior pastors were not only rare but in almost every example were appointed from within the church after the woman had gained the trust of the congregation. So I was turned down for a role I was willing to serve in, on the basis of my gifting, but then was not sought out for those roles for which many told me I was most suitable. I myself doubted my ability to be a senior pastor, for I felt I didn't fit the mould and was happy to serve in a variety of church roles. I had not been applying for senior pastor roles at churches with a stated theological position against female seniors. But even churches with no stated theological barrier to female senior pastors can be reluctant to employ women in the role. In Baptist churches in which the congregation votes to appoint pastors, there is often a concern that a minority might be upset, and so the appointment is viewed as divisive. Some years later, I was called as a senior pastor to a Baptist church in Sydney, but only after I had both attained a PhD and a public profile through my writing and podcast.[4]

In the National Church Life Survey (NCLS) Australian Leader Survey of 2021/22, the denominations in which greater proportions of women are in senior leadership roles were mainly those in which there is a model of married couples in senior leadership together. Out of the six denominations in which women represented more than a third of senior leaders, four were Pentecostal and one was the Salvation Army, all of which have a history of ministry couples. The remaining denomination was the Uniting Church, of which only some churches identify as evangelical. Meanwhile, the other major Protestant denominations have women in less than a quarter of their senior leadership roles with Anglicans at 24.5 percent, Baptists at 9.8 percent, and Presbyterians at 5.2 percent.[5]

Given that only some churches in these denominations have official theological positions against women in senior leadership, it seems probable that it's not only theological barriers that are keeping women out of these roles. Theology doesn't exist in a vacuum. Rather, it arises and is practised within existing contexts in all their complexity.

One complexity is to do with evangelical theology and practices about sexual desire and perceived risk. I have heard from many people that churches are often wary of hiring a woman as the second member of a pastoral team as this would lead to a team of one man and one woman who aren't married to each other. People are worried about how this looks, or about temptation for the man. And so, women are more likely to be the third hire, meaning that women are being overlooked for jobs at smaller churches. Behind this dynamic we can see the spectre of the Billy Graham Rule, with women cast as inevitable temptresses and men as unable to control their desires.[6] This is in itself a problem, given self-control is a fruit of the Spirit for all believers (Gal 5:23), but even more so for those in authority in the church, who are expected to be characterised by self-control (1 Tim 3:2). Instead of resigning ourselves

4. I cohost a podcast, *With All Due Respect*, with Anglican minister and academic Michael Jensen.

5. NCLS Research, "Women in Senior Leadership." Given women are excluded from ordained ministry in Presbyterian churches in Australia, their figure suggests an understanding of senior leadership beyond that of senior pastor.

6. The Billy Graham Rule was a rule followed by Graham in which he avoided any time alone with a woman who was not his relative.

to poor behaviour, we should instead be living out a different way within the church, breaking down the barriers between people, including that of gender (Gal 3:28).

## The Mistreatment of Women Ministers

In 2019, an American denomination that had been ordaining women for over a century released a video in which male pastors read the comments made to female pastors.[7] Some comments included sexual harassment and objectification. Others were belittling or hostile. When I saw it, I was struck by how similar it was to my personal experience.

I asked in several Australian Facebook groups for women in ministry the worst things said to them in the course of their ministry. These groups are predominantly evangelical and from several denominations. There was an immediate outpouring of grief and lament. Several strands were evident. One strand was to assume the woman's marriage and children would suffer due to her ministry. Another was to doubt her motivations or commitment to Scripture. Yet another was a whole range of sexually harassing remarks and behaviour. I have experienced sexual harassment myself, both in non-Christian and Christian contexts—it sadly hasn't, in my experience, made much difference in this regard.

In my experience, some of this mistreatment is the result of people feeling licenced by their theological disagreement to be aggressive toward women. But at other times it is meted out by those who claim to support women in ministry. A few years back, I was present at a forum of women in ministry called by my own denomination. Dismayed after hearing several stories, the director of ministries asked whether there was any woman there who had *never* experienced unfair working conditions on account of her gender. Not one raised her hand. These women were continuing in ministry despite being unpaid or underpaid, lacking job security or proper acknowledgment for their work. Churches were taking advantage of their desire to serve God. As I write this, many of their faces come to my mind, women whose perseverance I thank God for. Despite these difficulties, they have been faithful ministers for God, and often have advocated for and supported other women in invaluable ways.

My most disheartening experience was when I was working at a church in Sydney near the University of New South Wales, which has an

7. NC Conference, "Women in Ministry."

influential conservative evangelical student group. Each year as students from my church started university, I would brace myself for the moment at which they would be taken aside and told they were sinning for attending a church where I, a woman, was a pastor. Not one of the people who counselled these students in this way ever reached out to meet with me. I have often felt when interacting with those who disagree with my ordination that I am not considered a sister in Christ, or even fully human.

On the flip side, I regularly have men and women from across the denominational and theological spectrum reach out to encourage and support me. One such experience remains with me. I was in the middle of training for ministry and was starting to experience the difficulties of being a woman in ministry. I had begun to feel God was asking too much of me: not only was I a woman, but I was short and baby-faced. At the time I was also young, a shortcoming overcome now! I left chapel halfway through, crying, and was followed out by a male student. He asked me what the matter was, and I confided in him I was about to drop out and why. Despite holding different views from me on women's ministry, he quoted 1 Cor 1:27 to me, that God chose the foolish things of this world to shame the wise, and said this is precisely, Megan, why you should keep going. This was God-sent: these words cut through my fears and reminded me of the God who sees us differently and operates outside of the world's expectations.

## Benefits of Female Preachers and Pastors

I am hesitant to use a benefits model to justify women's service as pastors. If we believe that Scripture not only allows but encourages it, then a costs-benefits analysis shouldn't be needed to release women to be pastors. God has gifted women and we should not stand in their way. Nevertheless, it is not surprising to me, as someone who believes women pastoring aligns with God's design, that we see God's purposes met through women pastors.

Let me start with the most controversial area of women's pastoral service: preaching. I was myself a reluctant preacher. I remember the first time I had to speak in preaching class, to give a one sentence illustration from the front. I was so nervous that the lecturer remarked upon my nerves, for my whole body was visibly trembling. Why would God ask me and others to brave nerves and opposition in order to preach to mixed groups? I think because God wants us to hear from women on his word.

People often tell me how they are blessed by hearing a different perspective in sermons given by women. Madeline Mandall, an Australian Baptist, did some recent research with Australian Baptist female preachers on their experiences and points out three benefits of having female preachers. The first is that women can highlight women's experiences and perspectives in the Bible and in our society in ways men can't.[8] It often takes female preachers speaking to mixed audiences for the wisdom of women to find its way to the wider church. I think for instance of a 2020 sermon by Erica Mandi Manga in which she related her own experiences with menstruation to bring out the significance of the experiences of the bleeding woman in Luke 8.[9] This is an overt example of female related experience, but of course the wisdom women have to offer is more pervasive, and draws from a multitude of different experiences.

The second strength is resilience. Women are resilient, sadly because they've usually faced opposition to their call.[10] The impact of the opposition women face in ministry is part of what they bring to ministry. Women go through a refining process within ministry. Far from seeking power, they are met at every turn with disappointment, sacrifice, and mistreatment. Most female senior pastors I know express surprise to be in the role. It was not part of their career plan. I said myself, during my ordination interviews, that I did not intend on becoming a senior pastor—famous last words, as it turned out. Through hardship and opposition, women demonstrate and pursue a cross-shaped ministry.

This strength is paradoxical. Perhaps it may be that as women are given greater opportunities in ministry, they become more tempted to power and privilege. Yet this also reminds us that people bring the entirety of who they are into ministry. Women bring to ministry their experiences of vulnerability, opposition, and hardship. They also therefore bring hard-won resilience, empathy, and true humility. Pastoral ministry is enriched by the diversity of people who enter it.

A difficulty with the resilience required is that we miss out on the gifts and service of women who have, for various reasons, been unable to overcome the barriers and opposition. For myself, I know that a major reason for my resilience has been continual support from family and colleagues. For a woman without significant support from her family,

8. Mandall, "I Am Preac(her)," 40.

9. Manga, "Why Did Jesus Feed?"

10. Mandall, "I Am Preac(her)," 41.

church, and pastoral colleagues, the story is often very different. And it is the church that misses out.

The third strength mentioned by Mandall captures the women's experience that as preachers, they contribute both their spiritual gifting as members of Christ's body, but also their own unique experiences and insights as women, alongside all the God-given diversity found in the church. We need to recognise the value of each member of Christ's body in all their God-given uniqueness, and strive for this to have impact within every ministry of the church. To silo women off to some ministries diminishes their impact for God's kingdom.

As one of the few Australian evangelical women with a public voice, I'm constantly hearing from women about the failures of their churches to give them a healthy context in which to grow in their faith. I also hear from men who are frustrated that they cannot experience all the gifts women have to bring. My attempts to share their concerns in the public arena, as one of the few women able to do so, are sometimes met with welcome. But they are also at times met with rejection, as if I have overstepped the unwritten boundaries in which my presence as a female pastor will be tolerated. I need to remember that like most humans I have a negativity bias, holding on more to discouragement instead of encouragement. I thank God for the many people who have encouraged me, and I am reminded yet again of the importance of encouraging women to counteract the discouragement.

## The System Discourages Women

When I left theological college, accepted as an ordination candidate with first class honours degree in hand, I was full of hope about the future of my ministry. The recipient of awards and praise, I expected difficulties but believed I was living in a moment of change.

The first major difficulty was finding paid pastoral employment. While most men from my cohort had such employment already lined up, and were even fast tracked into senior pastoral roles, I continued working as a casual receptionist for some months. In my first role I oversaw a congregation within a larger church, but I was only paid for ten hours a week, even though I worked many more. So I took up casual work at a theological college as well. If I had been a single woman, I might well have left ministry at this point, due to insecure finances in an expensive city.

That's when I started a PhD. I had been prayerfully considering this because others had pointed out this seemed a good stewardship of my gifts. However, I was also at an age at which it was a good time to start a family. I took leave due to the birth of my first child, and then again for my second (neither being supported by any sort of parental leave), so I withdrew from postgraduate study. Not a single person asked me how they could support me to continue my study, as something to which God had called me. Instead, I was praised for "putting my family first." Meanwhile, when my church rang up our denomination to find out what the policy was for my parental leave, they were told there wasn't one.

Some difficulties as a woman in ministry are due to overt opposition, but others are due to culture and a resulting system that fails to remove barriers for women. Take one example: in my denomination, the current guidelines for parental leave simply state it should be "in line with national legislation."[11] There is so much more that can be done in this area beyond legislation to better support women in ministry, and I am glad to state these are now under review.

For me two decades ago, it felt pointless to continue to pursue postgraduate education, given the limited employment opportunities for women.[12] I did not expect to attain more seniority than an associate role, and I even doubted whether I would ever have a full-time ministry role. I also thought it would be unlikely I was given a permanent faculty role. I resigned myself to less financial security for my family. I remained faithful to my calling in my contexts, hardly allowing myself to imagine that God might call me into other roles or arenas. So I withdrew from further study for almost a decade, until both my biological children were in school.[13] At the time, though, I was unsure that I would ever come back to it.

## The Public Evangelical Woman

So how did it come to be that I now have a PhD in theology, I copartner in a podcast and online platform for Australian evangelicals, and serve as a senior pastor? Perhaps the simplest answer is, once again, I heard

11. Baptist Churches, *Remuneration Recommendations*, 4.

12. See Martin et al., "Women in Theological Education."

13. I also have a non-biological daughter who joined my family when she was a teenager.

the call of God and answered it to the best of my ability. When my two biological children were both at school, I felt again that call to do a PhD, even though I doubted it would result in any kind of stable employment. I felt I must honour God with the ability he had given me, even if I couldn't see where it would lead. So with my children at school, I started a PhD. Little did I know that another child would join my family during this PhD candidature, a teenager whose mum, our friend, had died. This time parental leave was available, showing the changes that have occurred.

Also, around 2017 the #metoo movement, calling out sexual harassment, led to a growing acknowledgment of the abuse women also experienced in churches. As I thought about my own experiences and those of other women, I saw the desperate need for a public evangelical female voice in Australia. In prayer, I said that if this was what God desired me to do, to smooth my path and make this possible. I hardly knew how this could occur. But I started saying yes to anything that could enable this. A chance throwaway line led to Anglican male minister and academic Michael Jensen proposing we do a podcast together, and his connections gave it credibility and profile. This would develop even further into an ongoing project together that also has an online platform. What was extraordinary about this even starting was that Michael and I held different views on gender. And yet, together we have been able to work as a team in the service of Christ.

God's call on my life required creativity and courage. At first I had thought my acceptance of limitations on my ministry spoke of humility and being content with where God had placed me. I had lost hope. Looking back now, I see that I had accepted something I believed to be unjust, and in doing so I contributed to continuing injustice toward other women. I had misunderstood humility. Remember how reluctant a preacher I was? I overcame my nerves through praying every time I came to preach that God would be with me, and that God would be glorified. The more I focused on God, and the less on how I came across to others, the more I was able in God's strength to do.

I ask forgiveness for when I have failed to speak up for other women. It is too easy to divide up following Jesus by gender, to ask women to become servants like Jesus, and ask men to take courageous action like Jesus. Yet Jesus's call on our lives demands *both* from all disciples, regardless of gender. We need both humility and courage to prevent service from becoming oppression and bold action from becoming oppressive. For myself, I thought through what opportunities I did have, and how I could use these in God's service. I started saying yes where I would have said no before. I became aware of the incredible blessing I had in a family who had supported me fully in my ministry and a context in which more was open to me than other contexts, and I was convicted to use these advantages to speak up for other women who were in more difficult places than myself.

My public ministry is the one in which I have felt most that I am required to dance backward in heels. There is the double bind of female leadership: gender expectations for women (be warm, be friendly, be accommodating) are in tension with leadership expectations (be strong, be assertive, be direct). Women can't be too strong. But they can't be too sweet either. This applies even more so in Christian settings in which such expectations are given spiritual weight. Fail at these expectations, and it's made out that you're disobeying God or are unfit for ministry. The public evangelical woman is watched carefully and judged when she fails to fit into a very narrow scope of behaviour. She is required to overcome greater difficulties with greater competence, always with a smile.

So then, why have I and other women persevered? In one word: Christ. Christian service has never been measured by how easy it is. Indeed, Jesus told us to expect troubles (John 16:33). I have watched woman after woman struggle with these difficulties but have also seen that when women have been given opportunity to serve, they make a rich contribution to the kingdom. As Carolyn Custis James asks, "Will the whole church benefit from women's gifts and contributions, or will the body of Christ attempt to fulfill a mission that dwarfs our resources without the full participation of half the church?"[14]

This is my challenge to all in the evangelical church: do we accept the obstacles put in the way of women's contributions, or do we instead seek to remove them? Do we instead encourage and empower women in their service, knowing that in doing so we enable them in the service of the gospel? For my part, I am determined to be an advocate and mentor. And if you are a woman thinking of pastoral or related ministry, let me encourage you that you are not a problem or an optional extra, but an integral part of God's plan for the mission of the church.

14. James, *Half the Church*, 41.

## Bibliography


Baptist Churches of NSW & ACT. *Remuneration Recommendations 2025*. September 2024. https://nswactbaptists.org.au/wp-content/uploads/2024/10/Remuneration-Recommendations-2025.pdf.

Grey, Jacqueline N. "Torn Stockings and Enculturation: Women Pastors in the Australian Assemblies of God." *Australasian Pentecostal Studies* 5/6 (2002). https://aps-journal.com/index.php/APS/article/view/51/48.

James, Carolyn Custis. *Half the Church: Recapturing God's Global Vision for Women*. Grand Rapids: Zondervan, 2010.

Mandall, Madeline. "I Am Preac(her), Hear Me Roar: Unique Strengths and Characteristics of Australian Baptist Women Preachers." Unpublished BMin honours thesis, Australian College of Theology, 2023.

Manga, Erica Mandi. "Why Did Jesus Feed a Dead Girl? (Luke 8:40–56)." Barneys, February 23, 2020. https://www.barneys.org.au/talks/why-did-jesus-feed-a-dead-girl/.

Martin, Kara, et al. "Women in Theological Education in the ACT in Twenty-First Century Australia." In *Theological Education in Australia: Foundations, Current Practices and Future Options*, edited by Andrew Bain and Ian Hussey, 160–74. Eugene, OR: Wipf & Stock, 2018.

NC Conference of The UMC. "Women in Ministry." Vimeo, May 13, 2019. https://vimeo.com/335862568.

NCLS Research. "Women in Senior Leadership in Their Local Church." June 2025. https://www.ncls.org.au/articles/women-in-senior-leadership-in-their-local-church/.

Powell, Ruth, et al. *Church Pulse Check 2021 to 2024: Estimates of Australian Church Attendance, Faith Commitments and Churches Across Denominations*. NCLS Occasional Paper 61. NCLS Research, 2025.

Thaves, Bob. *Frank and Ernest*. Image #69155. May 5, 1982. https://www.frankandernest.com/search/index.php?iid=69155.

# The Pastor's Husband as Helper

David C. Ray

It was not long ago when the penny dropped for me on what my role is in the church. As the husband of a pastor, I am *the pastor's helper*. To get to this point, there was no snap decision but rather a long and winding road through the lives of the Rays over the last thirty years. It is a journey, not a destination. A narrative, not a recipe.

My story centres on one key question: What does "mutual submission in reverence to Christ" (Eph 5:21) look like in practice?

Long before I met my wife, Suzie, I had rejected the idea that leaders in the church had to be male. I had seen strong women in action and experienced how they were every bit as capable as men, perhaps more so. It made no sense to me that Paul was writing to me today to tell me that women had to be silent in church or submit to a man. Paul was "wrong," so I thought, admittedly with no biblical foundation. For I was stubborn and rebellious; I had a lot to learn.

It was obvious from the first time I saw Suzie serving in Christian ministry that she was meant for the role of pastor. There were three little kids, no older than four, and she was running a Christmas party for them in a park. Their parents were not too far away but certainly not involved. I was the observer. She had games, food, stories, and presents for them all. I recall they "beautified" her hair, which was so funny—it took ages to remove the bubbles, ties, and knots! It wasn't a huge turnout, but there was Suzie's calling. They loved every minute of it. So did I!

Suzie moved to inner-city Melbourne and turned up at a small Presbyterian church nearby. The minister there had been praying for someone to take on children's ministry, particularly as his children made up a quorum for a Sunday School program. Here was Suzie's calling! I soon followed and we enjoyed serving the children and youth program there. It meant so much to the minister and his family and soon more families came. We married as Presbyterians and enjoyed our first few years of marriage in that church.

Of course, that would have been the end of Suzie's ministry. A motion to discontinue female eldership had recently passed, which greatly disappointed us. At the same time, Suzie and I were missing out on weekly teaching due to our children's ministry involvement. We visited an evening service at a nearby Anglican church and came across an ordained woman. I'd heard this had happened in the US but hadn't realised that it was allowed in Australia. Anyway, here was Suzie's calling. Whether she realised that at the time, I do not know, but I recall thinking that might be a possibility.

It was interesting that Suzie herself had held patriarchal leanings into early adulthood. Earlier in our marriage she often referred to me, the husband, as the one who lays his life down for her (see Eph 5:25), taking it to mean I was somehow the leader of our marriage. I, on the other hand, had understood this expectation as the husband's duty of modern-day chivalry rather than any sort of authority structure within a marriage. In any case, it still made no sense to me that someone could be gifted emotionally and intellectually to lead or to follow and yet their gender would place a firm restriction on the opportunities they could pursue. As a male, this had worked in my favour from time to time, but I could see it was inherently unjust.

After six and a half years of marriage, we were eventually blessed with our first child. As the first child amongst our friendship group, our daughter was surrounded by supportive people, both family and friends, who shaped her into the person she is today. And Suzie was freed up to minister the grace of God, Father, Son, and Spirit, both within and beyond our home, in fulfilment of God-given talents. And I thought something along the lines of this: "If God gave to them the same gift as to us after believing in the Lord Jesus Christ, who was I that I could stand in God's way?" (Acts 11:17). After a few years, Suzie took up theological studies while working in banking.

Meanwhile, I had been working as an accountant for the best part of two decades but always felt unsettled in this role. Taking a retrenchment package, I also explored theological studies with ordained ministry in mind. I spent a couple of years as a student minister at a parish and completed every unit on the ordination path.

After learning the hard way that not all ministers in the church shared a positive view of women in ministry, Suzie was finally accepted at her first parish placement, heavily pregnant with our second child! A year later she was ordained.

Suzie's ordination into the priesthood was a cause for great celebration, but inside I felt a great sense of loss. I tried my best to hide it, but I'm sure plenty of people knew I was dying on the inside:

——

*How lovely she is.*
*Adorned in white.*
*Pure. Beaming.*
*Saunters, centre aisle*
*of that heavenly hall*
*on her special day*

*at her ordination.*
*Jammed in the pew.*
*Alone. Forlorn.*
*Watching her leave me,*
*as if I had given*
*my own bride away.*

——

This was a day of mixed emotions for me and one I am not likely to forget. Of course, I was thrilled for Suzie, but I felt like I had been left behind.

I had expected to be transformed into an art piece, worthy of "higher service" in the church. Despite my fervent prayers, I was met with only silence. Invisible brush strokes at best. And being male didn't help. Deep in my heart, I knew that I was not a suitable candidate. I never applied for candidature.

Eventually I began to understand what had happened on ordination day. I had lost nothing. Suzie was never mine to own—she was always God's own. God would use her whatever way he wished. And God would do the same with me. Her ordination didn't diminish our marriage, it enriched it.

My theological training was not wasted. It did become a platform for me to explore my interest in literature, language, and culture, first through biblical studies and later through the liberal arts. There I eventually learned the biblical foundations for my conviction that men and women alike are called to Christian ministry leadership.

As Suzie had only worked as a school chaplain for a few years after ordination, I never really had the experience of being a pastor's husband until she was called to the parish at which she had done her placement. It was fifty kilometres from home and there was no housing available near the parish, so we just made do with the travel. But the role of pastor's husband was just a Sunday "job."

A couple of years later, Suzie was called to a parish in Northern Territory. This was no great surprise to me. We had visited early in our theological training and thought it was a place we could enjoy. After I recommended Darwin as a holiday destination once again, Suzie asked, "Should we see if we might be able visit the bishop?" While she was expecting an emphatic No!, I calmly replied, "Yeah, sure." About six months later, Suzie was commissioned as rector of a parish in the low socioeconomic area of its northern suburbs.

What I had not yet appreciated was that I had also been sent up north as the pastor's husband. Assuming there would be no opportunity for me to teach or research from Darwin, I took it as a sign that I should put on a brave accountant's face once again and return to the workforce. Besides, I didn't have time to be the pastor's husband, nor did I see any value in that role. I had more important stuff to do. Or did I?

In hindsight, returning to work as an accountant was a big mistake. Although I did make some positive contributions, I couldn't contain the great frustration of being a researcher trapped in an accountant's body. To alleviate that frustration, I took an opportunity to tutor online at my old theological college for a couple of years alongside full-time work and editing my thesis for publication, as well as taking on the Sunday role of pastor's husband. But this gave me less and less time to do research and I became more and more resentful and harder to live with and work with. I felt just as stubborn and rebellious as I was in my early twenties. After a few years, that pathway came to a dead end. Once again, I was an empty canvas asking God to paint me. And once again, I cried out in earnest.

It was Ambrose of Milan, a fourth-century bishop of all people, who responded to me through my reading of *On the Duties of the Clergy*. Ambrose argues that we should avoid anger becoming sin by maintaining a tranquil disposition:

> Indignation is a terrible incentive to sin. It disorders the mind to such an extent as to leave no room for reason. The first thing, therefore, to aim at, if possible, is to make tranquillity of character our natural disposition by constant practice.[1]

And I thought to myself, "Even though I am not clergy, that's good advice. But how can I practise tranquillity of character?" The answer was in the ensuing chapter 44:

> Everyone ought to apply himself to the duties suited to his character.[2]

Part of the argument related to the tendency of men to simply follow their fathers, doing whatever their father did, rather than take up a ministry calling. That was not directly applicable to me. But there was something else that I had to recognise. I could no longer work in my profession as an accountant as such duties no longer suited my character. Perhaps it had always been thus. I had been stubborn and rebellious but perhaps one of the reasons for that was that I was vocationally displaced. My attempts to substitute that vocation were in vain. Now I had to find duties that aligned with my character.

In the beginning, according to Genesis, the woman is fashioned by God to be "helper" for the man (Gen 2:18, 20–23). One can see how this story has been interpreted as setting up a pecking order in family and society generally. But this misses the point of using the term *helper*. Everywhere else the term is personified, it refers to God as helper of his people. God helps Moses, who names one of his own sons Eliezar, literally "My El (God) is helper" (see Exod 18:4). In the Song of Moses, God is referred to as helper three times for the sake of his people (Deut 33:7, 26, 29). God is called upon many times in the Psalms to be helper (Pss 20:3; 33:20; 70:6; 89:20; 115:9–11; 121:1–2; 124:8; 146:5).

We might extend this brief study to the New Testament. The Greek term for advocate or helper might be best represented by the phrase "the one called beside." This is similar to woman fashioned "from the side" (not the "rib") of the man in Gen 2:21. The one "called beside" is actually used to describe, first, the Spirit, sent from the Father and through the Son, as our "helper" (John 14:16, 26), and second, Jesus Christ the

1. Ambrose, *Duties*, 1.21.90.
2. Ambrose, *Duties*, 1.44.

Righteous One as our "advocate" (1 John 2:1). A helper is then surely a companion for Christian ministry and, most importantly, someone who is called.

So I am now helper to Suzie as pastor and perform tasks that are suited with my character and enable me to practise tranquillity. And Suzie as pastor enables me to pursue my interests in research and fitness because our lifestyle now allows for that. I believe I am settling into the role of the pastor's helper. It is another form of "habitus" or office.

Suzie needs all sorts of help. Sometimes with the jobs no one else wants to do—fixing toilet seats, cleaning the bins, picking up stock and doing the checkout at the food pantry program, opening up for the tradies, fixing the PA. Sometimes with activities in which I have something to offer—mowing the field and doing the edges (hard work up in the tropics), running a Bible study, listening to someone who is suffering or in need, preaching a sermon. Whatever it is, it is ministry to which I have been called. For whatever reason, I have landed in this position for which I praise God.

What does it look like to be the helper as the pastor's husband? It is simply to be "the one called beside" my wife. Put simply, I am called to her side so that she is never alone in her ministry. Her ministry is to serve others. *My ministry is to serve her.*

Now I can well imagine readers feeling quite repulsed at that statement: *my ministry is to serve her*. From pastors' wives, who were in no way called to be at the side of their husband but rather did it out of marital obligation, even against their will, there must have been a great sense of loss in giving up their dreams and hopes in favour of their husband. From others, the idea that one spouse is called to support another is submission par excellence. These are fair and reasonable reactions. God knows I felt it too.

But every married couple with an ordained spouse must negotiate their own way through ministry together. We have been placed together in marriage so that God the Father might be glorified through Christ in us. We owe it to God to work out together what that might mean in practical terms. *This is precisely why marriage should be equally yoked.*

May I encourage you to meditate on what "mutual submission in reverence to Christ" means in marriage? Or in any relationship for that matter. I see this as partners in life, brought together by God, with eyes fixed on Jesus.

Suzie spent years working as a chaplain and then an assistant priest while I studied and researched—there may have been a breadwinner, but no head, if by that we mean "boss." We raised our children together—there was no head of that either. And now, as I come to realise that it is better for me to glorify God through my research and volunteer work, we have decided that we are going to work this way to allow Suzie to use her gifts of leadership and teaching. Service in marriage requires only mutual submission to Christ, the one who came not to be served but to serve and to make his life a ransom for many (Mark 10:45).

But not all pastors are married, nor does one need to be married to be in ministry; single people can and should pursue ordained ministry. Given this, we as a church could think of ways relationships other than that of spouse might also be the helper. The helper might be applied to other types of relationships in ministry, like sisters or friends too. Other marriages will look different to mine and might turn to different people as their helpers. The helper cannot be codified into canon law. On the contrary, relationships that are equally yoked are the firmament over which the Spirit can move with great power in the church of Christ. *The success of a minister-helper relationship depends on how those partners can mutually submit to Christ with the aim of glorifying God.*

Very brave women and men forged a path for the ordination of women today (and for clerical shirts which fit their waist and bust!). Now it is going to take very courageous ministry men to accept a "lowly" position, just as many ministry women have, and recognise that taking on the role of helper is to be filled with the Spirit, encouraging one another and praising God in reverence to Christ and mutual submission to one another (Eph 5:18–21). I hope more men reflect theologically on the role of helper and take on that role willingly. I maintain my earlier view that women are every bit as capable as men in leading the church of Christ and, given the challenges the church faces today, perhaps more so.

I wish also to make special mention of men who are dating (or showing interest in) unmarried women who are aspirants, candidates, or ministers and pastors. I was particularly taken by seeing Suzie so passionate in teaching her Sunday School children about the love of Jesus. May I suggest that seeing a woman dedicate themselves to teaching others about Christ as saviour and example is most attractive!

It is perhaps ironic that I now realise husbands serving as helper to female clergy is a ministry that mirrors Suzie's earlier conviction—that, in loving one's wife, the husband lays down his life for his wife as Christ laid his life down for the church (Eph 5:25). That being so, *the role of helper* is perhaps the highest calling on this earth, of course not in the world's eyes, but in the eye of the Almighty God, *our Helper*.

## Bibliography

Ambrose of Milan. *On the Duties of the Clergy, Book 1*. Translated by H. de Romestin et al. In *The Nicene and Post-Nicene Fathers*, 2nd ser., edited by Philip Schaff and Henry Wace, 10:1–43. Buffalo, NY: Christian Literature, 1893.

# Hope on a Tightrope

## *When the Church You Love Doesn't Let Women Preach*

Leisa Aitken

Many Christians I speak to are conflicted about their church. They love the community, but at the same time are saddened or frustrated by the absence of women preaching during regular Sunday services. You may be one of those, or it may be good friends of yours who feel this. This chapter is about how to hold the difficult tightrope balance of love for those who think differently to ourselves. You may be reading this book to explore your own thoughts on this issue, or be convinced one way or the other. I invite you to walk that way of love. As it is my own conviction that the Bible supports both men and women preaching to mixed congregations, this chapter is also about how to hold an active hope that things can change.

About five years ago I found myself in a situation I hadn't expected. After twenty-five years in churches where women were encouraged to preach (and I was regularly on the preaching roster), we moved to a church where women's solo preaching was not permitted. It was hard to find a church at that time—with teaching that resonated, a sense of belonging in the community, and opportunities to serve that expressed our gifts and passions. In a previous era of my life, I would have added a suitable children's church or youth group. There's no perfect church, right? For me, that women couldn't preach was something I would just have to cope with, at least for the time being.

This church includes people who have strongly held views on each side of this debate—both for and against women preaching on Sunday. What I hold even more strongly than my view that women can preach is that loving those who think differently to us is crucial. I don't use the word *crucial* lightly—it comes from *crux*, meaning "cross." I do think that it is part of "carrying our cross" to be not just tolerant of, but downright loving toward those with whom we differ. This is harder than it sounds, and yet so important. As Jesus said, "Everyone will know that you are my disciples, if you love one another" (John 13:35). And as the apostle Paul enthused, "If I have the gift of prophecy and can fathom all mysteries and all knowledge, and if I have a faith that can move mountains, but do not have love, I am nothing" (1 Cor 13:2).

And this led to me asking an important question. I'm a clinical psychologist, so I wondered:

## What Are the Psychological Reasons We Struggle to Be in Community with Those Who Hold Different Views?

The reasons we struggle with this are all "common sense" and yet it can be hard to face up to them in ourselves.

We all have an innate human desire to belong and tend to categorise people into in-groups (like us) and out-groups (not like us). In churches, our views on disputed issues, such as women preaching, can become markers for what in-group we fit into. Psychological research shows that even if we pride ourselves on our intention to love everyone, it is simply easier to like people who agree with us, but a struggle when their beliefs differ. This is not just at a conscious level—it is quite subliminal too. For example, psychologists asked one group of participants to listen to a live recording of a stand-up comedian. They were told that the live audience they could hear laughing were university students like themselves (an in-group). Sure enough, the presence of this canned laughter had the impact of increasing the participants' laughter. However, another group listening to the same comedy routine were told that the canned laughter was from people with very different political beliefs to their own (an out-group). This group barely laughed and rated the comedian as less funny than those who heard the in-group laughing—all happening below conscious awareness.[1]

These identity markers are powerful. It's easy to slip into seeing those who differ as the *other* or the *opposition*. Our minds lean toward fast, yet

1. Platow et al., "It's Not Funny."

biased stereotypes far more than we would like to admit.[2] It is harder work to do slow, complex, nuanced thinking about issues or people, but this is the bedrock of wisdom and flourishing relationships. This instinct for quick judgments can easily turn complex issues into boundary markers. For example, too easily the conviction that women can preach to men is taken as proof that one lacks a high view of Scripture, folded into a broader package deal of assumptions. I know from my own experience that these accusations can be very frustrating! This reality means it is important for those who believe the Bible encourages women's preaching ministry to mixed groups to be able to clearly articulate the reasons we hold this position. It is not enough to simply borrow the thinking of those we are close to or admire—this applies no matter what our position! We must get out our Bibles and do the hard work of reading and thinking through the issue of women's roles in church ourselves.

These debates are not just intellectual differences—they stir deep emotions and shape real lives. Many women feel frustrated, ranging from irritation to deep anger, at the patriarchal systems they see in the church. They may have missed opportunities in ministry. They see women whom they know to be wise and gifted teachers sitting quietly in the congregation while a male preacher gives an uninspiring sermon. More subtly, women may recognise a diminished sense of self, such as an instinct to self-silence in the presence of male church leaders (I was shocked recently to notice how often I do this myself), and under-functioning in expressing their gifts.

Such costs create a heavy emotional weight to the challenge of loving those who think differently. These wounds call for a process of forgiveness, beginning, as always, in our own hearts. I had to actively work on forgiveness toward a senior minister who, many years ago, indicated that my husband's job at the church was at stake if I began the university course I had enrolled in. Instead, he insisted I run the church playgroup, despite me telling him that my gifts were in teaching adults and I was hopeless with small children! I did find a way to do the degree later. The wounds can come from other women too. At a ministry wives conference it was a group of women who, once they found out I preached in my church, made it clear that they considered me doctrinally unsound. I felt like an outsider for the whole weekend. I had to do the hard work of not allowing hurt and anger to win. I still see those women from time to time,

2. Kahneman, *Thinking, Fast and Slow*.

and I am trying to be genuinely warm and friendly, as I know they are working to serve Jesus in their own frameworks.

Which brings me to an important point. As followers of Jesus, our truest belonging is not as part of any in-group, whatever its framework, but in Jesus himself. He challenges us to not merely tolerate but actively love those with whom we differ. Paul urged the early churches to resist factions and division (1 Cor 1:10–12 and Gal 5:19–21). Whatever our beliefs on women preaching, we are still family in Christ, reading the Bible through different lenses but equally beloved. The reality is we all read Scripture through the lenses we've inherited, shaped by years of sermons, the church tradition we are in and the theologians it prefers, and our own life experience. None of us comes without bias (even though some seem not to realise this). We do well to practise *epistemic humility*—that is, acknowledging that we cannot know anything perfectly or completely. I try to remember the limits of my own perspective, as well as viewing others as also doing the best they can to honour God through the lenses they wear. Romans 14:4 steadies me: "Who are you to judge someone else's servant? To their own master they stand or fall. And they will stand, for the Lord is able to make them stand." It reminds me that each of us is finally only accountable to God, softening my temptation to judge.

True emotional and relational maturity is shown in our capacity to define our own beliefs clearly, without attacking, withdrawing, or demanding someone else changes. We can express our own carefully thought-through position with gentleness and respect. As we speak with those who hold different views, we can be curious as to how it is they have come to hold their position. Genuine curiosity can help us to resist any nasty labels about them we might whisper inside our minds. We also may need to resist any derogatory comments about them we voice to those who already agree with us. Such conversations create a triangle, which casts the third person as the enemy or outsider, and breeds factions and fractures in a community. Of course, we will discuss the issues with those with whom we agree, but let's be deeply respectful to those with whom we disagree, even when they are not present. Easier said than done! Let us love those who think differently while still holding hope for change.

## How Does Psychological Research on Hope Engage Us in Creating Possibilities for Women's Voices in the Future?

If you find yourself struggling to have hope for hearing women's voices preaching in church, there are four questions on which you might like to reflect.

### 1. What Are the Meaningful Possibilities I Can Look Forward To?

Hope involves the belief that the future has meaningful possibilities. To better understand this, we must delve into each word: why might allowing women to preach be *meaningful* and what *possibilities* do you see?

#### *A. Why Might Women Being Able to Teach in Church Be Meaningful and Important?*

Maybe some of the reasons include:

- Scripture teaches that women and men are called to lead and serve based on call and gifting.
- Opening more ministries to women will enable more people to be reached with the message of Jesus.
- Women's voices are valuable—we offer different perspectives as we have had different life experiences.
- Women are more likely to draw out the role of the many women written about in Scripture.
- Preaching by women helps dismantle patriarchal structures, not just institutionally but also psychologically.

There may be others that are important to you. All of these can be expressed by women preaching from the pulpit; however, if we find ourselves in a church where women cannot preach to mixed congregations, they can also be lived out in many other possible ways.

#### *B. What Possibilities Are There?*

Reframing possibilities is an important part of holding onto hope. If formal preaching is not possible, other avenues for those with a gift of teaching often remain open: teaching in small groups, leading Bible studies, speaking at women's retreats, writing devotionals, publishing sermons online, or mentoring the next generation of women leaders. These expressions may not be preaching at church on Sundays, but they can still reflect much of what is meaningful as listed above. We can support women who do find ways to teach publicly: listen to women's sermons online and buy and read books by female theologians and authors. Promote them! There are so many rich resources from women. For myself, I am thankful to have had wonderful opportunities of being asked to preach in other churches, give talks at schools, and write for Christian journals, even when I was unable to preach in my own church.

These ideas may be somewhat frustrating for some, as they are often female voices being heard from the edges rather than the centre. However, even in more extreme patriarchal times, God used these seemingly peripheral platforms powerfully. Think of Hagar the slave woman, cast out to the desert by the great patriarch Abraham, and yet she is the first to name God as *El Roi*, "the God who sees me" (Gen 16:13); Esther rises as a national saviour, "for such as time as this" (Esth 4:14); Mary, a young Jewish girl chosen to bear God's son; or the women who were the first witnesses of the resurrection and evangelists—the list goes on. We shouldn't underestimate the opportunities God gives us to have a voice or teach his ways in many aspects of life, even if they are not centre stage.

In some churches with strong doctrinal views about women, these alternate possibilities may be all that will realistically happen, at least for the near future. Depending on our own stance, we each have to decide: do we move to a church where women's preaching is encouraged, or do we accept that these other possibilities are enough?

## 2. Coping Agency: How Do I Stay Poised to Act and Cope in the Meantime?

Of course, if we do think it is important, we can be actively pursuing women preaching in church when the time is right. If we truly hope for anything in life, then we will want to act to make it happen and be poised to take up opportunities as they arise. In psychological jargon this is *latent agency*, a determination to act to make a difference that also involves waiting well and coping with disappointment and frustration without bitterness or giving up.

### *A. Am I Clear About What I Need to Do to Fulfill My Hope, Even If It Is Playing the Long Game?*

If you have a teaching gift yourself, there is always a possibility that in the future you may preach, so you can cultivate your sense of agency by deepening your theological education. There are some excellent online courses and podcasts. Or, like me, you may love devouring theology books; I listen to audiobooks by theologians on every car trip. It may be refining your communication gifts; I joined a local group for professional speakers. Seeking supportive networks beyond your own church might be helpful. There are great interdenominational online preaching collectives that can empower you to act without waiting for institutional permission. You may not want to preach yourself, but to see other gifted women do this. Having agency also means discerning when the time is right to speak your convictions within your own system, being willing to have prayerful, informed, persuasive conversations with those in leadership.

### *B. How Do We Best Manage Our Frustrations in the Waiting?*

Hope, by definition, involves waiting and that is very difficult for most of us. In our age of instant responses, we are not used to patient perseverance. One of my favourite verses for thinking about this is Rom 8:22–25:

> We know that the whole creation has been groaning as in the pains of childbirth right up to the present time. Not only so, but we ourselves, who have the firstfruits of the Spirit, groan inwardly as we wait eagerly for our adoption to sonship, the redemption of our bodies. For in this hope we were saved. But hope that is seen is no hope at all. Who hopes for what they already have? But if we hope for what we do not yet have, we wait for it patiently.

Paul uses the imagery of birth pains, a decidedly female metaphor, to encapsulate both the frustration of our present, as well as the patient waiting needed to have hope. Childbirth is a visceral image of the coexistence of both painful suffering and anticipation of joy! In this passage, Paul is using *hope* in a technical sense—we could call it *capital-H* Hope; the specific and certain Christian Hope, based on God's promise of the new creation, a future age of love, joy, peace, justice, beauty, and communion with God. Our small-*h* hopes in life now are somewhat different as they are uncertain. And yet ultimately, all of our everyday hopes in this life are resonances or brief instances of that heavenly Hope. And these smaller hopes—including hope for women preaching—also require their own patient waiting.

Persevering as we wait in hope is like balancing on a psychologically difficult tightrope. We could tip too far down one side and go in all guns blazing to convince everyone that women should preach to mixed congregations. But our expectations for rapid change might be unrealistic and we can alienate people with our intensity and get frustrated ourselves. Alternatively, if we decide to wait it out too quietly, then nothing will change and we can simply become apathetic. We need to stay poised to act where we can, aware of the pulls in each direction, but be smart about the timing of speaking up. So much of wisdom is about timing!

How do we wait without growing bitter? As real tightrope walkers will attest, the key is to keep looking straight ahead. Fix your eyes on what Jesus has called *you* to do—to love him and use your gifts to serve the people in your community in the ways you can. It may be very slow progress as you explore the possibilities mentioned above that work for you, but you can head in the right direction, one spirit-led step at a time. If we look around too much and focus on what we think others "should" do, we can lose our foothold. If I am going to speak up about the role of women, I don't want it to come from a place of judgment or coercion of others, but from my own conviction of its rightness, goodness, and capacity to bless the church. I remind myself of Paul's words: "Be completely humble and gentle; be patient, bearing with one another in love. Make every effort to keep the unity of the Spirit through the bond of peace" (Eph 4:2–4).

### 3. Trusted Relationships: Loaning and Borrowing Hope

Hope flourishes in community. We are so often dependent on others to encourage us and to provide opportunities to bring about what we hope for. You could say that we often need to "borrow hope" from those around us. If you would like to preach, then stay connected with those who affirm your gifts. Whether it's a spiritual mentor, a group of like-minded peers, or a pastor who offers informal preaching opportunities, these trusted relationships provide encouragement, feedback, and emotional holding. They remind us that we are not alone—and that God often works through small, faithful partnerships before larger change emerges. Keep encouraging women whom you know are gifted teachers. Loan them some hope.

## 4. For Those Who Would Love to See Women Preaching at Their Church on Sunday, What Hope-Filled Glimpses of the Future Do We See in the Bible and in the Church for Women?

Finally, the *feeling* of hope comes alive when we catch sight of glimpses of what we hope for: men and women as true partners expressing their gifts for the building up of God's church. When we see just small tastes of this happening, the emotional aspect of hope begins to rise up and we feel the flicker of excitement for what might one day be.

Sometimes these glimpses can be found in looking backward through time. This could be from reading about women with impactful voices who witness to Jesus in the Bible. For example, female apostles (Junia), prophets (Philip's daughters), evangelists/gospel workers (Euodia, Syntyche, Phoebe), teacher-pastors (Priscilla), and disciples (the female witnesses to the resurrection). Or even further back in time—being inspired by the lives of many women speaking with godly courage in the Old Testament.

As I have searched the past for glimpses of this hope, I have also found myself at the feet of some of the great women of the early church. Macrina the Younger is one of my heroes. She lived in the fourth century in Cappadocia (now Turkey) and was the older sister of several foundational theologians of the church, including Gregory of Nyssa and Basil the Great, both shapers of the Nicene Creed. Although she lived in a deeply patriarchal society and was never behind a church pulpit per se, her wisdom commanded respect and she had a profound theological influence on her siblings. She established a monastic community of women, including a hospice for travellers and the sick, and her brothers and those in her community had profound respect for her insightful Bible teaching. Gregory of Nyssa's important theological book *On the Soul and Resurrection* is written as a dialogue between Macrina and Gregory where Macrina is recognised as his teacher. It's pretty extraordinary for the fourth century! In this everyday exchange, brother and sister draw each other deeper into the mystery of God. It embodies Gregory's conviction that men and women *together* constitute the image of God. Gregory states that God "devised for his image the distinction of male and female, which has no reference to the divine archetype."[3] So Gregory argues that there is neither male nor female in God, rather the full perfection of God's image is found in the combination of both, since the human race is represented in both.

Sometimes glimpses happen in the present. What women do you know who embody the gift of teaching in ways that inspire you in your unique setting? For me, one such woman is Rev. Dr. Joanna Collicutt McGrath. She is, like me, a clinical psychologist—in fact, she was my PhD supervisor, necessitating for me many wonderful trips to Oxford. She is also an Anglican minister and university lecturer who brings academic psychology and theology together in her preaching and writing in a way that is intellectually rich, deeply wise, and—here's the bit where she really inspires me—understandable. A favourite of mine is her book *Jesus and the Gospel Women*; well worth any woman reading to be captivated by the deep empathy and high value that Jesus shows the women he meets. It has psychological insights and profound reflections on theological themes throughout the Old and New testaments and *Pride and Prejudice* woven through. Often Joanna's teaching makes me smile in recognition, in a way that only listening to another woman's voice can do. Over the years, I've found her to be more than just a beautiful person and mentor, but a glimpse for me of what is yet possible.

Other glimpses may be of those we don't necessarily know personally but we hear about. Stories of other women who persisted and eventually preached, or congregations flourishing under female leadership, can offer glimpses of the future God may still bring. They are like spiritual signposts, reminding women that their longing to preach is not misplaced or futile, but part of a larger story still unfolding in the church.

Sometimes these glimpses come from looking forward, as we anticipate the new creation. We see that ultimately all of these past and present glimpses are in fact tastes of the future coming to infuse the now. In the new creation, the enmity that fractured relationships in Eden will be replaced by love and shared purpose. Every voice, male and female, will join together in the song, "To him who sits on the throne and the Lamb be praise and honour and glory and power, for ever and ever" (Rev 5:13). One of my heroes, Jürgen Moltmann (author of the brilliant *Theology of Hope*) has expressed it like this:

3. Gregory, *On the Making of Man*, 16.14.

> In the new creation the contradictions and conflicts between men and women are overcome, because the whole creation is transfigured into the fellowship of the triune God. There is no domination and subordination any more, but mutual recognition and joy in the other.[4]

A few months ago, after five years of waiting and actively hoping, I glimpsed something of this new creation breaking into our church. Our senior minister stood before us all and explained that he felt that the time had come: women would no longer only team preach with a man, but would be free to preach in their own right. I knew he had been treading carefully for some time, trying to ensure unity in his staff team, who held a range of positions, and discerning when the congregation may be ready for this next step. He clearly and carefully explained his position from the Bible and acknowledged the strong emotions from every side. His words were humble and deeply moving. We could feel the weight of it. From my point of view, his courage, hard-won, had cleared space for women to express their gifts as equal coworkers in Christ. This may not yet come in your church, but you can choose the way of hope: to embrace those who differ, search out possibilities, wait with patient and active agency, and have eyes to not only see but even to become the glimpses of God's yes for women.

## Bibliography

Gregory of Nyssa. *On the Making of Man*. Translated by W. Moore and H. A. Wilson. In *The Nicene and Post-Nicene Fathers*, 2nd ser., edited by Philip Schaff and Henry Wace, 5:387–475. Buffalo, NY: Christian Literature, 1893.

Kahneman, Daniel. *Thinking, Fast and Slow*. New York: Farrar, Straus and Giroux, 2011.

McGrath, Joanna Collicutt. *Jesus and the Gospel Women*. London: SPCK, 2009.

Moltmann, Jürgen. *The Coming of God: Christian Eschatology*. Translated by Margaret Kohl. Minneapolis: Fortress, 1966.

Platow, Michael, et al. "'It's Not Funny If They're Laughing': Self-Categorization, Social Influence, and Responses to Canned Laughter." *Journal of Experimental Social Psychology* 4 (2005) 542–50.

4. Moltmann, *Coming of God*, 259.

# FAQs and What's Next for You

# Frequently Asked Questions

## *Complementarianism, Egalitarianism, Culture, and the Bible*

Erica Mandi Manga (née Hamence)

The issue of women preaching has followed me like a shadow my entire Christian journey, and throughout my nearly twenty years of ministry. I became a Christian in a primarily complementarian context. I first worked as an Anglican minister in an egalitarian church in Melbourne. Then I moved to a "soft complementarian"[1] church in Sydney, where I preached. In that latter role, I was constantly asked to explain my position on women preaching to congregants. Some asked out of curiosity, others with outright hostility.

This chapter is a collection of the most frequently asked questions I encountered. We start by unpacking common terms, and then we turn to common objections to women leading churches or preaching to mixed congregations.

### What's Complementarianism, What's Egalitarianism, and What's the Difference?

As soon as you start thinking about what women and men can do in and outside the church you are likely to come across the terms *complementarian* and *egalitarian*. Although these are by no means the only terms

1. More on this later.

that are relevant, they are the main ways that Western Christians group themselves on the topic.

That is not to say that it is essential for Christians to subscribe to either of them; many Christians do not find these terms helpful. However, given how prominent these terms are, it is worth being across them.[2]

## In a Nutshell, Complementarianism Is the Conviction That:

- God made men and women for partnership in his plans for the world (Gen 1:26–28).
- Partnership has two main components: similarity and difference (complementarity).

  The similarity can be found in the fact that both, male and female, are "made in the image of God" (Gen 1:27). For most complementarians, this is what conveys that men and women are equal in "essence."

  The difference aspect can be found in that male and female are distinct from one another. Again, Gen 1:27 might be a reference point: why else would the author specify that *both* male *and* female are made in God's image?
- This complementarity carries into the family unit.

  In particular, complementarity entails that the husband is the "head" (taken to mean "leader") of his wife (based on Eph 5, for example), and that wives ought to submit to their husbands' authority.
- This complementarity carries into church ministry.

  In particular, complementarity entails that their differences make it appropriate to distinguish different roles for men and women within the church, with the role of elder reserved for men (based on 1 Tim 2:11–15 and 3:1–7, for example).

2. I am aiming to give fair representation to both groups. However, it is necessary to generalise. Not every complementarian or egalitarian will articulate their beliefs exactly the way I articulate them here.

## In a Nutshell, Egalitarianism Is the Conviction That:

- God made men and women for partnership in his plans for the world (Gen 1:26–28), giving them a shared commission and dignity (both being made in the image of God).
- Although men and women are distinct from each other (egalitarians also believe men and women are complementary), what they have in common cannot be overlooked. For example, the first woman is made from the first man (or "human"). The fact that she is not made from some other material underscores this fundamental sameness of being.
- Hierarchy between women and men is an expression of sin in the world, from the fall (for example, Gen 3:16). Scripture does not affirm that there should be hierarchy between men and women.
- Because God has not instituted hierarchy between man and woman, the husband is not the authority of the wife, and the wife is not subordinate to the husband. Instead, they function as equals (based on Eph 5, for example). Gender does not determine what one is able to do in the church.

One of the key differences between these groups is their view on 1 Tim 2:11–15. For many complementarians, this passage is the grounds for prohibiting all women, everywhere and always, from preaching, teaching, and exercising authority over men. What they consider to constitute each of these elements (preaching, teaching, authority, and even the definition of men) can vary, as we will explore further below.

Egalitarians, on the other hand, do not believe that 1 Tim 2 prohibits all women, everywhere and always, from these activities. Like complementarians, there will be a variety of ways in which they reach their positions.

### How Did They Get There?

A big part of why the issue of women in (preaching) ministry is so contested is because it's not *just* about how we read 1 Tim 2:11–15. Although there *are* important interpretive aspects at play, those interpretations don't occur in a vacuum. Instead, they are shaped by the presuppositions and conclusions each person has made about other issues.

You could think of this as a puzzle. Complementarians are putting different pieces together and coming up with a different final picture to egalitarians. They are emphasising different passages, interpreting those passages differently, and perceiving different stakes compared to egalitarians.

Back in the age before the internet had more than two websites, Choose Your Own Adventure books were all the rage for tweens. At the end of each chapter you'd be presented with two options. Choosing one option would lead you to another chapter that would then present you another two options and so on, until finally you reached some dramatic end point. Had you made a different choice anywhere in that chain of events, you would have reached a completely different conclusion.

To extend the choose-your-own-adventure analogy, it's not that egalitarians and complementarians are coming to the same chapter and simply choosing different options, but they have *already* chosen many other different options in previous chapters, and that's how they are ending up in such different places.

Why does this matter? Why should we spend time understanding how each group has reached their conclusions?

Well, for one, it helps us not to ascribe bad faith to anyone who has landed on a different conclusion to ours. It is not *necessarily* that they are biased or bigoted. Whether they are aware of them or not, they have likely reached that conclusion based on a number of different choices, and we should seek to understand those.

Second, unpicking the path for how different conclusions are reached should help us be appropriately thoughtful as we make our own way toward a conclusion.

And last, by understanding both sides better, we will all be enabled to discuss in terms that are more intelligible to each other.

So, what are some of those different choices that have led complementarians and egalitarians to different conclusions?

Here's a short list of some of them:

- Difference vs. commonality
- Gender as primary vs. gender as secondary
- Hierarchy vs. mutuality
- Roles vs. relationship
- Plain reading vs. contextual reading

## Difference vs. Commonality

Complementarians and egalitarians *both* believe there are differences between men and women, as well as some similarity, as we saw before.

However, broadly speaking, complementarians emphasise difference more than similarity. Conversely, egalitarians emphasise similarity more than difference.

Not only are men and women distinct, complementarians say, but this distinctness needs to be reflected in men and women playing different roles in relation to each other at home and at church. Not only ought men and women to play different roles, but those roles should be organised hierarchically, with men playing a role that is variously described as "initiative-taking," "leadership," and "primary," and women variously described as "helpers," "following," and "submissive."

Egalitarians, on the other hand, hold that the differences between men and women do not require hierarchy. They are also more likely to emphasise commonality between women and men (and when they do recognise difference, they are less likely to attach hierarchical value to those differences). When it comes to a passage like Gen 1:26–28, they emphasise that the image of God is not differentiated along gender lines (with men having one kind of image of God and women having another), nor is the image of God expressed differently (men do not get one task and women a separate one). Instead, what they see in Gen 1:26–28 is a *shared* task that cannot be completed without cooperation.

## Gender as Primary vs. Gender as Secondary

Connected to this is a disagreement about the place of gender in Christian living. Complementarians might be described as holding a "gender is primary" view. That is, they would likely see gender as a fundamental element that must colour every interaction in the church and family. In contrast, egalitarians would likely see gender as *one* relevant factor amongst many others.

We are more likely to find complementarians talking about different roles for men and women, and at times encouraging men and women to develop different character traits from one another. Essentially, from this point of view gender is an overlay to everything a person does, a lens through which maturity and godliness ought to be expressed. You might imagine a complementarian asking the question, "How do I show womanly or manly kindness?" for example.

Whereas we are more likely to find egalitarians asking the question, "How do I show kindness like Christ?" You could call this view "gender is secondary." In other words, egalitarians do not believe gender dictates or defines all the expressions of a person's faith, whereas complementarians are more likely to suggest that it should.

These differences in priority affect the stakes for complementarians and egalitarians in the debate around women's participation in the church. Complementarians are likely to see greater danger where men and women do not sufficiently distinguish themselves, and egalitarians are likely to see greater danger when men and women are kept apart, as it threatens their ideal of partnership in ministry.

## Hierarchy vs. Mutuality

One crucial element of complementarianism is that it conceives of a hierarchical (or asymmetrical) relationship between men and women, with men holding authority and women following. Most complementarians would insist that this hierarchy is compatible with equality, maintaining that what the Bible teaches is *functional* hierarchy but *ontological* equality (that is, equality on the "being" level and equality before God, but not the "doing" level or in relation to each other).

In contrast, egalitarians would say that, in Christ, men and women are equal in *every sense*, and hierarchy on the ground of gender alone is incompatible with this. They would also be concerned that gender-based hierarchy introduces a dangerous power imbalance into the relationship between husband and wife and across the church more broadly.[3]

Complementarians and egalitarians are also likely to differ on what verses within the same passage they deem relevant. Consider Paul's instructions to the church and to households in Eph 5. Egalitarians are more likely to see it as significant that Eph 5:21 instructs believers to submit to one another, framing submission as something that may happen non-hierarchically and multi-directionally. That is, submission in the context of Eph 5 is not a response to a unilateral authority but simply a continuation of Paul's instructions in Eph 5:1–2, that Christians "walk in the way

3. We do not have the space to explore this further. However, as an anti-domestic and family violence advocate, I want to acknowledge that this is a real issue worthy of serious consideration.

of love." Complementarians, on the other hand, are likely to emphasise Eph 5:22–24, in which Paul refers to the husband using the metaphor of a "head" and exhorts wives to submit to their husbands. Thus, they would argue, the command to "submit to one another" in verse 21 is qualified by what comes after it, offering a kind of caveat: submit to one another within these ordered relationships (such that husbands need not submit to their wives).

## Roles vs. Relationship

Closely connected to the issue of mutuality and hierarchy is how each group articulates the husband-wife relationship. Complementarians are more likely to speak of husbands and wives as each having a distinct "role" to play in relation to each other. There's a lot bundled up in the concept of roles. A roles-based framework would suggest that husbands should "stay in their lane," doing things like providing, protecting, and leading, and wives should correspondingly commit to submit, nurture, and follow, for example. Returning to Eph 5:22–24, complementarians will speak of "headship"—conceiving of a totalising role for husbands that carries a sense of authority to everything he does in connection with his wife.

Egalitarians, on the other hand, are less likely to see distinct roles for husbands and wives and more likely to conceive of their obligations to each other as grounded in mutual love, care, and respect. The ways they relate would be more influenced by the unique personality, capacity, skills, and gifts of each partner. In other words, the relationship is idiosyncratic, particular to the two people within it, rather than governed by standards that apply to all husbands and all wives.

Egalitarians are likely to dispute the meaning of the metaphor "head" in this context. They are also likely to question the breadth of its application, suggesting that it is one metaphor among many.

## Plain Reading vs. Contextual Reading

If someone were to make a bingo card for phrases that arise in the context of the women-in-ministry debate, you could safely predict that one phrase would come up more than any other: "You're ignoring the plain reading of the text."

If this means nothing to you, let me explain:

When it comes to 1 Tim 2:11–15, complementarians are more likely to believe that their reading of the text is a "plain reading." A plain reading is one that accepts and respects God's word as it stands, that doesn't attempt to manipulate God's word to mean something else in service of a more palatable reading.

In 1 Tim 2:12 Paul writes, "I do not permit a woman to teach or to assume authority over a man; she must be quiet." Thus, complementarians might say, it's simple. Paul said women are not allowed to teach or have authority over men, and any interpretation that differs from that is simply the result of people refusing to accept God's command.

Egalitarians would say that no reading is as simple as that, no matter what passage. And that in this instance "plain reading" equates to "whatever I thought at first glance without thinking too much about it." This, they say, is not doing justice to the text. Rather, one should consider carefully various possibilities for what it might mean, and what faithful application of it looks like.

What is caught up in this is also a question of what principles underpin our interpretations of the Bible. Is it acceptable to dismiss a biblical practice for cultural reasons but seek to hold on to an underlying principle, or to accept a different expression of it that fits with today's norms and practices? In the context of 1 Tim 2 we can observe several questions of this kind. For example, does 1 Tim 2:8 properly applied mean men everywhere should lift their hands when they pray today? What principles might help women work out if it is permissible to wear gold or pearls or designer clothing, given Paul's instructions in 1 Tim 2:9? How do we know which instructions apply across all cultures?

Complementarians are more likely to protest that it is suspicious to claim that biblical teaching can apply differently today. Egalitarians are more likely to argue that they are doing nothing more than good exegesis and thoughtful application.

## Bringing It All Together

What you should see now is that each of the above points of difference builds on the one before. If you believe one premise, another becomes more plausible. It would not make much sense to believe in distinct roles for men and women but reject an emphasis on gendered differences, for example.

What all of this means is that when complementarians and egalitarians come to read passages like 1 Tim 2:11–15 and Eph 5:21–24, they "see" different things, and certain readings of those passages become more persuasive as a result.

It also helps to explain why complementarians and egalitarians perceive different dangers in each other's interpretations.

## But Wait, There's More!

What we have just sketched is the two camps in their broadest possible senses.

But as you likely know, it is not just across those two camps that we find significant points of difference; even *within* each camp there are differences.

It is possible to sketch those differences across a spectrum. At one end of the spectrum we have "soft" complementarians, and at the other end of the spectrum we have "hard." This is mostly a reference to differences in practice rather than conviction. Both would largely agree about the elements we considered above but have different ways of putting them into practice.

A soft complementarian senior minister may allow women to preach and may be positive about how women's voices shape the church, but he will likely believe that those women preach "under" his authority, and that it would not be appropriate for men to be "under" a woman's authority. In a soft complementarian church women might lead services, teach, lead Bible studies, and exercise significant influence, but could not be the senior minister.

A hard complementarian church might prohibit women from service leading, and leading Bible studies. They might also prohibit women from teaching male youth of a certain age.

A spectrum is harder to perceive within egalitarian churches. This does not necessarily mean that egalitarian churches will always have women in leadership. Some egalitarian churches believe that women can and should preach and lead, but do not prioritise this conviction. Sometimes a commitment to being "gender blind" has made it difficult for women to be supported or mentored actively, given the additional challenges many women face. In fact, in some cases, women in complementarian churches have reported that their churches have done more to support and enable women for ministry (but not senior ministry leadership) than their egalitarian counterparts.

## Do Female Preachers Just Want Power?

Other iterations of this question include:

- Why can't you just be happy serving in some other way?
- Are you resisting submitting to God's commands?
- Are you just disobeying God?

Most women in ministry are serving simply because they have an earnest desire to serve God as best they can. Instead of recognising and commending this earnestness, questions of this kind view these women and their motivations with suspicion. This question effectively says to women whose desire is to serve God, "Aren't you just serving yourself?"

The assumption underlying these questions is that the female preacher insists on preaching to mixed audiences *despite* knowing that God's word says she should not. It assumes that she does not have the strength or forbearance or sacrificial attitude required to abstain. She is not willing to sublimate her desires to God's will.

I have now been in paid ministry for eighteen years, and I was in lay ministry for approximately five years before that. I have personally never met a female preacher like this. Instead, the women I know who preach to mixed audiences are some of the most well-practiced in these skills of forbearance and sacrifice. Often, this is by virtue of the challenges women in ministry face. Women who preach, especially in denominations or dioceses in which it is not well accepted, face regular criticism and scepticism. They are often ostracised by fellow ministers. They are often willing to serve in places where they know they will not receive praise or recognition. They are often fully aware that they could receive much greater professional acclaim and "success" in a secular environment.

To share personally, after the last sermon I preached at the church in which I serve, I was told that some attendees had discussed among themselves how they would simply "try not to listen" to me whilst I was preaching. This is not the first time I have heard such a thing, or even the worst thing I have heard, just the most recent.

Would a woman wanting power continue with such things?

We should see a deep irony here; women's desire to *serve* is cast as a desire for *power*. And we should recognise that when men seek to lead, they are not often treated with such suspicion. When men lead, it is often viewed as sacrificial. It's often framed as nobly giving up the power and riches that an alternative career path might have offered. It's worth asking: how did this double standard come about, in which men's ministry is seen as humble, and women's as proud?

## Are People Who Support Women Preaching Just Worldly?

How will we know we have not just given in to the world's perspective on gender? Is it not possible that people who support women preaching have been more influenced by feminism than the Bible?

To some extent, this question is understandable. Christians are often taught to be "countercultural," seeing it as nearly synonymous with being godly. In contrast, anything that aligns too closely with the mainstream is considered potentially "worldly" and ungodly.

And we might agree that feminism has become more accepted in the mainstream. It is more prominent in our conversations and media, for example. So, the argument goes, if you're arguing for women to have a more significant public role in the church, you're going *with* the grain of society, and those who argue for more restrictions on the roles of women are going *against* it. And that must mean you value acceptability more than obedience, the world's opinion more than God's.

Though understandable, under a closer look, this view falls apart.

For one, Christians are not always and only called to be countercultural, as if God's will were for us to oppose the values of the world, no matter what they are. First and foremost, Christians are called to be like God. In many instances, that will look like going against the prevailing values of our society. And we should be willing to face the challenges that come from that. But it is unsound to say that where we do not find ourselves on the opposite side of an issue to the world that we are necessarily being worldly. We need to do more thinking to establish if that is the case, especially where Christian teaching has shaped our society.

But more importantly, it is important not to overstate where the world is on gender equality. The fear about worldliness is based on an assumption that the world is a place of equality between women and men.

However, a quick look at any gender equality statistics, just for Australia, shows that this is a fantasy.

In Australia, one or more women are murdered every week by a current or former male partner. Half of Australian women have been sexually harassed.[4] Women do not earn the same as men, in any field.[5] Women's health is not taken seriously, with two thirds of women experiencing discrimination in healthcare.[6] When Australia elected its first female prime minister, she was on the receiving end of enormous sexist commentary.[7] Women do more housework than men, and express greater dissatisfaction with this than their male partners.[8]

So then, imagine you were an alien, coming to earth and surveying Australia. As part of your studies, you come across the statistics outlined above. Would you conclude that we live by "egalitarian" values when it comes to gender? Or would you conclude that there exists in Australia a gender hierarchy where men receive better positions and pay in the workplace, and better treatment in interpersonal relationships?

It's hard to see how our surrounding culture is consistent with an egalitarian or feminist view of gender.

Here is what this means. Just as egalitarians and those who support women preaching need to examine themselves and evaluate whether they value culture over the Bible, so, too, do complementarians.

In fact, given that gender inequality has been a deep and lasting feature of our society, complementarians should ask: how do I know *I* am not just going with what culture says about men and women?

Of course, this question of culture applies not just to society as a whole, but also to the communities to which we belong. All of us need to ask: Have I simply gone with what I was taught to believe by my church or Christian community?

What are the stakes for me if I differ from the majority on the issue of women teaching? What have I gained by going with the majority, and what do I lose if I do not? Is that what has influenced my view more than just my good faith engagement with God's word? It may be that it has not,

4. Australian Government, "Status of Women."

5. The pay gap is 11.9 percent, but is greater when it comes to CEOs and business. See Australian Government, "Status of Women."

6. National Women's Health Advisory, *#EndGenderBias Survey*, 4.

7. Kernot, "Julia Gillard Hits Back."

8. Wilkins et al., *Household, Income*, 104; Family Friendly Workplaces, *National Working Families Report*, 5, 14.

in which case, that is great! But let's all examine ourselves seriously and ask the question.

## Bibliography

Australian Government. "Status of Women Report Card 2025." March 8, 2025. https://genderequality.gov.au/status-women-report-cards/2025-report-card.

Family Friendly Workplaces. *National Working Families Report 2024: The Impact of Work and Care on Australian Families.* Deloitte, 2024.

Kernot, Cheryl. "Julia Gillard Hits Back at a Long History of Sexism in Parliament." The Conversation, October 9, 2012. https://theconversation.com/julia-gillard-hits-back-at-a-long-history-of-sexism-in-parliament-10071.

National Women's Health Advisory Council. *#EndGenderBias Survey Summary Report.* Canberra: Department of Health and Aged Care, 2024. https://www.health.gov.au/sites/default/files/2024-03/endgenderbias-survey-results-summary-report_0.pdf.

Wilkins, Roger, et al. *The Household, Income and Labour Dynamics in Australia Survey: Selected Findings from Waves 1 to 20.* Victoria: Melbourne Institute, 2022. https://melbourneinstitute.unimelb.edu.au/__data/assets/pdf_file/0011/4382057/HILDA_Statistical_Report_2022.pdf.

# Epilogue

Anna Boxwell

*I WRITE THIS EPILOGUE for women readers who may be considering what serving God could look like in their life, including going into ministry. If that's not you, I'd love for you to listen in. As the preceding chapters have shown, we don't exist alone. We need all of God's people, men and women together, working to support one another in unleashing our gifts in service to Christ's body in all of life.*

Having read this book, what's next for you?

There's a hill near my house with a beautiful walking track. From the top, you can see across the valley where I live, and over to the mountains beyond. Walking up there lifts my eyes off the day to day and helps me to see clearly. If I could go walk and pray with you up Mt. Taylor to hear your hopes for your life and ministry, these are some things I would say to you.

I am full of hope in the beauty and power of gospel witness that can emerge when women and men work together. God's purpose is for men and women to serve him in partnership so that the message of Jesus Christ will reach the ends of the earth. That purpose was marred by human sin. But it is such a refreshing contrast when discipleship and evangelism in local churches are carried out by women and men in genuine partnership, when women and men use their wisdom and insight together in governance boards. No jostling, no self-conscious second guessing, no minimising or hiding of God-given gifts.

But if you're a woman, you may be counting the cost, not only of a life of ministry, but also the cost of ministry as a woman. Navigating this path means wrestling not only with the usual demands of gospel work, but also with the realities of being a woman in spaces where your presence and leadership may be questioned, undervalued, or misunderstood, even by people who are supportive of women in ministry.

Any Christian is called to contend for the gospel of Jesus Christ. But as a woman in ministry myself, I also need to do the intangible work of contending for my validity as a pastor. I call this the double contending.

I tell you this not to draw attention to my experience so much as to expand your imagination: your sisters in ministry probably have similar experiences, and if you are reading this as a woman prayerfully considering going into ministry yourself, know that it's worth it and I am doing anything I can to pave the way for you. It won't be easy. We want women to be released from the burden of "double contending" so you're free to contend for the good news alongside your brothers.

Your desire to share of the hope, forgiveness, and life in Jesus Christ is not wrong. God's church needs you and your contribution. Notice, in prayerful conversation with trusted older Christians, your abilities, interests, and skills. In what areas do you need to learn or grow in knowledge and Christlikeness? Why not sign up to take a class—or degree—in theology? What are the opportunities where God could use you to build up your local church and share the good news with others? What are the needs and how might you meet them? What's it like in the community where God has planted you in your life, work, and church? What is God putting before you? God has created you uniquely, and there is a place for you in his church—perhaps in ways you haven't yet imagined.

Remember how Paul so naturally refers to his coworkers in Christ, for example in Phil 4:2–3 and Rom 16 and numerous other places? Remember the example of the prophets Anna and Simeon in the temple, praying and prophesying over baby Jesus (Luke 2:22–38)? Remember the women at the tomb who were told to "go and tell" (Matt 28)? Remember the people who first shared of Jesus's love with you? Who will you tell?

I long to see the church pull together for the sake of the health and holiness of the church, to the glory of God. Women and men are not in competition with one another; we get to joyfully serve together without taking on fallen-world patterns of relating. I want to see more women in ministry not merely so women can exercise their giftings but so that the body of Christ may be built up in healthy ways. We long for the church to stop looking at one another with suspicion and mistrust. Let's get on with the work God has set before us!

So take heart. We need all hands on deck, and God has equipped suitable men and women to be co-labourers in the gospel. We need one another as the body of Christ.

> For Christ's love compels us, because we are convinced that one died for all, and therefore all died. And he died for all, that those who live should no longer live for themselves but for him who died for them and was raised again. So from now on we regard no one from a worldly point of view. Though we once regarded Christ in this way, we do so no longer. (2 Cor 5:14–16)

Together, we can contend for the good news of Jesus Christ for a world that needs to meet him. May Christ's love compel you, too, to share the hope and life in Jesus Christ together with all our brothers and sisters.

www.ingramcontent.com/pod-product-compliance
Lightning Source LLC
LaVergne TN
LVHW050627100826
845148LV00011B/1763

*9798385263691*